THE
INNOVATION
ULTIMATUM

THE
INNOVATION
ULTIMATUM

HOW SIX STRATEGIC TECHNOLOGIES WILL RESHAPE EVERY BUSINESS IN THE 2020s

STEVE BROWN

WILEY

ISBN 9781119615422 (Hardcover)
ISBN 9781119615446 (ePDF)
ISBN 9781119615439 (ePub)

Cover image: © MATJAZ SLANIC/Getty Images
Cover design: Wiley

Printed in the United States of America

V10016518_122719

For my parents, who ultimately made everything possible for me.
For my lovely wife, who supported me every step of the way.
And for the inimitable Richard Tonn,
who so wanted to read this book but never saw it finished.

CONTENTS

FOREWORD
DON'T FEAR THE FUTURE . . .
PREPARE FOR IT

Would you like to know a secret about the future?

The future isn't fixed. There is not a single future that we are all running toward, helpless to do anything about. The future is built every day by the actions of people and organizations. This is why it is so important to be an active participant in the future. People should not be passive. No organization should sit back and let the future happen *to* them—that never ends well. The first step to becoming an active participant in your future is gaining knowledge, and this book is a great place to start.

All too often when people learn about the future it is cloaked in a shroud of fear and dread. Artificial Intelligence. Blockchain. Augmented Reality. The Internet of Things. 5G networks. Autonomous Machines. Each of these advances will reshape the world. No industry will be untouched. But these changes are not organization-ending events. These transformative technologies don't mean the end to your business or organization. They will however mean that you will need to adapt and to prepare your teams for change. By learning about these technologies today, understanding their possible and potential impact, you can prepare for tomorrow.

Once you have done this, then you can ask yourself and your organization: What is the future you want to build? What is the future you want to avoid? If you are reading this, I believe you know that you will have to do *something*. Organizations that ignore the future are the ones that find themselves disrupted, rudderless, and obsolete. This informed, active participation means that you get to decide your own future and then begin to stake out the prudent and pragmatic steps to get there.

Would you like to know another secret about the future?

Fear makes you stupid. When humans are fearful, their brains can only make one of three decisions: Fight. Flight. Freeze. We have all seen really poor business and life decisions that have been made during these three paralyzing states. Knowledge and informed commentary about the future can help to dispel this fear.

Beware of anyone who tells you that you should be scared of the future. Instantly be suspicious of anyone who tells you that because of some technology, the world will never be the same again and that you are powerless to do anything about it. Ultimately, what this person is trying to do is disempower you, to scare you into making poor decisions, or worse . . . to frighten you into inaction.

This is the power of Steve Brown's work as a futurist. He has spent years empowering organizations to make well informed decisions about the future. Sometimes they might be difficult decisions, but ultimately his goal is to give organizations the vision and perspective to not only plan for the future but get excited about it. This book is a valuable tool for people to become informed about the future and begin the necessary conversations about how to prepare for—and thrive in—the coming tomorrows.

Brian David Johnson, author and futurist

Arizona State University

INTRODUCTION
TO SURVIVE, EVERY COMPANY MUST BECOME A TECH COMPANY

Innovate—or die.

This business maxim has never been truer than it is today. Consumers are demanding and fickle. Their expectations are set by the best and most recent experiences they've had. They have no tolerance for companies that skate by and that don't constantly strive for excellence. Consumers expect brands not only to deliver, but surprise. There is a massive and rapidly widening gulf between the capabilities of companies that invest in technology and those that don't.

It is a time of reckoning. Emerging technologies will empower brave innovators to make giant leaps forward, while those without vision, courage, and agility will wither and perish. Winners will change the world.

The Innovation Ultimatum

It's no coincidence that most of the companies on the *Brand Z* list of the top 100 most valuable global brands invest heavily in technology to drive innovation into every aspect of their business: product development, operations, marketing, and customer service.

In the next decade, a suite of six strategic technologies—artificial intelligence (AI), Blockchain, the Internet of Things (IoT), augmented reality, autonomous machines, and 5G networks—will drive unprecedented innovation into products and services, creating entirely new business models along the way. Investment in information technology (IT) will be a strategic imperative for every company. Every company will become a technology company, and every company will become a data company. Business operations will be retooled using both process automation and worker augmentation.

Automation and Augmentation

Automation will speed business processes, improve quality, and reduce costs. Augmentation will elevate the capabilities of workers, blending machine and human intelligence. Artificial intelligence will assist us, partner with us, guide us, inspire us, and make us even more capable. We don't need to merge with technology to collaborate closely with it.

Product, Service, and Business-Model Innovation

New products and services are the best way to retain existing customers and gain new ones. In the next decade, expect significant innovation in products and services as technology becomes embedded inside anything and everything. Companies will use data, sensors, and machine intelligence to elevate business models and get paid more for their efforts, moving upward from products to services, services to experiences, and experiences to transformations.

The Innovator's Palette

In the coming years, we will see the broad deployment of six important technologies. Think of these technologies as six new colors being added to your business innovation palette. To some extent, your ability to innovate will only be limited by your imagination.

Six Technologies Intimately Connect the Digital and Physical Worlds

Each of these six technologies builds a bridge between the digital world and the physical world. Computing capabilities, and value created in the digital world, both advance exponentially. As we build ever more intimate connections between the digital and physical worlds, more of that value flows across the bridge to be experienced in the physical world.

Engineers have been building this bridge for several decades now. This, in itself, is not a new story. But the next decade will dramatically accelerate the building of the digital–physical bridge. Trillions of sensors will enable the digital world to understand what's happening in our physical world. Robots and other autonomous machines will enable the digital world to act within the physical world. Artificial intelligence will give digital devices eyes and ears so they can make sense of the world. Distributed ledgers and Blockchains, combined with arrays of sophisticated sensors, will track the movement of physical goods around the planet. Augmented reality will blend digital objects and information with our visual perception of the physical world. Finally, 5G networks and satellite constellations will tie everything together, allowing everything to connect with everything else.

This is an exciting (and daunting) time to be in business. Competition is fierce. Customers are never satisfied; neither are shareholders. In the 2020s, the companies that thrive will be the ones that never rest on their laurels. These companies will fully embrace every one of these six technologies and combine them in creative ways to leapfrog competition. Those that hesitate risk irrelevance. Nobody is immune, not even today's titans. Winners will create massive value in the digital domain and use the six technologies to bridge that value into the physical realm, streamlining operations, delighting customers, and creating exciting new products and services.

Winners Will Wield and Combine These Technologies Like Artists Use Color

The six technologies that are the focus of this book aren't all brand new. The term "artificial intelligence" was coined in the 1950s, the ideas behind the Internet of Things have been around since the last century, and Blockchains were first created more than a decade ago. For various reasons, each is only just coming to maturity. It is the creative combination of these technologies that will lead to breakthrough innovation. For example, IoT sensors are made exponentially more powerful with AI. Next-generation, massively scalable distributed ledger technology will combine with ubiquitous low-earth-orbit satellite networks to transform logistics and the supply chain.

As innovators seek to reimagine how they create value, serve customers, and operate their businesses, new technologies act like new colors in their creative palette. The most impressive innovations will be painted using a creative combination of many colors. *Uber* was created at the intersection of apps, GPS sensors, cloud services, and the gig economy.

Expect More Change in the Next 10 Years Than the Last 40

New technologies change the innovation landscape forever. Some technologies have a much larger impact than others. Since the 1980s, four major technological leaps defined the innovation landscape for business IT: the PC, the web, mobile, and the cloud. When IBM launched its personal computer in 1981, it kicked off an upward spiral of innovation and productivity. In the early 1990s, the rise of the web meant that every business had to open a new front door, online. Steve Jobs kicked off the mobile revolution in 2007 and put a portable supercomputer into the pockets and purses of billions of people around the world. Finally, the cloud computing era, which occurred concurrently with the mobile era, made it easier for companies to create digital value, scale it on demand, and innovate rapidly. Sure, there were other technologies that were stirred into the mix, but those were the big four. Four decades, four big leaps forward, four new colors in the innovation palette. In a single decade, the 2020s, six technologies will combine to fuel more innovation than in the last 40.

Should I Be Afraid or Excited?

From my time on the speaking circuit, I've learned that whenever I talk about future technology, particularly AI, it engenders a wide range of emotions in my audiences. Some people are energized and excited by the potential AI holds for humanity. Others are filled with fear. Most manage a healthy balance of both.

Technology has the potential to reshape humanity and propel it forward in giant leaps. AI may help us cure major diseases and unlock the secrets of the universe. Automation may also displace hundreds of millions of people from the workplace, and some tech luminaries warn that AI may ultimately destroy the human race.

Movies about aliens, killer robots, and pandemics sell tickets. Dystopian stories outsell utopian stories and strong stories are driven by conflict and drama. So, for decades, Hollywood has been fascinated by the darker side of technology's potential. Audiences love the spectacle of a *Terminator* stomping on human skulls, Mr. Anderson fighting Neo inside *The Matrix*, or Ava manipulating and killing her way out of captivity in *Ex Machina*. Directors want to tell a rollicking-good story; they're not there to accurately portray reality. We must recognize that our preconceptions and fears about technology are grounded in our exposure to these fictional stories. In part, this book is an attempt to counterbalance the Hollywood storytelling machine. Overall, technological advancement is a very positive force.

Our ancestors were afraid of telephones, televisions, and rock music. In the nineteenth century, people refused to ride trains believing that if your body moved faster than 30 miles per hour you would melt. Fire can warm a home or burn it to the ground. A split atom can power an entire city or devastate it. Technology is not the culprit; it's how we use it that matters. We must deploy technology responsibly, thoughtfully, and in a manner that benefits humans without posing *unreasonable* risks.

We are right to be cautious about the development of technology, but we must not fear it. Technology promises incredible potential to serve humanity. It may help us to address the challenges of climate change, eradicate diseases, improve transportation safety, eliminate fraud, limit waste, lower the cost of education, and deliver breakthroughs in the future of energy, materials science, and biology. Somebody reading this book—you, or your kids, or their kids—may have their lives saved by pharmaceuticals developed by a future AI. Should we deny you life because we've seen *The Terminator* a few too many times? We must retain healthy skepticism and ask tough questions about new technology, but remain open to the bounties it will bring. The six technologies described in this book will bring incredible innovation to every part or our lives. This is an exciting time to be alive! While automation will inevitably destroy some jobs, technology will create many new ones and elevate human work by taking on dull, routine tasks. New technology will create entire new career paths and make work more meaningful, challenging, creative, and rewarding.

Getting the Most Out of This Book

In the first part of this book, we cover each of the six technologies in turn: artificial intelligence, the Internet of Things, autonomous machines, Blockchains, augmented reality, and 5G networks. If you are already well-versed in these technologies, you might skip to the second part, but note that there are many stories included in these early chapters that demonstrate how these technologies are already being applied to solve real business problems.

In the second part, we review the high-level business implications of these technologies—automation strategies, the strategic importance of data, and the future of work.

In the third and final part of the book, we review specific examples of early innovation using the six technologies. Each chapter is focused on a particular industry. They describe the unique challenges of each industry, how technology is already solving real business problems in that industry, and the key lessons readers can learn and apply elsewhere.

No matter which industry you are in, I strongly encourage you to read this final section of the book. If you're in healthcare, read about manufacturing and transportation. If you're in retail, read about construction and supply chain, and so on. Steal ideas with pride. Lessons can always be learned from other industries. I hope you will read about something happening in another industry and think, "Well that's nothing like what we do, but it's given me a great idea. . . ."

Please read this book with a mind-set of exploring a world of possibility. Every businessperson, no matter their seniority, line of business, or role within a company, needs to understand the six technologies described in this book. Businesspeople don't need to understand the technical ins-and-outs of how these technologies work—that's a role for the IT department—but they must understand the practical and strategic implications of these technologies, and how their capabilities will evolve with time. Armed with these insights, business leaders can guide informed conversations with their teams as they build their medium- and long-range plans.

Collectively, these technologies will transform business operations, customer expectations, customer relationships, labor strategies, and the competitive landscape. No industry is immune. No company is exempt.

Don't Panic; Don't Wait; Get Help

Every business should prepare for widespread turmoil and change. Standing still is no longer an option, especially for industries that have stagnated for years, or decades.

Resist the temptation to panic. This level of change can feel overwhelming but remember that every company is in the same boat. By virtue of reading this book, you already have an advantage. That said, there is no time to waste. Don't wait to embrace the technologies described in this book. Start strategic discussions today. Connect your IT department with your strategic planners and task them to drive innovation across every aspect of your business. Fund pilots and try new approaches. And remember that unless you are a tech company, you can't be expected to understand and implement artificial intelligence and other technologies on your own. So, get help. Push your suppliers for solutions that embrace these technologies and deliver the capabilities you need. If they don't respond, find new suppliers.

To summarize: Don't panic. Don't wait. Get help.

Above all, prepare your organization to embrace change and get them excited about driving innovation into everything you do.

The Innovation Ultimatum is both a call to innovate for survival in a rapidly evolving competitive environment, and a moral imperative to use these six technologies to serve people, elevate work, and make a lasting, positive impact on the world. Let's dive in.

Part I

Six Technologies That Will Reshape Business in the Next Decade

1 Artificial Intelligence

Artificial intelligence (AI) is all around us. It underpins speech recognition, natural language processing (NLP), and machine vision. AI is behind the sophisticated spam filters that keep your inbox (mostly) free of junk mail. It flags unusual usage patterns on your credit card and assesses your credit score. It suggests tags for people in photos you post to Facebook. It offers intelligent suggestions when you use the search bar. AI is all around us, yet we have only scratched the surface of AI's future potential.

Like a femme fatale in a classic movie, AI seems simultaneously sexy and scary. While artificial intelligence may help us to unlock cures for diseases, discover new wonder materials, and predict the future, some people worry that it threatens human life as we know it, either economically or existentially.

What Is It and Why Is It Important?

Artificial intelligence is the umbrella term that describes the effort to mimic human skills and replicate human intelligence with machines. Various approaches have been used to build artificial intelligence over the years. In the 1980s and 1990s, "knowledge systems" were all the rage. Today, most modern AI uses a technique known as machine learning.

Machines learn from examples in the form of training data. Most machine learning systems are built with artificial neural networks (ANN), also known more simply as neural networks.

Electricity, Digital Computers, and Artificial Intelligence

About 120 years ago, electrification changed the world. Electricity refrigerates our food, washes our clothes, lights our homes, and powers our factories. Electricity transformed every industrial sector and now powers modern life.

Roughly 60 years ago, the first digital computers were built. Initially limited in their capability, computers evolved into powerful machines that brought us word processing, spreadsheets, the internet, video games, social media, streaming media, and smartphones. Like electricity before them, computers transformed business and changed our lives.

Artificial intelligence will have an impact as profound as both electrification and the digital computer. AI luminary Andrew Ng is the former chief scientist at Baidu, former lead of the Google Brain project, and now runs Landing.ai, a company that solves manufacturing problems using AI. In 2017, Ng observed, "Just as electricity transformed almost everything 100 years ago, today I actually have a hard time thinking of an industry that I don't think AI will transform in the next several years."

Artificial intelligence is a huge deal, worthy of the first and longest chapter of this book. Sundar Pichai, CEO at Google, once said, "AI is one of the most important things humanity is working on. It is more profound than, I dunno, electricity or fire." While hyperbolic, this statement from the head of one of the world's most powerful tech companies should make us all sit up and listen.

AI's hype is largely justified. Just as digital technology was a vital component of any successful business strategy in the 1990s and 2000s, so AI must be central to strategic plans of the 2020s.

The Next Era of Computing: Traditional Digital versus Artificial Intelligence

Artificial intelligence and traditional digital computers are complementary. Importantly, AI solves problems that are costly or impossible for traditional computers to solve. The two technologies will coexist and work side-by-side, each solving a different set of problems. For a language translation app on a smartphone, traditional computing presents an attractive interface, while AI handles voice recognition and language translation functions.

AI solves problems using a radically different approach from traditional computers. Traditional computers are programmed to solve problems. Programs apply a set of rules to data and compute results. Said another way, they take rules and data as input, and output results. AI solves problems without using preprogrammed rules. Machine learning, a popular form of AI, takes data and results as its input and infers rules as its output. Through a complex training process, AI finds patterns and associations between data and results and divines its own rules for how they connect. This trait lets us solve entirely new problems with AI. It's why AI can seem so magical: It solves problems we don't know how to solve ourselves.

To find complex associations in data and build rules, AIs must be trained with thousands or sometimes millions of examples. Today's AIs are not like human brains. While some of the organizing principles are the same, human children learning about the world don't have to see a million automobiles before they can recognize one and adorably yell the word "car."

A 1950s Concept and 1980s Algorithms Meet Modern Computing Horsepower

The term "artificial intelligence" was first coined in the 1950s. The core algorithms behind today's AIs were first proposed in the 1970s and popularized in the mid-1980s. But it was 2012 before the recent crop of AI breakthroughs began to appear. Why the quarter-century delay? Older computers lacked the performance to run AI applications. High-end graphics processors, GPUs from companies like Nvidia, eventually provided the computing horsepower needed. Their parallel number-crunching architectures, designed to create realistic video games, turn out to be pretty good for training an AI. As well as fast computers, AIs need training data to learn from. As digital storage costs fell and broadband speeds increased, data flooded in from many sources: billions of industrial sensors, millions of smart cameras, billions of people sharing trillions of photos and billions of videos, and trillions of clicks on social media. Users upload 500 hours of video to YouTube every minute and more than 1.2 billion photos to Google Photos every day (Source: Wikipedia).

With cheap, powerful computing, an avalanche of training data, and a small army of AI-savvy researchers and developers, artificial intelligence is now poised to solve myriad problems and create many exciting new capabilities.

What Can You Do with It?

Artificial intelligence can solve a wide variety of problems. Considering all the possible applications of AI can be overwhelming. I've found it helpful to cluster AI applications into eight broad categories:

1. Machine vision
2. Natural language processing (NLP) and voice platforms
3. Exploration and discovery
4. Better-informed decision-making
5. Predicting the future
6. Seeing the world through a new lens with super sensors
7. Solving complex problems by learning from experience
8. Creating and co-creating content

In all of these eight application categories, AI is used to find patterns and associations in data and to make statistical predictions. Each application uses this fundamental feature in different ways. Apply the associative capabilities of machine learning to images and you get machine vision; apply it to historical data and you get predictions; apply it to cursive text and you get handwriting recognition. In voice platforms, AIs trained on human speech determine what words you are saying. AIs trained on historical weather data are used to make predictions that inform the weather forecast.

Artificial intelligence finds important associations that we may not previously have discovered: the complex association between the molecular structure of a chemical compound and its physical properties, or the complex set of circumstances that lead to an outbreak of disease. This characteristic enables AI to solve problems that we don't yet know how to solve ourselves.

As we review each of the eight main applications of AI, think about how each one might impact your business, your life, and society at large.

Machine Vision: Computers Open Their Eyes

With the advent of artificial intelligence, machines have evolved eyes and ears. Computers can now see, hear, and "understand" something about the world that they inhabit. This understanding is still rudimentary. Computers can recognize an image of an apple and correctly categorize it with the five letters a-p-p-l-e, but they don't understand what an apple is, that it grew on a tree, or what it tastes like.

Machine vision has many interesting applications across a wide range of industries. Stocktaking robots audit shelf contents in grocery stores. Facial recognition algorithms turn faces into passwords. Agricultural robots spot-spray herbicide on weeds. Quality assurance AIs perform visual inspection on the manufacturing line. Autonomous machines— robots, drones, and self-driving vehicles—all rely on machine vision, too.

EarthNow, an ambitious startup funded by Bill Gates, Airbus, Softbank, and others, is a splendid example of machine vision's future potential. EarthNow will operate a constellation of satellites, each containing four powerful, high-definition cameras. The company's goal is essentially to create a real-time version of Google Earth, though with an important twist: Artificial intelligence, built into the satellites, runs applications to interpret camera images and add intelligent insight. These applications will reveal important details about activity on our planet.

A lightning strike in a remote location can start a devastating forest fire that rages out of control. Detection, rapid response, and early containment may save millions of acres of land from incineration, prevent damage to structures, and save lives. With EarthNow, global fire detection is just another application that runs on the satellites. The network becomes an eye in the sky that watches for fire starts and automatically alerts local authorities, 24/7/365.

EarthNow has proposed a range of other exciting applications for their satellite constellation. The system could provide real-time traffic information to city managers, real-time crop health information to farmers, and alert law enforcement or government agencies to illegal fishing, mining, and logging activity. Marine biologists will be able to track whale migration and volcanologists will monitor volcanic activity. Global asset tracking applications include tracking ships at sea, trucks on the road, planes in the air, and shipping containers in transit. Other applications include improved weather forecasting, law enforcement, and news coverage. EarthNow is a powerful platform that raises serious privacy concerns. This is why EarthNow chose to build machine learning capabilities into the satellites themselves. Users have very limited access to data from applications—real-time traffic data, the GPS locations of whales—but not the image data itself. The machine vision capabilities of the EarthNow platform present an exciting new set of opportunities for research scientists, public safety professionals, local governments, and a wide range of businesses.

Natural Language Processing and Voice Platforms

Human language is complex, powerful, and full of rich nuance. It's a tough task to build a computer than can "hear" spoken natural human language, break it down into its component parts, infer meaning and intent, and then act on that information to do something useful. Artificial intelligence is behind many incredible applications of natural language processing. It can find spelling and grammatical errors, translate from one language to another, review legal contracts, and summarize the important points of a report.

Natural language processing (NLP) is an umbrella term that describes a machine's ability to understand, process, and communicate using natural human language. NLP consists of two pieces: natural language understanding (NLU) and natural language generation (NLG). You can think of one as being language input and the other as language output. In more technical terms, NLU converts unstructured human language data to structured data that a computer can understand while NLG converts structured data to unstructured data in the form of human language. Artificial intelligence is essential to both NLU and NLG. Natural language processing sits at the heart of voice interfaces, language translation services, email sentiment analysis, and many other applications that involve human language.

Natural Language Understanding (NLU)

Computers that understand human language perform many useful business tasks. Sentiment detection assesses text to determine if it conveys positive or negative emotion, for example, to highlight positive online product reviews or surface negative customer emails that require a swift response. NLU is also used to detect profanity, hate speech, threats, abuse, and other conversation that may be deemed inappropriate.

Natural language understanding is used to analyze documents and provide decision support. Scriptbook, a startup from Antwerp, Belgium, reviews movie screenplays to predict their likely box office failure or success. The software helps studios to make greenlight decisions on scripts. Scriptbook analyzed the scripts of 62 movies released in 2015 and 2016. Thirty of these movies were box office successes; 32 were failures and lost money. Scriptbook's AI correctly predicted all 30 of the box office hits and correctly called 22 of the movies that were duds. With 52 correct calls made on 62 movies, the AI scored far better than the Hollywood moguls had. Scriptbook also uses NLU to predict a film's likely MPAA rating, the likeability of characters, and the countries where a movie will find most success, all based on its script.

LawGeex, an Israeli company, uses natural language processing to automate the review of legal contracts and nondisclosure agreements. LawGeex challenged 20 U.S.-trained lawyers to identify legal issues in five real-life nondisclosure agreements (NDAs), faster than their AI. The test was overseen by an independent lawyer and performed with input from legal experts and law professors. The lawyers took an average of 92 minutes to review all five NDAs and achieved an average accuracy rate of 85%. The LawGeex AI scored an accuracy of 94%, equal to the best lawyer's score, and completed the entire task in just 26 seconds. Lawyers that I've told about this AI are generally delighted. Reviewing NDAs is not a favorite part of their work and they are excited to offload routine tasks and focus more time on higher value, higher revenue work.

Natural language understanding speeds data entry. AIs identify email addresses, physical addresses, dates of birth, and phone numbers from nonstandard forms, automatically. This technology, sometimes combined with handwriting recognition (thanks again, AI!), makes short work of data entry.

Voice recognition combines speech-to-text capabilities with NLU. This technology automatically creates subtitles for videos and presentations. Microsoft now includes this capability with some versions of its PowerPoint application.

Natural Language Generation (NLG)

Computers with the ability to write or speak in natural human language are a huge breakthrough. AIs generate language either from source data or from source text. For example, an auto-generated weather report is created from weather forecast data, while a translation from one language to another is performed based on source text.

Natural language generation (NLG) has many valuable business applications. Language translation is an obvious one. Another is the automatic creation of summaries and abstracts. These might be summaries of financial reports, legal documents, operations reports, performance reviews, news articles, or medical records. NLG is combined with image recognition to automatically caption or describe images. This is a valuable function for people with visual impairment and also improves the quality of image searches.

In March 2014, the *Los Angeles Times* published a short story on an earthquake in Beverly Hills, California. The article described the location, time, and strength of the earthquake (4.4 on the Richter scale, if you're interested) and posted it to the *L.A. Times* website within three minutes of the earthquake. The article was written by a simple piece of software that sourced seismic data from the U.S. Geological Survey. This simple automation populated data into a prewritten template but demonstrates the power of automation. In a world of 24-hour news cycles and shrinking ad revenue, NLG frees human reporters to focus on higher-value stories and investigative journalism. More advanced automation now writes weather and traffic reports, summarizes business results, and covers sports events. Wordsmith, an automated reporting platform used by the Associated Press (AP), uses NLG to generate stories about minor league baseball games, college basketball, and quarterly corporate earnings reports. The AP claims that Wordsmith produces more than 4,400 corporate recaps each quarter, more than 15 times the number it could previously handle using a human writing staff. Wordsmith offers a glimpse of the more sophisticated NLG capabilities coming in the near future.

Simplish uses AI to convert complex text, with a vocabulary of more than 100,000 words, into simpler text with a vocabulary of less than 2,000 words. NLG will make complex language accessible to broader audiences with lower levels of education, for example, an academic text translated for lay people or children. Future NLP applications might provide comprehensive copyediting services or disrupt the businesses of companies like CliffsNotes.

Quillionz uses AI to automatically generate questions, quizzes, and assessments from a body of text. This provides an amazing aid for teachers, who can guide the AI to focus on particular keyword topics and automatically create multiple-choice questions.

There is a dark side to NLG technology. If we think that online fake news is a problem now, just wait until next-generation NLG is unleashed by the Russian troll farms. A human troll farm might create a hundred fake "news" articles in a day; a weaponized AI could pump out a million pieces of disinformation in a single hour. OpenAI claims to have created NLG software that writes such high-quality text that they have chosen to withhold its release, based on such concerns.

A 2015 survey of 352 leading AI experts by the University of Oxford predicted that AI will translate languages better than human translators by 2024, will write high-school-level essays by 2026, but won't write a best-selling novel until 2049. It's a giant leap from teenage essays to Tolkein, but the direction is clear. While we are a long way from the first Pulitzer Prize–winning novel written by AI, sophisticated NLG technology will soon create complex documents that rival human output.

Voice Agents

Voice agents like Apple Siri, Microsoft Cortana, Amazon Alexa, Samsung Bixby, and Google Assistant improve significantly every year. Some add new capabilities almost every week. Google claims their voice assistant is now available on more than a billion devices. These "conversational computing" or "digital dialogue" platforms will reshape the way we work and become an increasingly important part of our lives. Paradoxically, voice agents may become both our managers, and our subordinates, guiding our actions and performing our errands.

Voice interfaces are an important component of hands-free computing and a natural complement to augmented reality. Hands-free technology offers the prospect of "computing for the rest of us" and voice interfaces are valuable for people with impaired vision, for use in sterile clinical environments where physical interfaces aren't appropriate, and for the 80% of people who either work with their hands or in highly mobile environments.

Artificial intelligence—in the form of speech-to-text, NLU, NLG, and speech synthesis—underpins the operation of voice platforms. Continued advances in AI will make conversational computing sound more human. Future voice agents will engage in complex back-and-forth conversations, speak realistically, use human idioms, and even add fake breathing sounds and natural hesitations and pauses to make them sound more human. Google's Duplex technology and Microsoft Cortana have already made great strides and we should expect *major* breakthroughs in this area in the coming years.

As voice agents become more sophisticated, they will become everpresent in our lives and help us navigate our days. We will use them to make reservations, manage our calendars, run errands, place orders, troubleshoot problems, give advice, and even provide emotional support. Ultimately, a transactional conversation with a digital voice agent will become indistinguishable from one held with a human. This prospect has profound implications for those that work in customer service.

Exploration and Discovery

The New York Police Department (NYPD) uses PATTERNIZR, an AI-based discovery tool, to spot crime patterns. With more than 68,000 robberies, larcenies, and burglaries occurring in New York in 2018 alone, the NYPD will take all the help they can get. The NYPD is split into 77 separate precincts. PATTERNIZR, rolled out in December 2016 but only revealed to the public in early 2019, looks for crime patterns that span precincts. PATTERNIZR frees up human analysts to focus on more complex analysis tasks. Just like a human analyst, PATTERNIZR compares factors including method of entry, the type of items stolen, the distance between crimes, and so on. To eliminate racial bias, the system is not given the race of suspects. PATTERNIZR has already proven useful. For example, the AI found a link between crimes that spanned precincts that had not previously been flagged as connected. In two cases, a man used the threat of a syringe to steal a drill. The AI identified two other instances where a syringe was used as a threat in robberies. The NYPD used the information to locate the suspect and arrest him. He pleaded guilty to larceny and assault.

AI's predictive capabilities are a powerful tool for researchers. Material scientists use AI to predict the structures of materials that may have a desired set of physical properties. New alloys and compounds may be discovered as a result. AI-guided research could lead to the discovery and synthesis of new wonder materials such as room-temperature superconductors and high-efficiency battery electrolytes that would transform the energy sector and help to address the climate challenge. As we review in Chapter 10, pharmaceutical companies use a similar approach to help them discover new drugs. Predictive AI may help us discover therapeutic drugs that transform human health. How might AI boost your company's research efforts?

Better-Informed Decision-Making

Business analytics refine data to offer all manner of insights. Some use statistical techniques, some use heuristics, and many now leverage the power of AI to find associations in data, extract insights, and make recommendations. Intelligent decision support systems use such analytics to support data-driven decision-making. Credit agencies like Experian and credit card companies including American Express use machine learning to boost the speed and accuracy of credit approvals by crunching terabytes of consumer data. Some Customer Relationship Management (CRM) platforms use AI to intelligently prioritize leads. AI is used to guide recruitment decisions, spending decisions, investment decisions, purchase decisions, marketing decisions, design decisions, engineering decisions, and much more.

Mortgage companies use AI to assess loan risk and guide underwriting decisions. Underwriters make the near-Shakespearean decision of "to loan, or not to loan" with risk models built on historical data. An underwriter assesses risk using 10 to 15 data points about a prospective borrower: salary, credit score, debt-to-earnings ratio, and so on. Based on this assessment, the underwriter either gives the thumbs up or thumbs down. Limited data doesn't provide a full picture of a person's ability to repay a loan. There's more to a person than 10 to 15 data points. Underwriters use this narrow data set to limit complexity and manage their workload. An underwriting AI considers hundreds of data points about a person and finds complex associations that create a more nuanced picture of a prospective borrower. Zest Finance and Underwriter.ai claim their underwriting AIs find low-risk loan candidates who don't qualify with a traditional underwriting approach. The upside for mortgage companies: they sell more loans without increasing their risk.

Predicting the Future

AI offers us a crystal ball. When AI is applied to historical data, it finds patterns and complex associations that allow it to make high-quality predictions about what might happen next. AIs are used to predict disease outbreaks, assess actuarial risk, and predict future demand on the electric grid. Atidot, Quantemplate, and Analyze Re use AI to predict insurance risk.

Law enforcement uses AI to predict crime. PredPol is a collaboration between the Los Angeles Police Department (LAPD) and the University of California at Los Angeles (UCLA). PredPol predicts where and when serious crimes are most likely to happen. PredPol scientists claim the system has double the accuracy of human analysts. Importantly, the system only predicts the locations of future crimes, not the identities of people predicted to commit those crimes. We are still a long way from the precrime concept described in Philip K. Dick's *Minority Report*.

Most businesses need to make forecasts or predictions, and AI is just starting to scratch the surface in this space. AIs will power all manner of business planning systems: demand forecasts, risk analysis, design trends, and more.

Seeing the World through a New Lens with Super Sensors

Sensors, turbocharged by AI to create "super sensors," will lift the veil from the world, extend our existing five senses, and allow us to perceive the world more fully. Like the microscope before it, AI gives us a new lens to view the world through; a lens to experience the world in all its complexity and beauty. Super sensors will oversee business operations, monitor the operation of equipment, create new products, and provide us a more holistic view of people.

An exciting early example of super-sensing capabilities comes from the work of Dr. Dina Katabi, a professor and research lead at MIT's Computer Science and Artificial Intelligence Lab (CSAIL). Katabi's team has created a super sensor. What adds to the delight of this particular story is that it begins with *Star Wars* and ends with *Star Trek*.

As a child, Katabi was fascinated by the notion of "The Force" in the *Star Wars* movies. Her fascination persisted into adulthood. In *Star Wars*, Obi Wan Kenobi describes a mystical force that "surrounds us, penetrates us, and binds the galaxy together." As she considered the fictional notion of The Force, Katabi realized that a real force surrounds us all—electromagnetic energy. If you flap your arms up and down, you literally create a disturbance in that force. Katabi wondered if sensing electromagnetic energy would let her see the world in a new way.

Katabi's research team built a simple wall-mounted sensor and fitted it inside a room. The sensor emits and receives radio frequency (RF) signals, much like a Wi-Fi hotspot. RF signals tend to pass through walls but bounce back from people. The sensor picks up reflected RF signals and feeds data into a neural network that makes sense of the reflected signal data.

To train the AI, Dr. Katabi's team captured video of people moving around inside the room. The AI was fed the video and RF sensor data as parallel inputs. The AI found complex associations between the RF sensor data and the video images and eventually correlated the two. With this insight, the AI can determine what is happening inside the room from just the RF sensor data and can register when a person is standing, sitting, or lying down. Since RF signals pass through most walls, the

AI can "see" through them and also "see" in the dark. Amazing. Katabi plans to use the sensor to monitor elderly patients under care. The sensor instantly detects when patients suffer a fall and calls for help. Incredibly, the sensor also detects vital signs—a patient's breathing and heart rate—and their sleep state—awake, light sleep, deep sleep, and REM sleep. If you understand how well a person sleeps, you can tell a lot about their health. Disturbances in deep sleep can indicate depression or anxiety. Disturbances to REM sleep can indicate early-onset Alzheimer's. Alzheimer's is also indicated by repetitive patterns of movement or motion, which the sensor also detects. Changes in a person's gait can indicate the development of Parkinson's disease.

By applying AI to a low-cost, wall-mounted RF sensor, we can monitor vital signs, sleep states, falls, and provide clinical insight on the development of conditions that include Alzheimer's, COPD, Parkinson's, and depression. All without a single wire being attached to the patient. The system operates without using a camera, limiting privacy concerns. Patients are monitored with their full consent, comfortable in the knowledge that no video images are ever being gathered. The sensor enables clinicians to "see" a wealth of information, all gathered wirelessly. We started this story with *Star Wars* and ended up with the sick bay beds from *Star Trek*.

Super-sensing turbocharges simple sensors with AI to reveal more about our world. Google's "Project Soli" technology uses short-range radar signals and machine learning to detect fine-grain finger gestures. This approach will transform sliders, buttons, and twistable crowns on mobile and wearable devices into virtual controls. More super sensors are detailed in Chapter 10 on the future of healthcare. What other super sensors will we create? What super sensors will your business create?

Solving Complex Problems by Learning from Experience

Some challenges—optimizing a system with many variables or programming a robot to walk on two legs—are too difficult, too complicated, or too laborious to tackle with traditional computers. AI solves some of these tricky problems using a technique called reinforcement learning.

Reinforcement learning is a branch of machine learning that uses a system of digital rewards and punishments as part of its training process. Reinforcement learning systems solve previously intractable problems through an iterative process of experimentation. The AI tries a range of strategies and learns the best way to approach a problem through an intelligent form of trial and error. It's like harnessing digital evolution.

Reinforcement learning teaches computers to perform complex optimizations, control complex equipment, and to play games really, really well. In 2018, researchers trained an AI to play the classic Sega console game, *Sonic the Hedgehog*. *Sonic* has two simple controls: run and jump. An AI was trained with the video game display as input and the game controls as the output. In reinforcement learning, AIs have an additional input known as a reward function. As the AI trains it tries to optimize the reward function. Game points increase the reward, and the reward decreases substantially if Sonic loses a life. At first, the AI plays terribly. Over time, the AI optimizes its model to run and jump at just the right moment, score maximum points, and keep the adorable blue hedgehog alive. The AI does not learn based on simple timing; it learns from what is happening on the screen, so it can succeed on game levels it has not seen before.

The most regularly cited example of reinforcement learning is Deep-Mind's AlphaGo system. DeepMind, a subsidiary of Alphabet, built AlphaGo to play the ancient Chinese game of Go. Winning strategies for Go are opaque; even grand masters can't always describe why they choose some of the moves they make—they say the move just "feels right." There are more possible configurations for pieces on a Go game board than there are atoms in the universe. To build a machine that understands the nuances and subtle strategies of this complex game is a monumental challenge.

AlphaGo was not taught game strategies. It developed its own strategies through observation of many human versus human games. In March 2016, AlphaGo played 18-times world champion Lee Sedol, the best (human) Go player in the world. AlphaGo beat the legendary player, four games to one. To win, AlphaGo deployed several new strategies that went against hundreds of years of received wisdom among expert players. By observing AlphaGo's approach, human players have improved their play. This story offers an important lesson. Rather than consider AI a threat to our unique humanity and our value within the workplace, we might instead think of AI as a sophisticated partner, one that boosts our skills and that ultimately elevates our humanity.

In 2017, DeepMind's next machine, named AlphaGo Zero, became a master Go player by playing millions of games against itself inside a simulation. It developed game strategies through practice rather than by observing human play. AlphaGo Zero now thrashes the original Alpha-Go machine and is unassailable by all human grand masters.

Reinforcement learning isn't just used to play games. Researchers at Warsaw University used reinforcement learning to train bipedal robots to walk more efficiently. The AI that controls the robots varies the combinations of movements made by the robot's motors and experiments with different walking strategies. The robot's AI gains a small electronic reward for strategies that speed the overall efficiency and pace of the walk. With this approach, roboticists achieved more efficient and natural-looking walking motions for their robots. One robot learned to walk almost twice as fast as it could using the best initial walking strategy programmed by its human creator.

AI's ability to learn from experience is used to solve many business problems, including complex optimizations. AIs optimize traffic control systems, industrial chemical reactions, advertising bids, industrial automation, supply chain flow, product design, warehouse operations, inventory levels, yields, trading strategies, wind turbine controls, medication doses, smart grids, and commercial HVAC systems. Reinforcement learning also teaches AIs to drive. Like humans, AIs learn to drive by practicing. They drive real cars in real-world conditions but also drive millions of miles inside realistic software simulations. In part, *Tesla* AIs learn to drive from sensor data gathered while owners are driving.

Creating and Co-Creating Content

Computers now have the capacity for imagination. Artificial intelligence can compose music, paint pictures, and even write poetry. AI also co-creates content with humans: a partnership of digital intelligence with artists, designers, and engineers.

Most AIs create content using a relatively new AI approach known as Generative Adversarial Networks (GANs). The first GAN was built in 2014 by Ian Goodfellow, then a researcher at the Université de Montréal and now part of the Google Brain project. GANs link two AIs together in a sophisticated version of reinforcement learning where each AI trains the other. The AIs operate in an adversarial context: Each tries to catch the other out. Here's how it works. One AI is trained to create content and the other AI is trained to spot fake/generated content. Think of these AIs as a forger and an art detective. The detective, known as the discriminator AI, is initially trained with many real-world examples of "good" data (real content). The forger, known as a generator AI, tries to fool the discriminator by creating high-quality, realistic content. At first, the content created by the generator AI is terrible and the discriminator easily spots it as "fake." But the generator steadily improves until eventually the discriminator finds it harder to spot generated content. Over time, each AI gets better at its assigned task. While the relationship between the AIs is adversarial, the net result is that the discriminator acts as a coach to the generator AI, and the generator acts as a coach for the discriminator. Eventually, the generator AI creates incredible, high-quality content: images, videos, speech, music, prose, legal contracts, and engineering designs. GANs have even been used to automate the design of crowns for teeth.

GANs have incredible potential. They will fundamentally change the way we work. Within the next decade, many of you reading this book may partner with GAN-based AIs to co-create content and collaborate on business tasks.

While there are some worrying downsides to generative AI—most notably deepfakes—many applications offer incredible potential. The most powerful example of machines with an imagination today is generative design, a field pioneered by engineering design company Autodesk. Generative design is used extensively in engineering and architectural design. We discuss these applications further in Chapters 14 and 15. Generative design uses the imagination and content creation capabilities of GANs to generate hundreds or thousands of alternative design options from a single original design. Designers specify constraints—size, weight, cost, and so on—and the tool generates options and evaluates each one using simulation tools. The designer simply picks the option that best meets their needs—perhaps the one that's cheapest to make, easiest to manufacture, or has the lightest weight.

Generative AI will help to design lighter-weight aircraft, cars that are more resilient to crashes, and stronger, lighter robots. Generative architecture will improve the structural integrity and design of new buildings.

Researchers at the University of California, Berkeley, working in partnership with Glidewell Dental Lab, use GANs to design dental crowns. The AI uses digital x-rays of a patient's upper and lower jaw to design a crown that perfectly fills the gap in the patient's tooth line, optimizes bite contact, and looks aesthetically pleasing. Researchers claim that AI-generated crowns outperform those designed by humans. The approach should speed crown production, reduce costs, and free dentists to spend more time generating revenue by working in patients' mouths, rather than designing crowns on a CAD machine in a back office.

Generative AI is an example of a broader category of AI that I refer to as "collaborative AI." Collaborative AIs operate in partnership with humans in a creative process. Humanity's use of tools distinguishes us from most other species. Traditional tools are subordinate—we wield a hammer, drive a car, and program a computer. Collaborative AI changes our relationship with tools. They are no longer subordinate, they now co-create with us. Collaborative AIs aren't just tools, they're partners.

Collaborative AI will co-create visuals for presentations, advertisements, and marketing brochures. Collaborative email software will auto-compose responses. Collaborative management software will co-create plans for complex projects. Many job functions will benefit from collaborative AI in the coming years.

Future Uses of AI

In a fast-moving field, new use categories, beyond the eight listed earlier, are bound to emerge. GANs, a technique that's central to several of these application categories, were invented relatively recently. As research embraces techniques beyond deep learning—cause and effect AI, common sense AI, capsules, and others—artificial intelligence will solve even more business problems than it can today.

AI is a big deal. Every leader should pay close attention. Every organization must understand how AI will shape product development, business operations, customer service, and workforce management.

How AI Works

You don't have to understand how AI works to use it. But such insight can help you to understand the capabilities and limitations of today's technology. While the following description is designed to be accessible to nontechnical types, feel free to skip to the next section if it gets too far into the weeds for you.

Neural Networks, Training, and Models

Neural networks underpin most of today's artificial intelligence. They operate quite differently from traditional digital computers. Traditional computers are glorified adding machines. Neural nets are organized more like the highly interconnected structures found in our brains.

Neural nets are made up of connected "nodes," which act like neurons. Each node holds a numerical value. Unlike binary computers that work with zeros and ones, each node can have a range of values; the range depends on the application. Nodes are arranged into layers. The first layer is known as the input layer and the final layer is known as the output layer. All of the layers in between are known as hidden layers (see Figure 1.1).

Typically, the more layers there are, and the more nodes in each layer, the more capable the neural network. Neural networks with many layers are known as "deep" neural networks. This is where the term *deep learning* comes from.

Every node in the hidden layers has both inputs and outputs. Each node is connected to every node in the previous layer and every node in

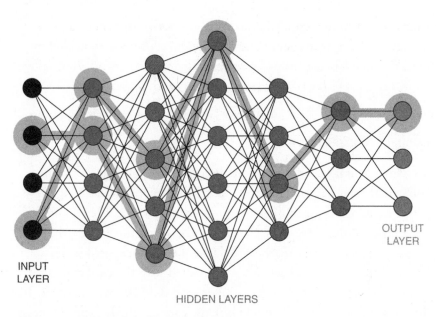

Figure 1.1 A simple neural network.

the next layer. The value of each node is influenced by the values of all
the nodes it is connected to in the previous layer. Here's the tricky bit:
some nodes have a stronger influence on the value of proceeding nodes
than others; their influence is weighted. The value of each node is the
weighted sum of the values of the previous nodes. These weightings are
determined during the training phase and collectively make up what is
known as "the model." The model determines the functionality of the
neural network: different weightings, different functionality. Information
passes across the network from the input layer to the output layer via this
complex web of weighted interconnections.

Neural networks are trained with a process known as backpropaga-
tion, or "backprop" as it's known in the business. The details of how
backprop works is beyond the scope of this book. At a high level,
backprop is a computationally intensive statistical approach that compares the desired output of a neural network with the actual output
and then tweaks the weightings in the network to improve the accuracy of results. When the right result is given, the weightings of all the
pathways through the neural network that lead to the correct result are

strengthened. If the result was incorrect, the pathways that lead to the incorrect result are weakened. Over time, with exposure to more and more data, the model becomes increasingly accurate. The network "learns" the correct complex associations between inputs and outputs.

Example: A Radiology AI

To train a neural network to read radiology charts and look for tumors, you would expose it to many example charts (the input), each tagged with a radiologist's diagnosis—tumor or no tumor (the desired output). The output of the network is a single number, the probability that an image contains a tumor. Each time the neural net is exposed to a new image, the output of the network is compared with the correct result. If an image of a tumor is presented, the result should be close to 100%. If there's no tumor the result should be close to zero. The backprop process is used to tweak the network's model (the weightings of the connections between the nodes), strengthening the weightings of links that lead to the correct result, and weakening those that don't. Once trained with enough data, the neural network will predict the right diagnosis with impressive accuracy. A more complex network might have several outputs. One could be the percentage chance of a tumor, another the probability of an embolism, another the probability of a broken bone, and so on.

If this all seems too difficult to understand, that's okay. The key thing to understand is that neural nets can infer how to perform tasks from examples, *without* the need of a domain expert to supply explicit rules on how to perform that task.

Radiologists train for many years to read x-rays, computer tomography (CT), magnetic resonance imaging (MRI), and positron emission tomography (PET) images. After medical school, radiologists do additional training, often involving a four-year residency. Some do additional specialization training after that. Reading images to look for tumors and other ailments uses all of the radiologist's skill, experience, and training. Yet this task is within the reach of a neural network. Given enough training data, an AI can be built with diagnostic abilities similar to those of a human radiologist, a person with about a decade of intense education behind them. As we train the neural network, we are essentially codifying the collective knowledge, and several decades of professional experience, from hundreds of thousands of radiologists. Their experience and diagnostic insight are captured in the model that's generated.

Some radiologists already use AI-based tools to offer a "second opinion" as they read charts. As the accuracy of these tools surpasses that of human radiologists on routine charts, radiologists will be able to focus their attention on more complex, higher-value, and more patient-centered tasks and procedures. The progress made in radiology portends the future for other branches of medicine. Machine learning will be applied to many other fields of medical diagnosis and pathology in the coming decade.

While training an AI requires serious amounts of computing performance to create a model, using that model requires significantly less performance. The process of using a model is known as inference. Often, training occurs on workstations or in the cloud, while inference occurs on devices. Most future computer chips will include inference engines, silicon accelerators optimized to run AI models with relative ease.

Pattern Recognition

Pattern recognition is a core capability of many AI systems, including the radiology example we just discussed. Pattern recognition has many applications and comes in a range of different flavors. It's not important that you remember all these different approaches. They are listed here only to illustrate some of the fundamental capabilities of machine learning. As you read through them, think about how such a capability might be used to solve business problems in your organization.

- **Classification.** AI can classify data into similar types. For example, the radiology AI classifies images as positive or negative. A similar approach might be used to do visual inspection and quality assurance in a manufacturing plant, or to identify spoiled or underripe fruit at a fruit-packing plant.
- **Clustering.** Marketing professionals use clustering algorithms to partition consumers into market segments that share similar

characteristics—buying habits, affluence level, and needs or desires. Recommendation engines use clustering, too. *Spotify* recommends songs that you might enjoy by analyzing historical listening habits. A clustering algorithm finds the complex relationships between songs and listeners. The clustering algorithm might see that I like songs A, B, C, and D, and that you like songs B, C, D, and E. It may conclude that it's probable you will enjoy song A and I might enjoy song E. Clustering is useful to deliver personalized experiences.

- **Regression analysis** finds patterns that describe relationships between pieces of data. For example, regression analysis might observe that if Event A happens, most of the time Event B follows. More complex relationships are found, too, such as "if Datapoint A is below a certain threshold, and Event B and Event C are not happening, then Event D is 46% more likely to occur." This approach is used to make predictions about the future with predictive analytics tools. Regression analysis is used by Walmart to predict how sales of certain food items are influenced by specific weather conditions.

- **Sequence labeling** is a pattern-recognition approach used in speech recognition, handwriting recognition, and gesture recognition. Sequence labeling is used to break sentences down into constituent words and phrases and to label them in a way that captures their context. For example, sequence labeling identifies which words are nouns, verbs, and proper names. Words are best interpreted in the broader context of a sentence. Sequence-labeling algorithms classify words within a sentence, or cursive letters within a handwritten word, by examining the broader context surrounding them.

- **Time-series prediction** is used in weather forecasting, stock market prediction, and to predict disasters. These algorithms analyze a set of historical data points and use that to project which data points might come next in a sequence.

These pattern-matching algorithms use complex mathematics to work their voodoo. You don't need to understand how pattern matching works, or even recall the names of all the various techniques listed above. What you do need to understand is that AI makes it easier for computers to understand the physical world, to make predictions, and to find complex relationships hidden inside data. These tasks are at the root of solving many business problems.

Beyond Deep Learning: The Future of Artificial Intelligence

Most of the AI breakthroughs in the 2010s were built on deep learning technology and neural networks. Dramatic advances in machine vision, natural language processing, prediction, and content generation resulted. And yet, industry luminaries debate whether AI is about to enter a golden age of rapid technological advancement, or rapidly stagnate.

Stagnation or Golden Age?

The argument for stagnation is that deep learning has severe limitations—training needs too many examples and takes too long, and while these AIs pull off some amazing tricks, they have no true understanding of the world. Deep learning is built on algorithms from the mid-1980s and neural network architectures developed in the 1960s. Once we have perfected the implementation of deep learning technology and solved all the problems that we can with it, there are no viable technologies in the pipeline to keep things rolling. The current era of AI deployment will grind to a halt. So goes the stagnation argument.

On the other side of the debate are those who point to promising research that could take AI in new directions and solve a new set of problems.

Capsule Networks

Capsule networks are the brainchild of Geoff Hinton, the creator of backprop and one of the fathers of deep learning. Capsules overcome some of deep learning's shortcomings. The difference between capsule networks and traditional convolutional neural networks is beyond the scope of this book, but capsules capture some level of understanding about the relationship between features in images, which makes image recognition engines more resilient and better at recognizing objects from many different angles.

Common Sense

AIs are trained to understand something about the world. Typical AIs operate within a bubble. They have no understanding of the way the world works. A lack of common sense limits their abilities. A household robot, on a search to find my reading glasses, should know that my desk and nightstand are good places to look first, and not inside the freezer.

Several organizations are trying to build AIs with common sense. They are building vast databases of the commonsense notions humans use to help them make high-quality decisions. For example, oranges are sweet, but lemons are sour. A tiger won't fit in a shoe box. Water is wet. Oil is viscous. If you overfeed a hamster, it will get fat. We often take this context for granted, but to an AI these notions are not obvious.

Researchers at the Allen Institute crowdsource commonsense insight using Amazon's Mechanical Turk platform. They use machine learning and statistical analysis to extract additional insights and understand the spatial, physical, emotional, and other relationships between things. For example, from a commonsense notion that "A girl ate a cookie," the system deduces that a cookie is a type of food and that a girl is bigger than a cookie. Allen Institute researchers estimate they need about a million human-sourced pieces of common sense to train their AIs.

The Cyc project, the world's longest-running AI project, takes a different approach. Since 1984, Doug Lenat and his team have hand coded more than 25 million pieces of commonsense knowledge in machine-usable form. Cyc knows things like "Every tree is a plant" and "Every plant dies eventually." From those pieces of information, it can deduce that every tree will die. Cycorp Company, Cyc's current developers, claims that half of the top 15 companies in the world use Cyc under license. Cyc is used in financial services, healthcare, energy, customer experience, the military, and intelligence.

As they mature, commonsense knowledge systems may help future AIs to answer more complex questions and assist humans in more meaningful ways.

Causal AIs

Causal AIs understand cause and effect, while deep learning systems work by finding correlations inside data. To reason, deep learning AIs find complex associations within data and assess the probabilities of association. Reasoning by association has proven adequate for today's simple AI solutions, but correlation does not imply causation. To create an AI with human-level intelligence, researchers will need far more capable machines. Some AI researchers, most notably Dr. Judea Pearl, believe that the best path forward for AI development is to design AIs that understand cause and effect. This would allow AIs to reason based on an understanding of causation. A deep learning AI associates events (A and B happen together) while a causal AI understands that one event caused the another (A caused B), and not the other way around (B caused A). The sophisticated machines needed to solve big problems like climate change will need to understand all of the causational relationships involved in highly complex systems. Causal AI will rely on the commonsense knowledge mentioned in the previous section to give it the vital context it needs for sound reasoning.

Neuromorphic Computers

Neuromorphic computers are inspired by the way brains work. Today's neural network designs are based on an understanding of neuroscience from the 1960s. Half a century later, we finally have the computing horsepower needed to implement these archaic machine models. The next time you ask Google Assistant or Alexa to play some Beatles music, remember that the foundation of the AI you're using was designed at the time when the Stones and The Beatles were first vying to be top of the charts. Neuromorphic computers, also referred to as cognitive computers, are based on a much more recent understanding of how the brain operates. Nodes are hyperconnected, their connections can change over time (in the same way that the human brain exhibits plasticity), and there is no separation between memory and processing functions.

Major research projects—the Human Brain Project in the European Union and the BRAIN (Brain Research through Advanced Innovative Neurotechnologies) initiative in the United States—seek to advance our understanding of the human brain, mapping and understanding brain function. These efforts, and others like them, push the boundaries of our understanding and offer new frameworks for the design of future neuromorphic computers. New computer chips, inspired by neuromorphic insights, may accelerate AI functions, reduced power consumption for AI tasks, and enable exciting new capabilities.

Whether it's capsule networks, neuromorphic computing, or common sense and causal AI, there are plenty of avenues of research that should fuel future advances in AI in the coming decades.

Narrow, General, and Super Intelligence

All of today's AI is considered to be "narrow" AI. The holy grail of AI research is the development of "general" and "super" AIs. Let's quickly review these three categories.

Artificial Narrow Intelligence (ANI)

Artificial Narrow Intelligence (ANI), also known as weak AI or vertical AI, refers to any AI that solves problems or performs tasks with a level of intelligence equivalent to, or higher than, a human, but only within a narrowly defined domain. Every AI available today, and every AI described in this book, is an example of narrow AI. Narrow AI is only good at the task it was designed for and useless at others. A chess-playing AI can't filter the spam from your email, and your spam filter can't play chess.

Artificial General Intelligence (AGI)

Artificial General Intelligence (AGI), also known as strong AI, describes AIs with the equivalent intelligence of a human being in any area of human expertise that you might imagine. An AGI can perform any intellectual task that a human can. Researchers continue to chip away at the problem of creating an AGI but currently have no clear plan for how such a feat might be achieved. AGIs aren't created by bolting together enough ANIs. It doesn't work that way. Never say never, but AGI, if we achieve it, is likely several decades in the future.

Artificial Super Intelligence (ASI)

Artificial Super Intelligence (ASI) is where things get really exciting, or really scary, depending on your viewpoint. ASI defines an intelligence that surpasses the intellectual ability, knowledge, creativity, wisdom, and social skills of the very best human brains in almost every field. An ASI could be just 1% smarter or a million times smarter than the smartest human. In theory, an ASI machine that we build could design future, more powerful machines that operate in a way we aren't able to comprehend. Once ASI is achieved, rapid, runaway advances could follow. If that idea makes you uncomfortable, you're not alone. Exemplars of the high-tech and scientific world—including Elon Musk, Bill Gates, and Stephen Hawking—have all spoken out on the dangers of artificial super intelligence. It's hard not to think of the movie *Terminator* when you think about the professed dangers of AI becoming self-aware and designing better versions of itself. How engineers develop narrow AIs today may inform the design of super AIs in the future. This is why research and engineering focused on transparent and unbiased AIs is so vital.

Strategies to Get You Started

Artificial intelligence holds huge potential and will drive successive waves of innovation throughout every industrial sector. As your organization starts to build out a comprehensive, multiyear AI strategy, here are a few places to start your thinking.

Make Predictions about Customers, Operations, and Trends

Use AI's predictive capabilities to forecast demand, streamline operations, target marketing efforts, predict trends, and influence the design of future products. Energy companies use AI to forecast demand for electricity. Fashion designers use AI to suggest fall colors for a couple of years from now. Equipment makers use AI to predict when their machines will fail so they can schedule preventative maintenance. What could AI predict for your business?

See More, Understand More, Make Better Decisions

Future super sensors may improve the safety of autonomous vehicles, become "the next CT-scan" in medicine, or give us all a sixth and seventh sense. Super sensors will smooth business operations, revolutionize human interfaces, and transform the products and services of the future.

Every company should lead a strategic discussion around the possibilities super sensors present. Determine how your company can use super sensors to get eyes on your business, gain insight on operations in real time, and use those insights to make high-quality, data-driven business decisions. Inspired by Google Soli technology, consider how you could build super sensors into your products to improve the human–machine interface. How might you see your customers in new ways with super sensors? What other insights might super sensors reveal about your business?

Build a Comprehensive Digital Voice Strategy

Every business should have a digital voice strategy. Voice platforms offer customers a new way to interact with your brand, will complement customer support capabilities, and can be helpful for employees who use their hands to perform their work or don't work in traditional office settings.

First, determine the goals for voice platforms within your organization. Find areas where information delivered via voice interfaces improves worker efficiency or boosts their collaboration. Ask what conversational capabilities your brand should create for existing customers, and how voice might be used to attract new customers. Consider the role of interactive, talking online ads, e.g., "Click to ask me questions about our latest model!" Explore how digital voice agents can reduce support costs and open new sales channels.

Customers always want more choice. When brands give us more choice, they honor our desire to be recognized as individuals. Consumers expect to interact with brands through many channels: face-to-face, phone, web, mobile app, social media, virtual reality, interactive augmented reality objects, chatbots, voice agents, and more. Each brand will offer as many of these choices as makes sense for them. A voice interface is a new front door to your business, and voice agents are ambassadors of your company's brand. You must secure that front door the same way you secure your website. And you need to teach your ambassador to always put your best foot forward.

Businesses will need to train their chatbots to interact with a "tone" that is consistent with their brand voice. Marketing departments will need to define appropriate design parameters: Should the voice agent strike a casual or a formal tone? Calm and efficient, or excited to serve? Serious, or with a sense of humor? Rated G for everyone, or more PG-13? Voice agents for Disney, Harley Davidson, and Moët & Chandon will sound very different from one another.

Decide where to develop your voice agents: in-house, using third-party frameworks, or on existing voice platforms. Google, Amazon, Apple, and other tech giants enable developers to create apps for their voice services. Google calls these apps "actions" while Amazon calls them "skills." The make-versus-buy decision will vary by brand. Most will build a presence on the major tech platforms. For competitive or security reasons, some brands may elect to build a dedicated voice agent that is embedded inside their apps and websites. Banks may prefer their own voice agents for security reasons. Bank of America's Erica virtual assistant is a good example.

The future of voice may become more open. Today's main voice platforms, Google Assistant and Amazon Alexa, resemble AOL and Compuserve, the walled garden online services of old. The rise of the internet, with open standard web pages and browsers, broke down the walls of the online services and opened up the online world to anyone who wanted to participate. Efforts like the Open Voice Network seek to build standards for online voice akin to HTML for webpages and enable brands to build their own voice capabilities. Time will tell if this will fell the initial duopoly of the tech giants.

Understand and Mitigate for Bias

When AIs are trained with data that represents examples of human behavior, they learn unwanted human biases that are reflected in that data.

Amazon receives a small mountain of job applications each week. To triage resumes, Amazon built an experimental AI to surface candidates worthy of an interview. There was only one problem. According to a report by Reuters, it quickly became clear that Amazon's AI was biased against women. The problem with the AI had nothing to do with the way it was coded. The AI reflected historical bias in Amazon's hiring process. The unconscious bias of hiring managers had been codified in the recommendations of the AI, which learned to favor male candidates. Amazon canceled the project before it was ever deployed and reviewed its hiring practices. Sometimes AI holds a mirror up to our own humanity.

We should hold our AIs to even higher standards than we hold ourselves, and should strive to create AIs that don't reflect negative human bias. The state of New Jersey built an AI as part of their plan to do away with the bail bonds system. Cash bail has been a part of the U.S. court system for centuries but is criticized for penalizing poorer defendants. According to a 2013 study by the Drug Policy Alliance of New Jersey, 75% of the New Jersey jail population were people awaiting trial. The average wait time for trial was 314 days. Almost 40% of the people awaiting trial were there because they couldn't afford $2,500 or less in bail. Under New Jersey law, everyone must be given bail, no matter the crime, so rich people always avoided jail and bail bondsmen made good money. In January 2017, the state of New Jersey replaced their bail system with an AI that created a public safety assessment (PSA) for each defendant. The PSA was used as a guide by judges. The PSA predicts the chance defendants will commit crime while awaiting trial and whether they will appear for their court date. The new system reduced the number of people in New Jersey jails awaiting trial by 30%. The AI was trained with information about 1.5 million previous defendants in 300 jurisdictions. Race and gender information was deliberately removed from the training data. Developers also removed all information on the name, education level, employment, income, and home address of defendants. Any of these data can be a proxy for race and gender and thus might disadvantage some demographic groups. The way we train our AIs matters. We should expect our AIs to operate ethically, fairly, and without bias. Leaders must ensure that their teams work hard to strip bias from all the AIs they build.

Gather Data Today to Feed Your AIs of the Future

AIs have a voracious appetite for data. Build data pipelines to source the data today that you will need to train the AIs of the future. Your AI strategy informs your data strategy. Your data strategy informs your sensor strategy, your partnership strategy, your hiring strategy, and your IT strategy. Figure out what data you will need and where you will get it from. Think of this as another strategic "make versus buy" decision.

Data storage is relatively cheap. You never know what operational, customer, market, and other insights tomorrow's AI might find hidden inside today's data. It goes without saying that every business should adhere to all relevant data privacy and data retention laws. Wherever possible, businesses should gather and archive as much data as possible, particularly data that comes from machine operations, sensors, and market research. Today's data is tomorrow's AI fuel.

Develop New Products and Services

Use AI to spark innovation across your entire product line. Enhance and simplify human interfaces using voice and super sensors. Create new value and build products that intelligently manage and maintain themselves. Use generative design to accelerate research, push the boundaries of product design, and speed service delivery. Marry human talent with collaborative AIs to build new service offerings at new price points.

Final Thoughts

At the beginning of the twentieth century, every business had to grapple with electrification. In the late twentieth century, every business had to understand and embrace digital technology. To remain competitive, every business must now build a comprehensive strategy that embraces artificial intelligence in every aspect of their operations. No exceptions. No delay.

2 Sensors and the Internet of Things (IoT)

The Internet of Things (IoT) is by no means a new concept. The term *Internet of Things* was first coined in 1999 by Kevin Ashton, a UK tech entrepreneur, and the basic concept was first demonstrated in the early 1980s. The broad idea of IoT has also been peddled under a variety of names: ubiquitous computing, machine-to-machine (M2M), the Internet of Everything, ambient intelligence, and a few more besides.

While IoT has been around for a while, the 2020s will be the decade of widespread IoT adoption. Spending on IoT technology in the next decade will dwarf all previous deployments. IoT will reshape every industry on the planet. It will streamline business processes, create new value, improve customer service, make infrastructure more responsive, reduce maintenance costs, shift business models, and speed process automation.

IoT is set to transform almost every business, every city, and every home in the developed world. Ultimately, it will transform the lives of everyone on the planet. All of the main ingredients needed to make the Internet of Things viable are now in place: low-cost sensors, cheap computing, widely available connectivity, cloud storage, low-cost compact batteries, energy harvesting technology, and standards to connect all the pieces together.

Cheap, Tiny Computers and 100 Trillion Sensors Make Everything Smart and Connected

The idea behind the Internet of Things is that everything—objects, infrastructure, machinery, appliances, devices, perhaps ultimately our bodies—will be infused with sensors and connected to digital intelligence. Connected cameras, connected cars, smart thermostats, industrial equipment, smart traffic signals, wearables, connected jet engines, and connected toothbrushes are all examples of the Internet of Things.

The Internet of Things builds a bridge between the physical and the digital worlds. Information flows back and forth across that bridge, from atom to bits, and from bits to atoms. Sensors allow the digital world to understand what is happening in the physical world and actuators enable the digital world to act within the physical world. For example, a moisture sensor allows an algorithm to detect when the soil is dry, and a connected sprinkler (an actuator) enables the algorithm to turn on the water. These connections between the physical and the digital worlds enable us to create smart, interactive objects, to build responsive infrastructure that optimizes the use of precious resources, and to augment and semi-automate business operations.

Cheap, Tiny Computers Transform the Economics of Connecting Everything

Decades of massive capital investment by semiconductor companies has paved the way for the production of tiny, cheap silicon chips that will populate the Internet of Things. Today, you can buy a computer for five dollars. The Raspberry Pi Zero has similar computing performance to a laptop from the mid-1990s that cost thousands of dollars. In 2018, IBM showed experimental chips they claim have the equivalent compute performance of Intel 486 microprocessors that powered $3,000 PCs in the late 1980s and early 1990s. These tiny slivers of silicon are smaller than a grain of salt, and IBM claims they will cost less than 10 cents to make in volume production.

Connected computing intelligence is now a cheap ingredient that we can stir into the recipe for every product and every piece of infrastructure. Intelligence and connectivity can be integrated at near-zero marginal cost.

100 Trillion Sensors Connect the Digital and Physical Worlds

Billions of sensors are sold inside smartphones each year. The average smartphone bristles with a multitude of sensors: accelerometers and a gyroscope to track motion, GPS to track location, a proximity sensor, a microphone, a magnetometer (compass), and two or more cameras. Many smartphones also include air pressure sensors, temperature and humidity sensors, heart rate sensors, gesture sensors, fingerprint sensors, facial recognition sensors, and more. The volume economics of the smartphone sector have driven down the prices of all these sensors.

Trillions of cheap, tiny sensors will be deployed in the coming decade. Steve Whalley is the former chief strategy officer of, and now a strategic advisor to, the SEMI-MEMS and Sensors Industry Group, an industry body that advises companies on the future of sensors. He is also an old friend. When I asked Steve about his expectations for future sensor demand, he told me, "Sensors will experience rapid growth in the coming decade as they provide the data that feeds the AIs that provide real insights and value in products. The deployment of 5G networks to enable greater bandwidth, speed, and lower latencies for new products will unleash an explosion of traditional and new sensors in the next five years and usher in the era of 'Smart Everything.'"

Enterprise software company SAP estimates that by 2030 the world will be filled with 100 trillion sensors. That's more than 12,000 sensors for each person on earth.

Sensors enable us to make the world "programmable." By bridging the digital and the physical, they allow us to write programs that can respond when things happen in the physical world; programs that manage precious resources and allow the world to operate more smoothly and efficiently. By sensing human activity, sensors enable us to make the world more responsive to human needs and wants.

What Can You Do with It?

Cheap, abundant computing and sensors will be used to build smart, connected products and responsive infrastructure. Wearable technology will give people superpowers. Analytics, fed by data from trillions of sensors, will improve business decision-making and boost operational efficiency. Internet of Things technology will lead to an explosion of product and business model innovation.

Get Eyes on Your Business with a Suite of Sensors

Sensors are an essential component of any future business innovation strategy. You can't manage what you don't measure. Sensors allow us to take action, in near real time, when and where we sense it is needed.

In the future, we will use vast networks of sensors to measure, manage, and improve almost every aspect of human activity. Sensors will provide insight into everything from local air pollution levels, to vineyard operations, to the mechanical stress on bridges. By understanding more about the world, we can intervene where needed to fix problems and improve the way things work.

Sensors measure the physical world so we can make decisions that are informed by data. For example, rugby and American football coaches use accelerometers embedded in mouth guards to understand the forces involved in impacts. Real-time data from mouth guards allows coaches and medics to assess the risk of concussion and take appropriate action. Over time, the data enables researchers to improve their understanding of the correlation between impacts and concussion.

Some sensors are dumb. Some are smart. Dumb sensors include accelerometers, temperature sensors, and gyroscopes. These sensors measure some aspect of the physical world and turn it into numbers that a computer can understand. For example, a GPS sensor outputs two numbers that describe longitude and latitude. A microphone outputs a stream of numbers that represent the waveforms of sounds. Smart sensors detect more complex events and information than dumb sensors. A smart sensor uses built-in intelligence to interpret the information it gathers. For example, a smart camera is a combination of a traditional digital camera and image-recognition software that interprets the images it captures. Retailers use smart cameras to measure the foot traffic a store receives, and how it varies over time. Cities use smart cameras to count cars, trucks, and vans in traffic surveys, a boring, laborious effort previously performed by people. Intel has demonstrated a smart camera that uses artificial intelligence to spot abandoned luggage at train stations. It recognizes and tracks both people and luggage and establishes relationships between them. If a person walks away from their luggage for more than a few seconds, the smart camera triggers a security alert. Smart microphones, deployed in a forest, can listen for the signature sound of a chainsaw and text alerts (and GPS coordinates) to a forest ranger looking for illegal logging activity.

Build Service Portals: Smart Objects Create New Revenue Streams

In the 2020s, many of the objects in our lives will become far more intelligent than they are today. Smart, connected objects will make economic sense and provide important benefits to both consumers and manufacturers.

When we make an object smart and connected, it becomes a "service portal," a device through which digital value and services can flow. When you embed intelligence inside an object, it evolves from being a simple "dumb" product and gains the potential to become a service offering. New business models can be built around these smart, connected objects.

A simple illustration of this concept is the notion of a smart, connected teddy bear. Many kids grow up with a teddy bear, or something similar. You probably still remember the name of your favorite soft toy. The primary function of a traditional (dumb) teddy bear is to provide comfort to a child. A smart connected bear could be fitted with a range of sensors: a small camera in its eye, a microphone in its ear, and a speaker in its mouth. Set aside the obvious privacy issues this raises for now. We will address that concern in a moment. Focus first on the new possibilities this creates. If the bear's camera captures the image of a book page, optical character recognition and text-to-voice software will allow the bear to read the words aloud. Our smart teddy bear can now read a book to a child. Bedtime stories are an important time for parents to bond with their children. The smart bear would not replace this vital interaction. But our bear might offer a child something that his or her parents cannot. The bear could use a cloud-based language translation algorithm to translate text into another language. A book written in English could be read aloud to your child in French. Or Mandarin Chinese. Or Arabic. Or whatever language you might choose. Klingon, perhaps? Children can now learn new languages from the bear. The bear becomes a service portal through which language training services are sold.

Back to the privacy question. The bear's camera system could be designed with the camera and character recognition software in a completely closed system. No images would ever be stored, and the sealed camera subsystem would *only* output text, no images. Privacy could be fully protected. Again, though, this is offered as a thought exercise, not as a product proposal.

Our bear can now teach new languages, skills that will improve the quality of a child's life. A parent is no longer buying a product. At a minimum, they are buying language-translation services through the bear. Ultimately, if their child sticks with it, what the parent is buying is a transformation, a transformation of their child into a linguist. Any economics major will explain that you can charge exponentially more as you travel up the classic hierarchy of raw materials, piece parts, products, services, experiences, and ultimately transformations. The bear illustrates the potential for IoT technology to help businesses make more money by delivering more value and capability to customers.

How much is the smart bear worth? $199? $499? More? Rather than sell the bear to you for $199, a manufacturer might let it go for the low, low price of $49. The catch: you have to sign up for the basic English-language reading service at $3.99 per month. For languages services, you can choose the European language pack that includes French, German, Spanish, and Italian for another $4.99 per month. Chinese, Japanese, and Arabic might be available at $1.99 each per month. Klingon could be thrown in for free if you buy any two language packs. You get the idea. Smart objects create the potential for new pricing models.

Our smart bear could offer a range of other services beyond reading books. It could tell a child the weather forecast, teach them simple mathematics, or answer simple questions about the world. It could track a child's speech and reading development over time. A smart, connected object can be a portal to multiple services.

Think about which new services, experiences, or transformations you could sell to your customers through service portals of your own. Think about which new customers you might reach with such devices.

A service portal initially built to solve one problem can later be provisioned with a wide range of additional services that monetize the initial investment. It's important to establish an early beachhead position for smart objects, perhaps by offering heavily discounted initial hardware. Early winners can monetize their investment by selling a suite of services and charging access fees to others. For example, if toy company Fisher Price built a popular book-reading bear, they could sell access to the bear to Johnson & Johnson. A parent might be able to order a new box of diapers by talking to the bear, and Fisher Price might take a cut of that sale. The smart bear might gain an entire app store. Apple charges 30% for all the apps that go through its app store; forward-looking manufacturers may be able to create similar money-making machines with service portals of their own.

Selling access to your customers can be a dicey proposition. It raises the critical issues of trust and privacy, a topic that's especially sensitive when you're talking about children. In part, I picked the example of the smart bear as a way to highlight the issue. Any business that develops smart objects must guard their customers' privacy and ensure that new services are offered on an "opt-in" basis. Customers should always remain in control. If you provide enough value, are clear on the benefits you're offering, and are 100% transparent on the data you're asking customers to share in return for value, customers will generally sign up. Fall short on any of these and you're asking for trouble.

Our smart bear concept is not far-fetched. Connected toy company, Cognitoys, has already built a successful service portal. The Cognitoys Dinosaur is an educational toy designed for kids aged between five and nine years old. There's no screen and no camera. Just an eight-inch-tall plastic dinosaur called Dino with a push-button belly. Dino tells stories, has simple conversations, cracks age-appropriate jokes, teaches mathematics, plays games, and even remembers your child's favorite color. If Dino senses that a child is scared or sad, it will encourage them to talk to an adult and attempt to cheer them up with a joke. It's an impressive, but relatively simple piece of equipment. If you were to take a hammer to Dino and sift through his shattered debris, you'd find a button, a microphone, a speaker, and a fairly basic computer with integrated Wi-Fi connectivity. These components are encased in a piece of green dinosaur-shaped plastic. The hardware is simple and relatively inexpensive; the bill of materials might be no more than 10 dollars. The magic of Dino is not physical. All the clever conversational software resides on IBM's Watson cognitive computing service, built in the cloud. Cognitoys' investment is highly scalable. Digital value scales at near-zero marginal cost. If the majority of the value you deliver is digital, marginal cost is low and high volume quickly leads to high margins as development costs are recouped. Dino's digital component could scale to many other toys: a talking fire engine, a talking unicorn, or a talking backpack.

New Business Models

Smart, connected objects transform business models. Let's review real-world examples from the healthcare and insurance industries.

Beam Dental created a smart, connected toothbrush that logs how often and how effectively you brush your teeth. It's like a Fitbit for your mouth. What might sound like a novelty item actually has the potential to be a major disruptor in dental insurance.

People with good dental health need fewer expensive dental interventions like fillings, root canals, and all the other painful stuff that fills our nightmares. Because Beam Dental can remotely monitor each patient's brushing habits and see that they brush their teeth properly morning and night, they know they are a lower risk. That reduced risk allows Beam Dental to offer dental insurance premiums that they claim are 10–25% lower than their competition. That's a breakthrough. Beam Dental doesn't sell the smart toothbrush as a standalone item. Importantly, it's offered as part of a full dental health service that includes as much toothpaste and floss as you need and personalized oral health tips delivered through a companion app. Beam Dental has built their business model around reducing their risk by increasing their customer's use of preventative dental care measures. This is a revolution in thinking for the dental industry. Beam Dental customers are buying an entire dental wellness system that includes the smart toothbrush, dental hygiene supplies, remote monitoring, insurance, and dental health services. How can you repackage your offerings in new ways?

Semioticons, a research consortium, is developing a home health diagnostic product named the Wize Mirror with funding from the European Union Commissions on ICT for health. This high-tech mirror bristles with sensors—including 3-D scanners, multispectral cameras, and gas sensors—to measure the general health of its users. The smart mirror monitors facial expressions to look for signs of stress, anxiety, or depression. 3-D scanners measure the shape of a person's face and track it over time, a good proxy for weight loss or gain. The mirror reviews complexions, looking for pale, jaundiced, or flushed faces. Multispectral cameras measure heart rate and hemoglobin levels in the blood. A gas analyzer measures the breath to monitor blood sugar levels, drinking, and smoking. Each health check takes about a minute. Results are displayed on the mirror, which also acts as a screen. Ultimately, the mirror will provide health and lifestyle advice based on its observations.

Insurance companies use sensors to measure rather than model risk. Typically, auto insurance premiums reflect the risk each customer presents based on their driving record, address, gender, age, occupation, and car model. From these data points, algorithms model the statistical chance of a claim, and premiums are set accordingly. Progressive's Snapshot product is a small wireless device that plugs into a standard connector in your car, usually found underneath the dashboard near the steering column. The connector shares real-time data about your steering, acceleration, and braking. Snapshot, which is about half the size of a packet of cigarettes, monitors your driving habits and measures your risk as a driver, rather than modeling it based on historical statistical data. Progressive rewards careful drivers with lower premiums and claims that premiums for customers using Snapshot are up to 30% cheaper.

American Family, another U.S.-based insurance company, formed an alliance with Alphabet's Nest division to better manage their home insurance risk. American Family provides a Nest Protect smoke detector to their home insurance customers. These smoke detectors can be monitored remotely. Customers that regularly replace back-up batteries in their smoke detector and maintain the smoke monitoring service are rewarded with lower premiums. American Family knows the detectors are in good working order, and thus the risk of undetected fire is lower.

Service portals, in the form of smart objects, will create a whole new set of business models and will birth millions of exciting new services. As the price of computing and connectivity continues to drop, expect many smart, connected objects to inhabit our lives: connected washing machines, pill bottles, pillows, shoes, rings, cars, exercise equipment, wine bottles, staplers, dog collars, collection boxes, parking meters, garbage cans, and so on.

Every business should consider their service portal strategy. Portals can deliver services to customers, employees, and business partners. Market leaders will build their own portals, while followers will strike deals to deliver services through the portals of others. What will your service portal strategy be? Just because your business hasn't built such devices in the past is no good reason for not building them in the future.

Consider a wide spectrum of possible smart objects. On one end of the spectrum are objects that are 100% physical and that have no digital footprint: "dumb" objects. At the other extreme of the spectrum are objects where the value being delivered is almost 100% digital. They have little or no physical form, for example, a QR code printed on a newspaper page that links you to an app, a web page, or some other kind of digital value. Most smart objects exist somewhere in the middle two-thirds of the spectrum, some more focused toward physical value and others more focused on digital. The Cognitoys Dinosaur is closer to the digital end of the spectrum since its physical characteristics are mostly unrelated to the value delivered through it. The dinosaur could perform its function just as well in the form of a fluffy blue cube, a mirror, or any form appealing to a child. Smart objects closer to the physical end of the spectrum have digital value that is tightly connected to their physical function and form. For example, high-end cars now include smart headlights that use sensors and digital intelligence to direct their light beams around oncoming traffic. Drivers can keep their high beams on at all times without dazzling other drivers. The digital value of these smart headlights is tightly coupled with their physical form.

My friend Dr. David Rose works at MIT's Media Lab. David's team created several objects that illustrate this idea of digital value being deeply embedded into an object's physical form and function. He calls these objects "enchanted objects." A connected umbrella has a handle that glows when the local weather forecast calls for rain. A connected billfold wallet links to its owner's bank account. A variable-strength hinge makes the wallet harder and harder to open as the person's bank account dwindles, giving them tangible and immediate feedback on their spending ability. In both of these cases, digital value enhances the physical value provided by the object and is linked to the object's function.

Build Responsive Infrastructure with Control Loops

The Internet of Things allows us to build intelligent infrastructure. Sensors gather data from the physical world; the output from those sensors is interpreted in the digital world, and then action is taken based on that interpretation. This process of "sense, interpret, act" occurs in a never-ending loop, known as a control loop. Decision logic makes sense of the data and determines whether any action should be taken. Actions are taken by algorithms (perhaps an AI), autonomous machines (perhaps a robot), or humans. For example:

- An algorithm triggers the creation of an electronic purchase order.
- A robot is instructed to move an object from one place to another.
- A restaurant waiter receives an instruction on his smartwatch to deliver meals from the kitchen to table 3.

In this way, the digital world is given limited agency over the physical world. It makes decisions based on prewritten rules created by humans.

Let's consider how IoT technology might make a garden sprinkler system more intelligent. Rather than operating on a simple timer, our sprinkler system uses a moisture sensor embedded in the soil. A small computer in the sprinkler interprets the data from the moisture sensor and compares it against a predetermined threshold value. When the threshold level is reached, signaling that the soil is dry and needs watering, the computer activates the sprinkler. A smarter system, connected to the local weather forecast via an internet connection, would only trigger if rain isn't forecast within the hour.

Control loops can be very simple, as for our garden sprinkler system, or they can be very complex. Complex control loops are used to automate manufacturing lines, control nuclear power stations, and optimize traffic flow in major cities. Some control loops, like our sprinkler, might be navigated just a couple of times a day—on, off, on, off. Other control loops occur hundreds of times a second. The navigation system on an autonomous drone measures its position in space several hundred times a second, making tiny adjustments to the speed of its rotors to maintain its course and speed under blustery wind conditions. Some industrial control applications operate with control loops that occur thousands of times a second. Industrial turbines measure internal conditions and adjust gas intake and turbine speed to optimize fuel consumption and performance.

Many IoT applications are fundamentally about the optimization of control loops. Each time, you sense the world and then make a decision. That decision is usually an attempt to optimize for some kind of result. The seemingly simple, but vitally important, question is: What result should we optimize for?

Our sprinkler system is currently being optimized around two primary factors:

1. Minimize water usage
2. Optimize soil moisture levels to promote plant health

To illustrate the point, let's have some fun and imagine an unnecessarily sophisticated sprinkler system. First, let's optimize our sprinkler to minimize inconvenience to people enjoying or working in the garden. Many of us remember a time in our life when we were happily minding our own business, relaxing in the sunshine on a lovely lawn, only to be surprised by a torrent of water from an ill-timed sprinkler. After the swearing is over and we've dashed to safety, we inevitably wonder if somebody, somewhere designed the sprinkler system to do that to us on purpose.

A simpler design might only water at night. A better system would use a smart camera to sense when the garden is not in use. The ultimate (and entirely over the top) system could mount cameras in the garden, or on a drone, and use image recognition technology to understand which species of plants are located where. The watering system would optimize water delivery for each individual plant and monitor plant health over time.

The point of this exercise is to illustrate that control loops can become as complicated and sophisticated as you want (and can afford) and that the key is to decide what end results you are optimizing for.

Beyond Productivity and Efficiency: Optimize Your Business at a Higher Level

For 30 or 40 years, businesses used computers to optimize productivity and efficiency. Computers boosted office productivity and computer control made factories more efficient and boosted quality by bringing precision and repeatability to business processes. Most of the productivity gains that can be had from traditional client-server computing and automation have already been realized. Any remaining improvements will be incremental and are unlikely to be revolutionary.

The Internet of Things, coupled with cloud computing, Blockchain technology, and artificial intelligence, will lead to huge breakthroughs in business process improvement and product innovation in the coming decade. Automation will yield further advances in productivity, efficiency, and sustainability. The capabilities of the Internet of Things reach far beyond those of traditional client-server computing. The IoT creates far more intimate connections between the digital and physical worlds. The more intimately we connect the digital with the physical, the more value and capability can flow from the exponentially improving digital world into the physical world that we inhabit.

What we optimize for really matters. With IoT, system engineers can set higher goals for the automated IT systems that they build. We explore this notion more fully in Chapter 7 when we review the strategy and philosophy of automation.

Make Higher-Quality Decisions with Analytics

Powerful computers can ingest vast amounts of complex information gathered from a wide array of disparate sources. Algorithms spot patterns in this data and make informed decisions accordingly. Often these patterns are so complex, or spread across such vast troves of data, that they are impossible for humans to see. The class of software that finds these patterns and helps us make sense of complex data is known as analytics. Analytics are key to unlocking the full value of the IoT and business process automation.

Analytics guide the operations of many businesses. Analytics are used to design election campaigns, make Netflix and Spotify recommendations, assess credit worthiness, and set the pricing of flights and hotels. In the coming decades, turbocharged by artificial intelligence, analytics will become the "brains" behind many business operations. Smart sensors will understand what's happening in the business in real time, and analytics tools will make well-informed, lightning-fast, data-driven business decisions in response.

Understand the Four Main Flavors of Analytics

There are four main categories of analytics. Each answers a fundamentally different question. These questions are: "What happened?," "Why did it happen?," "What may happen?," and "What should we do?" The answers to these questions have tremendous business value. Let's explore each of these types of analytics in turn to understand how they can be used to make business operations run more smoothly and efficiently.

Descriptive Analytics

Descriptive analytics analyze historical data to help us understand the answer to the question "What happened?" They typically offer insight into the operation of complex systems: the flow of a city's transport network, the performance of a jet engine, or the operation of a large call center. Descriptive analytics turn raw data into information and insights that help people to make decisions, for example, highlighting rush-hour traffic and accident hotspots to help city planners redesign interchanges and improve public safety.

Diagnostic Analytics

Diagnostic analytics dig deeper than descriptive analytics and help people answer "Why did it happen?" Digital marketers use diagnostic analytics to crunch through social media data—posts, shares, likes, tweets, retweets, and mentions—to figure out which messages, channels, or campaign strategies worked best on previous marketing campaigns. Logistics companies use diagnostic analytics to understand their delivery efficiency. UPS analyzed the efficiency of the routes their truck drivers were taking using diagnostic analytics. They revealed that routes that require trucks to take fewer left-hand turns are generally more efficient. As a result, UPS route-mapping software now chooses routes that minimize the number of left-hand turns needed.

Predictive Analytics

Predictive analytics help you understand "What may happen?" This software attempts to predict what is likely to happen next, based on a deep understanding of what happened before. Predictive analytics have many powerful business applications. Restaurant chains use analytics to predict how busy each restaurant is likely to be on an hourly basis. These insights inform staffing levels and shift timing. Obvious data sources for these analytics include historical demand patterns and an annual events calendar. A restaurant is likely to be busier on Valentine's Day and St. Patrick's Day, but quieter during Ramadan and Lent or on a Tuesday night early in the new year. Predictive analytics factor in weather forecasts and scour social media and the web to ingest the event schedules of nearby entertainment venues, and correlate events against previous demand spikes.

Predictive analytics finds patterns of human behavior that are hidden inside massive sets of data. Walmart used predictive analytics to correlate local weather data with sales data from checkouts at every one of their stores. Walmart data scientists found that under a specific set of weather conditions, people visited the store looking to buy berries. Analytics software revealed a surge in demand whenever the weather was clear, sunny, with a light breeze and temperatures below 80°F (27°C). Acting on this insight, Walmart positions berries more prominently and boosts advertising when these weather conditions are predicted. It reduces stocks in unfavorable conditions. Incredibly, Walmart saw berry sales triple in some locations. A 10% sales uplift is a big deal in retail; a 300% boost is monumental! Walmart's analytics discovered that people are more likely to buy steak when the wind is above average, it's not raining, and the temperature is warm, but not hot. Ground beef, presumably to make burgers, sells better in warmer temperatures, low winds, and mostly sunny weather. When they spot these forecasted conditions, Walmart analytics automatically trigger the release of local ads focused on hamburgers. That results in a spike in ground beef sales of up to 18%! Understanding subtle patterns in human behavior with predictive analytics has a tremendous impact on sales for a major retailer like Walmart.

Prescriptive Analytics

Prescriptive analytics build on all the previous levels of analytics to answer the question "What should we do?" This is perhaps the most powerful of all the four main types of analytics as it begins to shift decision-making into software. In the coming decades, prescriptive analytics, fed by vast troves of data, will quietly, efficiently make many of the decisions that underpin the world that we live in. Businesses use prescriptive analytics to help them design products, set pricing, smooth business processes, and optimize the efficiency and effectiveness of their employees by guiding them on what tasks to do next. Italy's largest bank, UniCredit, uses prescriptive analytics to make better lending decisions and optimize its capital. Oil and gas companies use prescriptive analytics to help them decide where to frack and how to optimize the fracking process. Aurora Healthcare, an organization that spans 15 hospitals, employs 6,300 people, and serves 1.2 million customers, analyzed 10 years of clinical treatment data and patient outcomes so that they could offer near-real-time treatment recommendations to their doctors based on a patient's diagnosis and history. As a result, they were able to improve healthcare outcomes and reduce readmission rates by 10%, saving $6 million each year (Source: Datafloq).

Every business should have an analytics strategy and find ways to use analytics to help them make higher-quality decisions in every business process.

The Internet of People: Wearables and Hearables

When applied to people, Internet of Things technology enables us to enhance our capabilities and quantify our personal health and activity. Popular wearables focused on health and fitness measure activity and create feedback loops that encourage healthy behaviors.

Wearable technology will spread beyond the wrist and find a place on our heads, in our ears, on our fingers, and ultimately inside our bodies. Augmented and virtual reality headsets are discussed in Chapter 5, so we will skip them here.

A hearable is a smart, connected device that fits on or in your ear. Some wireless headphones already connect to voice assistant services. Future hearables will combine microphones with earphones to augment our hearing. Intelligent hearables will process sound and optimize it for us, protecting our ears in loud environments, applying personalized audio equalization (bass, treble, and mid), and filtering noise. Smart noise cancellation offers the prospect of being able to selectively remove sounds we don't wish to hear—babies crying at the mall, the rumble of an office air conditioner, or the screech of a subway train—while preserving the sounds we don't want to miss. Hearables may also enhance hearing for those who need it: first responders listening for survivors, hunters tracking animals, law enforcement chasing bad guys, or people at the back of a room listening to under-amplified public speakers. Hearables might also offer the ability to replay the last 10 seconds of sound in case you missed something, or to edit the voices of friends and family. Who wouldn't want to make their boss's voice sound like Darth Vader? Hearables will also translate languages in near real time. Waverly Labs' Pilot in-ear wireless headphones can translate 16 languages in near real-time with impressive accuracy.

For those people who have ever found themselves shouting directly into the ear of people next to them at loud concerts, hearables offer the prospect of being connected into personal audio networks. Temporary, private audio networks could be formed that capture speech with bone-conduction microphones in the ear and transfer them to friends who can hear you no matter the volume of the death metal band on stage. Teamwork at the supermarket would also get easier, too. "Hey honey, please grab some bread and ham and meet me in the cereal aisle."

Some hearables will measure biometric information from our ears, gathering heart rate, blood pressure, temperature, ECG, and even blood oxygen levels. Hearable accelerometers can measure movement and activity. Biometrics can be useful for authentication and security. Your heart rhythm, gait, and ear shape form a unique signature that could be used to authenticate access to devices and services, much the same way that an Apple Watch can sign you into a MacBook. NEC claims they can measure the reflection of sound waves in the ear canal and determine the unique shape of an individual ear with greater than 99% accuracy. When combined with other biometric signatures to further boost accuracy, this could provide a new root of trust for security applications that require continuous authentication. Goodbye and good riddance, passwords.

Advances in printed sensors and electronics deployed on flexible substrates will open up new platforms for wearable and medical devices in the coming decade. Future wearables will make today's products seem quaint by comparison. Researchers at MindX are hard at work developing mind-reading smart glasses that sense eye movement and brain waves to figure out where you're looking and what you're thinking. They could offer a new interface and be particularly useful for performing visual searches. Sana has built soon-to-be-FDA-certified smart goggles that promote relaxation and eliminate chronic pain using patterns of sounds and light to modulate brain waves. The goggles monitor brain activity in a closed-loop biofeedback system that learns how to reduce or eliminate pain when worn for as little as 16 minutes. Clinical trials are under way for the treatment of fibromyalgia, neuropathic pain, oncology pain, opioid misuse disorder, and severe pain.

Future wearables that combine advanced materials, sensors, and artificial intelligence to perform super-sensing will redefine the wearable landscape.

Strategies to Get Eyes on Your Business and Act on Events in Real Time

Every organization should have a comprehensive sensor strategy. The first step to building any automation strategy is to create a sensor strategy. If you don't have a sensor strategy, start today. Get eyes on your business operations and gather the data you need to automate or semi-automate decisions.

Use sensors to detect important business events so that you can act on them in near real time, speeding operations and delighting customers in the process. For centuries, bells attached to the doors of stores have alerted shopkeepers to the arrival of customers. Modern sensors can detect important business events that require immediate attention: a restaurant customer's drink being empty, a fire caused by a lightning strike, a package clearing customs, or a PR disaster unfolding on Twitter.

Starbucks in China uses the store's Wi-Fi hotspot as a sensor. Wi-Fi hotspots regularly sniff the airwaves for devices that want to connect to them. Even devices that don't connect share limited information about themselves, a unique identifier known as a MAC address. Starbucks uses the Wi-Fi hotspot to count the number of phones it can see. Most people have one phone, so the phone count is a good proxy for the number of customers in the store at any given time. Starbucks uses this information to control the music system in the store. When the store is quiet, they play more relaxing music designed to encourage customers to linger longer and maybe order a second drink or a slice of cake. When the store is busy, they increase the tempo and volume of the music, hoping to encourage people to grab and go. This approach has had a material impact on their business.

Most business events can be detected with the right sensor strategy. Detect as many business events as you can—customer-related events, operational events, employee-related events—and make your business more responsive and more efficient as a result.

3 Autonomous Machines—Robots, Cobots, Drones, and Self-Driving Vehicles

AI-powered machines will work alongside humans in almost every industrial sector. They will reshape the world of work and will fundamentally transform our transportation system.

What Are They and Why Are They Important?

Strictly speaking, autonomous machines are just another application of AI, but their impact on society will be so profound that they are worthy of their own short chapter.

Autonomous machines—robots, drones, and "self-driving" transportation—use sophisticated sensors and digital intelligence to make informed decisions about how they move through and interact with the world. AI gives machines agency, the ability to make their own decisions.

Autonomous machines come in many shapes, sizes, and formats. Some will fit in the palm of your hand; some are the size of a building. Some stay put, some have wheels, some have arms and legs, some can fly, and some carry cargo or passengers inside them.

Modern robots use AI to sense their environment and adapt to it intelligently, for example, sidestepping obstacles, catching a ball, or driving safely through a crowded street. Collaborative robots, dubbed "cobots," are specifically designed to work safely alongside humans. Autonomous vehicles, or colloquially self-driving cars and trucks, are just robots with wheels and a space to put people or cargo.

Flying robots, better known as drones, are mostly piloted by remote control today. AI will fill our skies will all manner of fully autonomous working drones, some of them large enough to carry human passengers.

Robots, cobots, drones, passenger drones, and autonomous cars, trucks, ships, and planes are all subcategories of fully autonomous machines. Over the next decade, our world will be flooded with millions of autonomous machines. Many are already here. Robots work tirelessly in Amazon warehouses, drones transfer organ transplants between hospitals, and self-driving trucks trundle safely along our freeways.

What Can They Do?

The term robot was first coined by Josef Čapek back in the 1920s. It's derived from the Slavic word "robota," which means forced laborer. "Visionary" videos from the 1950s showed robots wandering the middle-class homes of the 1980s and '90s, cleaning, tidying, and serving drinks. Sadly, that vision never came to pass, and I still don't have a robotic butler to make my martinis. Instead, robots spent most of the last century confined to the pages of science fiction novels. At best, they were relegated to repetitive manufacturing jobs inside our factories and trapped inside cages. To keep workers protected, unseeing industrial robots toiled behind steel safety fences.

Robots Escape Their Cages and Safely Share Our World

Machine vision liberated robots from their cages. Advanced vision and other sensory capabilities enable smart robots to perform more sophisticated tasks than classic, dumb robots. Powered by AI, smart robots can sense and navigate through their surroundings. They can take evasive action to avoid obstacles, which means they can safely coexist in the same spaces as humans. This makes them exponentially more useful.

We are entering a new golden age of robotics. Robots now shake cocktails on cruise ships, flip burgers, teach people to ballroom dance, count pills in pharmacies, park cars, build homes, and harvest fruit.

A large dairy or arable farm in the nineteenth century employed hundreds but can now be operated by just a few people. In the twenty-first century, advanced robots and artificial intelligence will continue to automate food production. Farm dogs will soon have new teammates: robots and drones.

Some farming is still very labor-intensive. Twentieth-century mechanization was suited to the harvesting of crops like wheat, corn, barley, oats, soy, and cotton because these crops ripen consistently and can be harvested all at once. Some plants grow at varying rates and can only be harvested when ready. Most fruit is delicate, and each piece requires judgment to determine if it is ripe and ready to be picked. Thus, most fruit and leafy green vegetables are still harvested by hand, usually by migrant labor. With the poor availability of human labor to pick fruit, farmers are turning to sophisticated robots with powerful machine vision. A number of startups—including Dogtooth in the UK, Octinion in Belgium, Harvest CROO robotics, and Agrobot—are trying to build robots that can pick strawberries. Agrobot CEO and founder, Juan Bravo, told me, "it is not hard to design a robot to do a task on the farm. The challenge is to make it cost-effective, simple, robust, and reliable." Robocrop's robot picks raspberries. The robot peers through the canopy of leaves that surrounds a fruit, assesses its ripeness, and then gently picks it from the plant without bruising it. Fruit harvesting robots work 24/7, and importantly are happy to work at night. Fruit, particularly soft berries like strawberries, are best harvested at night when cooler conditions reduce bruising. Sweeper's robot picks peppers, and FFRobotics and Abundant robotics build machines to pick apples. Plant breeders are working to develop plants that are easier for robots to harvest, for example, researchers at the University of Florida have bred a tree with a large, open canopy and with apples on long stems that are easier for robots to pick.

Swiss start-up company ecoRobotix sells a fully autonomous farm robot powered by a large solar panel mounted on its back. The robot uses GPS and computer vision to navigate a field for up to 12 hours a day without a human operator. It roams the field to identify and zap weeds, either with a small, directed spray of herbicide, or with a spinning cutting tool. ecoRobotix claims their robot uses 20 times less herbicide than a traditional approach, improves soil health, and boosts yields because no herbicide is left on crops. John Deere, maker of some of the most highly respected (and wonderfully bright green and yellow) agricultural machinery in the world, has invested heavily to develop smart, connected, and semiautonomous farm equipment. Their Autotrack Universal 200 system can steer a tractor, a combine harvester, or a sprayer. This frees the farmer to monitor and control equipment operations rather than having to drive. For example, the farmer might set the depth at which seeds are planted or tweak the amount of fertilizer being sprayed onto a crop.

John Deere has a wonderful view of how humans and machines should work together in the fields. I spoke with Joel Hergenreter, head of strategy for embedded solutions at John Deere. He told me that John Deere considers the human–machine connection to be central to success in the fields, in the same way that the relationship between the farmer, plough, and horse was central to farming 200 years ago. John Deere plans to build machines that become a farmer's trusted partners: partners that relieve stress, help the farmer to achieve more, and make the farmer a better steward of the land. John Deere believes in the unique human "sensors" the farmer has and seeks to build a powerful partnership between human and machine intelligence. An experienced farm hand uses their sense of smell, their eyesight, their hearing, and their sense of vibration to monitor what's going on while sitting in the cab of farm equipment. John Deere wants to build equipment that pays as much attention to the farmer as the farmer has to pay attention to the equipment. This is a great way to think about human–machine symbiosis that should inspire every other innovator.

Combine harvesters must periodically be unloaded as they harvest crops. Every time you stop to unload, you're wasting time and money. John Deere designed a system to unload the combine as it harvests. When a tractor is driven close to the combine, the combine automatically takes control over it. It steers the tractor, matches speeds, and aligns the tractor's trailer to receive crops. The combine unloads its harvested crop without stopping. When the trailer is full, the tractor is released, separates from the combine, and its operator drives the tractor away to unload the cargo. In large farms, several tractors and trailers service one continually operating combine so that it works constantly during harvest.

It's not a big stretch to see how most of the farming system could ultimately become autonomous. First steps in this direction have already been taken. A research project in the UK, named the Hands-Free Hectare, successfully harvested a hectare (about 2.5 acres) of barley. What made this project so special is that they planted, tended, and harvested four and a half tons of barley using only autonomous vehicles and drones. Not a single human hand touched the crop during the entire growing cycle. The team's goal was to show that by embracing autonomy, open technology, and standard farm equipment, farming can be achieved at scale without having to resort to ever-bigger pieces of farm equipment. Heavy machinery can compact the soil, which reduces soil health and slows plant growth. The team envisions a future of high-resolution, precision farming where individual plants are each given exactly the care that they need to optimize growth and crop yield. To celebrate their success, the researchers used the barley to make beer.

Gigantic robots are being developed to provide grid-level storage for renewable energy. SoftBank invested $110 million in Energy Vault, a startup that plans to build autonomous brick-lifting cranes that lift 35-ton composite bricks to store electricity as potential energy. The robots will lower the bricks to power generators and feed energy back into the grid when it's needed. Each skyscraper-sized tower stores up to 80 MWh and can deliver 4 to 8 MW of continuous power discharge for 8 to 16 hours, enough to power 5,000 homes.

Robots will automate some jobs, particularly repetitive, boring, and dangerous work. But for the foreseeable future, humans will still play an important role in physical work. Robots still have significant limitations; Some, but not all, will be overcome with time.

Robotic dexterity is a notoriously difficult challenge. OpenAI researchers used reinforcement learning to train a robotic hand to manipulate a colored cube. Researchers first created a digital simulation to accurately model the physics of the hand and cube—the exact physical dimensions of the hand, the articulation of the finger joints, the pull of gravity, the weight of the cube, the friction of materials, and so on. Researchers trained a neural network to manipulate the digits of the simulated robot hand. The AI was given the goal of manipulating the cube into a desired orientation. Inside the simulation, the AI controlled the jointed fingers of the robotic hand and tried to reach the goal. When it was successful, the AI was rewarded. The AI was given a negative reward for mistakes, such as dropping the cube. This reward function is an input to the neural network. The AI tries to increase the reward function with time. Once the robot hand successfully oriented the cube, it was given a new goal—a new, randomly chosen orientation. This training occurred entirely inside the simulation. Practice makes perfect, and this AI practiced and learned. Through the course of the training, researchers changed key variables of the simulated environment at random: the strength of gravity, the mass of the cube, the starting position of the hand, and so on. Each combination of variables essentially created a slightly different version of "reality" within the simulation: a new version of the laws of physics. In each different "reality," the AI learned how to achieve its goals. With time, the AI became resilient to changes in these environmental conditions.

The researchers ran this simulation for the equivalent of 100 years (if it had been run in real time on an actual robot). Once trained, the researchers disconnected the AI from the simulation and connected it to an actual, physical robot hand. The AI instantly achieved impressive results. To the AI, the real physical environment was just another variation of the simulation. The AI was resilient enough to adapt to new environments on the fly and wasn't fazed by differences between the physics of the simulated and real-world environments. The AI was so resilient that it adapted quickly when the cube was replaced by a new shape, a cylinder. The OpenAI researchers showed that while robotic dexterity remains challenging, AI, in the form of reinforcement learning, will likely bring significant advances in the coming decade.

Despite these advances, human dexterity is still light years ahead of robots. Human hands are incredible. Twenty-seven bones, 34 muscles, millions of nerve endings, opposable thumbs, and fine motor control enable us to grasp and manipulate delicate objects with ease. Our hands are an incredible feat of evolution. Robotic dexterity doesn't even come close.

Drones Fill Our Skies and Do Real Work

Drones can do a lot more than take cool photos of the top of your house. Recent technological advances—ultra-efficient electric motors, high-capacity batteries, low-cost sensors, and sophisticated flight control systems—have made drones an affordable and powerful tool suited to use in many industrial sectors. Drones survey construction sites, spray pesticide on fields, inspect equipment, map archaeological digs, fight fires, plant trees, survey dams, deliver packages, inspect bridges, and save lives. Drones have become twenty-first-century workhorses.

Drones vary wildly in their size, form, and function. Some are powerful enough to lift a full-grown man from the ocean, some have arms that allow them to interact with the world, some spray liquids onto crops. The tiniest drones are mostly developed for covert surveillance while the largest drones are big enough to carry several human passengers. Most drones use four or more rotors to maneuver and hover in place; some use a fixed wing design to travel long distances using less energy. Passenger drones use many redundant rotors to increase safety.

If you're not sure what to get your errant niece or nephew for their birthday this year, there's always a flamethrower drone. In China, maintenance crews use flamethrower drones to clear debris from high-voltage power lines. This saves a high-risk climb to remove troublesome trash. Today, these drones are controlled by workers on the ground. With advances in machine vision and connectivity, drones like these are poised to lose their remote controls and become fully autonomous. In the future, teams of autonomous drones may live on the power lines, performing visual inspections, alerting the power company of issues, and dealing with debris automatically.

Autonomous drones have many useful applications. A small platoon of security drones can patrol an area to look for intruders, poachers, or safety hazards. These autonomous drones return to their charging cradles when their batteries get low and work in teams to ensure there's always at least one drone on duty at any given time.

Farming drones survey crop and soil health and do active work in the fields. Crop spraying by drones is estimated to be five times as fast as traditional methods. Precision control using GPS location and 3-D cameras optimizes the flight path and flies drones at a prescribed height, no matter the topography of the land or the varying height of crops, to ensure an even coating on the plants below, which uses less pesticide and fertilizer, saving money and reducing chemical runoff.

DroneSeed, based in Seattle, builds drones for precision forestry. Their drones plant tree seedlings to reforest areas after fire or harvest. They are particularly useful for areas that are difficult to access, such as steep hillsides. Each large drone carries a 57-pound payload of seeds. They fire seeds into the ground like a flying paintball gun. Each seed is enclosed inside a small capsule of nutrients that protects it as it enters the soil and then nourishes it as it starts to grow. DroneSeed's vision is to make reforestation scalable through automation. Their goal is to develop a solution that can reverse the massive deforestation that has occurred in the last decades. Deforestation is a significant contributor to global warming. Planting millions of trees to sequester carbon from the atmosphere will be an important part of the fight against climate change. DroneSeed claims that while a good human tree planter can plant about 800 trees in a day across about 2 acres, a single operator working with a swarm of 15 drones can do the equivalent of 360 manual hours of tree planting in a single day.

Chinese company Walkera builds drones to fight fires in high-rises. Their Zhun drone shoots fire-retardant foam and launches fire-suppression missiles into burning apartments to extinguish flames. Firefighters on the ground control the drone to deliver rapid response containment measures. In the future, fire-fighting drones will operate autonomously and work in partnership with human firefighters.

Ultimately, a global air-traffic-control system will be needed to manage drone and robot traffic as they travel the planet; 5G networks will likely be a key enabler for such a network.

Autonomous Vehicles Upset the Apple Cart

Autonomous vehicles will change human mobility forever, improving safety, increasing access, reducing cost, and shifting cars from a product we own to a service we use. AI will control all manner of vehicles, from personal transportation units, to cars, trucks, planes, passenger drones, and ships. We will explore the impact of autonomous vehicles in Chapter 11.

Autonomous vehicles will change the face of our cities, transform the logistics industry, and put some people out of work. Autonomous vehicles will also create a new platform on which new services will be delivered, creating new companies and new jobs in the process.

Strategies for Success

Automate, Semi-Automate, and Elevate Human Work

As AI boosts the capabilities of robots, drones, and other autonomous machines, they will offload more physical work from humans. Every business should keep a close eye on the trajectory of autonomous machine technologies. Look for strategic intersections with business operations and build strategies to automate dangerous, repetitive, and demanding physical work wherever possible.

Significant advances in AI and robot mechanics are needed before robot dexterity and capability rivals that of human beings. In the near and medium term, humans will maintain a healthy lead over robots in jobs that require delicate physical manipulation of objects or tools. Longer term, dexterity will cease to be a uniquely human capability. People should plan their careers accordingly.

Most automation will involve the semi-automation of business processes. Rather than using automation to replace human jobs, the goal of semi-automation is to build human–machine partnerships and elevate the work of humans. Successful business automation projects will allow your employees to contribute at a higher level, create more value for the company, and do more satisfying work. We explore these ideas in greater depth in Chapter 7 when we review the philosophy of automation.

4 Distributed Ledgers and Blockchains

Blockchain technology, first thought to be somewhat esoteric and useful only as the underpinnings of obscure cryptocurrencies like Bitcoin, has emerged as one of the most compelling new technologies of our time. Blockchain is disruptive to the status quo, with the potential to reshape the economics of entire industries. In other words, Blockchain is a big deal.

Beyond Cryptocurrencies: Why Blockchain Is a Big Deal

Blockchain technology will decentralize power structures, reduce transaction costs, improve traceability, secure data and assets, increase transparency, enable new value creation, and construct new incentive and funding models. Blockchains have profound implications for every business, including yours.

Blockchain will birth new products, new services, and possibly new industries. It will transform everything from healthcare records to real-estate transactions and touch everything from digital voting booths to shipping containers. Blockchain will transform the financial services sector and strip intermediaries and brokers from transactions. Some of those intermediaries may be your existing suppliers or customers. Some might be working inside your company. One of them might be you.

I often compare the rise of Blockchain technology to that of HTML (Hypertext Markup Language), the technology that kickstarted the web revolution and ignited the internet era. While they are very different technologies, Blockchain has the potential for a similar level of impact and market penetration as HTML. Powerful foundational technologies take time for their impact to be felt. The world's first web page went live on August 6, 1991, but it was several years before the titans of a new industry began to emerge: Yahoo! in 1994, eBay in 1995, and Google in 1996. Facebook didn't show up until 2004. It's now unthinkable for a company to exist and operate without a web presence. The web reaches more than 4 billion people and has created trillions of dollars of value. Newspapers are filled with stories of major retailers closing their doors forever and Amazon, founded in 1994, made Jeff Bezos the richest man on the planet. HTML changed how billions of people communicate, learn, play, buy, work, and thrive. Without HTML there would be no Pinterest, Wikipedia, or YouTube. Netflix might still be shipping you Blu-ray discs through the mail. The web created hundreds of millions of jobs and powered the IT sector to a $5 trillion global industry. When Tim Berners-Lee first created HTML, he could have had no idea of the incredible innovation he was to unleash. Blockchain technology has similar potential to underpin tectonic shifts and to fell industry titans.

Blockchain is to trust and transactions as HTML is to information and the web. Like HTML, the impact of Blockchain technology will grow steadily over time until it eventually becomes a vital component in the operations of every business. Mighty businesses, including big, established internet companies, could be shaken to their core. More than a decade into the Blockchain era, it's still too early to determine how disruptive Blockchain technology might eventually be. Early pioneering developers, working on the web when it was little more than a clickable online magazine, would have had their minds blown by Skype, Kayak, PayPal, and Dropbox.

Learning about new technology can sometimes be like eating our vegetables. We learn about it because we should, even when we would rather learn about more exciting stuff like augmented reality and flying cars. Like HTML before it, Blockchain technology sits in the "dull-but-important" category. You don't need to understand the details of how Blockchains work, but you should understand what Blockchains make possible. Make yourself comfortable. It's time to eat your technology broccoli.

Blockchain 101

Blockchain technology is an example of distributed ledger technology (DLT). Since Blockchains are the most widely talked about DLTs, we will use the term Blockchain as a proxy for DLT throughout this book. Toward the end of the chapter, we briefly explore other types of DLT beyond Blockchains.

What Is a Blockchain?

Simply put, a Blockchain is just a fancy database for storing information. The database is special because it's immutable, which means that once you put information into it, it can't be changed. Information stored in a Blockchain is time stamped, so you know when it was added.

A Blockchain acts as an electronic agreement machine. It gives multiple people, or multiple organizations, a programmatic way of coming to agreement on what is true. That truth might be about who owes who what money, where goods reside in a supply chain, or whether there are any liens on a property.

Blockchains can store financial transaction data, healthcare records, shipping manifests, marriage certificates, title deeds—any type of data that must be recorded in a trusted fashion. Blockchains give us a digital method to establish truth and trust in a world of distrust.

Distributed and Decentralized

Blockchains store records in a distributed ledger. In a financial setting that ledger might record that an amount of money moved from person A to person B on a particular date and time. Blockchains don't have a single, central data repository. Each of the participants in a Blockchain network keeps a local copy of all the data. Data is decentralized and distributed across all the "nodes" of the network. This massive redundancy is one of the things that makes Blockchains nearly impossible to hack. The price of this approach is that it also makes Blockchains a less efficient way of storing information.

Information in a Blockchain is stored in blocks. These blocks are linked together in a chain. By now, more observant readers will have figured out where the name "Blockchain" comes from. The links between blocks are made using military-grade encryption. Now let's dive deeper, and if it gets too much for you, you at least tried to eat your broccoli and are excused to skip to the next section on how Blockchain is used to solve business problems.

Immutability and Truth

When a new block of data is added to the end of a Blockchain, all of the computers connected in the Blockchain network race to solve a complex cryptographic puzzle. The solution to this puzzle, known as a hash, is used to link the new block of data to the end of the chain in a secure manner. It requires a significant amount of computational power to solve these puzzles. This is by design. The new block is only added to the chain once enough computers on the network agree on the solution to the cryptographic puzzle, the hash. The process by which this occurs is known as the consensus mechanism. This process is designed to stop any one person or organization from adding bogus information to the Blockchain. Earlier in this chapter, I suggested that a Blockchain acts as an "agreement machine." The consensus mechanism is the computational busy work involved in the operation of this agreement machine. It allows consensus to be built on what is true, which allows information to be stored in a trusted way. This process is a little esoteric and can be hard to understand, but it is the heart of the way that truth is established electronically. Different Blockchains have different consensus mechanisms. Some are optimized for transaction speed—which means more blocks can be added to the chain each second—while others are optimized for high security.

When blocks are added to the chain, the process involved is a bit like knitting, at least in my mind. The hash of each block is tied back to the previous block, a bit like a stitch links back to a previous stitch in knitting. If you drop a stitch and don't immediately realize your error, you have to unpick all the stitches you made, fix the dropped stitch, and redo your work. If a nefarious actor tries to alter data stored somewhere on a Blockchain, they would need to "unpick" all of the military-grade encryption that links blocks together, make the change, and then reconstruct all the blocks and hashes before the next block of data is added to the chain. Even if bad guys could muster enough computer power to do this, they would be defeated by the consensus mechanism and the distributed nature of the Blockchain. Each node on the Blockchain network holds its own copy of the Blockchain data. To alter data stored in the Blockchain would require you to hack a majority of the computers in the Blockchain network, simultaneously, and to recalculate all the encryption codes for all the data, perfectly, and do it near instantly before anybody noticed. The bottom line is that data stored in a Blockchain is immutable and nearly impossible to hack. Information can be trusted, and it gives us a digital method to establish and preserve truth.

Cryptocurrencies, Tokens, Smart Contracts, and dApps

Like all technologies, Blockchain technology evolves over time, adding new features and capabilities along the way. The first Blockchain was built to underpin the Bitcoin cryptocurrency. It was a simple distributed ledger with limited features. First-generation Blockchains were designed purely for cryptocurrencies and payment. Think of them as Blockchain 1.0.

Second generation Blockchain technology (aka Blockchain 2.0 technology) adds a feature known as smart contracts. Smart contracts capture the business rules of an agreement, including transaction details and penalties, as computer code stored within the Blockchain. This code executes automatically when preagreed conditions are met. The result is a self-executing contract that automatically enforces contract obligations. Smart contracts remove intermediaries from business processes and speed business operations. Blockchain companies use smart contracts to build distributed applications, known as dApps, which we will discuss shortly.

Third generation Blockchains (Blockchain 3.0 technology) have additional features that improve transaction speeds, reduce energy consumption, and make it easier to build distributed apps (dApps). Blockchain 3.0 technology offers developers a highly scalable platform to build powerful applications. Examples of third-generation Blockchains include EOS, Aion, Tron, and Cardano.

Let's explore cryptocurrencies, tokens, smart contracts, and dApps in more detail.

Cryptocurrencies and Tokens

Cryptocurrencies like Bitcoin, Litecoin, or Dogecoin are virtual currencies that use cryptography to secure their underlying operations. Strong security makes them hard to counterfeit. Each cryptocurrency is built on top of an associated Blockchain, which stores the details on each transaction of the cryptocurrency. The account balance of each person or entity that holds cryptocurrency is stored on the chain, together with a full history of all payments and transactions ever made.

When new blocks of data are added to a Blockchain, computer nodes on the Blockchain network secure the data by solving difficult cryptographic puzzles. This effort takes time and consumes energy. To reward nodes for their participation, the first node to crack the cryptographic puzzle and create the hash is given a small amount of cryptocurrency by the network. This cryptocurrency is also known as a token. On the Bitcoin Blockchain the tokens are Bitcoins. On the Ethereum Blockchain those tokens are known as Ether. This incentive increases the transaction speed of the network. Since only the first node to solve the problem gets the reward, the race to crack codes is always on! This process is known as mining. Some nodes participate in a Blockchain network purely for the purposes of being rewarded for mining tokens.

An important duality exists here. The cryptocurrency exists on top of the Blockchain. And the function of the Blockchain is underpinned by the reward of cryptocurrency.

One of the things that makes Blockchains interesting is their power to shift the economic incentives and behavior with tokens. We explore this concept more fully in the section on token economics.

Many people ask why cryptocurrencies and tokens are ascribed value. The answer is the same as for fiat currencies like the British pound or the U.S. dollar. Currencies are based on a promise and a belief in the stability, strength, and economic power of the institution that backs them. The value of a currency is determined by the market. Currency only has true value when it is exchanged for something of value in the marketplace. The value of cryptocurrencies is also determined by the market. Crypto-exchanges trade cryptocurrencies for traditional fiat currencies, the same way that currency exchanges trade dollars for pounds. This is how we see the dollar value of Bitcoins rise and fall. The value of a cryptocurrency associated with any given Blockchain is based on the perceived value created on top of that Blockchain. If the market values the platform that you have built on your Blockchain, they'll value your token. The more value you create, the more your tokens are worth. Owning a token is like owning a share in the Blockchain-based platform. As with the money supply, the total number of tokens that are available affects the individual value of each token.

Smart Contracts

Classic contracts are an agreement on paper that is enforceable by law. Smart contracts are agreements stored on a Blockchain that are enforced by code.

Second and third generation Blockchain platforms, such as Ethereum, Neo, and HyperLedger, include smart contract capabilities. Business rules or contract logic can be embedded inside them as code. Smart contracts automatically execute a transaction once predetermined conditions are met. Examples of automated transactions include:

- A mortgage loan is funded once required insurance is purchased for a property.
- Money is transferred from a home buyer to a seller once a title deed is transferred into the buyer's name.
- Ownership for a block of shares is transferred when payment is received.

Smart contracts speed and simplify transactions by turning the validation and execution of contracts into simple computer code. Long term, this will reduce or remove the need for third parties who bring added trust to the contract process, including notaries, brokers, clearing houses, escrow, and title insurance.

London-based legal tech firm Mattereum built a platform to manage the sale, lease, or partitioning of physical assets using legally enforceable smart contracts. Mattereum is a collaboration between lawyers, software developers, and investor William Shatner. Yes, *the* William Shatner. Fresh from his success with travel brokerage Priceline, Shatner is now hooked on all things Blockchain and crypto. Mattereum's goal is to bridge the gap between smart contracts and actual legal contracts. They want to build the infrastructure needed to enable what they call the "Internet of agreements." Mattereum's approach is to establish legal title over assets, a concept that is universal across almost all jurisdictions globally. The Mattereum platform establishes a chain of custody and uses smart contracts to move ownership of assets from one entity to another. This approach enables easy resolution of legal disputes. This chain of custody approach underpins all global supply chains.

Distributed Apps (dApps)

Modern Blockchains include features that make it easier to build distributed apps, commonly known as dApps. Blockchain platforms like Ethereum mask the complexity of distributed ledgers to let businesses focus on building applications. We explore many examples of dApps throughout this chapter.

Establishing Truth in a Trustless World

Blockchain technology enables trust to be established between two parties that don't know each other. Most financial transactions today involve intermediaries: banks help you pay your bills, escrow companies hold funds for pending transactions, clearing houses handle the buying and selling of shares. These intermediaries validate the identities and trust-worthiness of buyers and sellers to reduce the risk of those transactions not going to plan. They broker the deals and mitigate for a lack of trust between strangers.

Vast amounts of money are made in the intermediary business. Mortgage brokers, stock brokers, insurance brokers, stock exchanges, credit card companies, and title companies get paid to bring an added level of safety to transactions. This "trust industry" reduces the risk of transactions by acting as a trusted third party and guarantor that creates trust wher ever trust is needed. In a world built on Blockchain technology, trust is established electronically. This diminishes the value of the trust industry. Entities that exist purely to add trust to transactions, and that provide no other value, may no longer be needed.

Shifting Incentives with Token Economics

The value of the tokens associated with any given Blockchain is in direct proportion to the value that is created on top of that Blockchain. If people value your platform, they'll value your token.

As previously mentioned, tokens reward those who contribute the computing resources needed to underpin a Blockchain's cryptographic operations. Additional tokens are given to people who add value to the platform by contributing data or other resources. For example, DTube, a Blockchain-based competitor to YouTube, and Steemit, a distributed social network, reward users for posting popular content. People who discover cool content and vote for it early, before it becomes broadly popular, are rewarded as curators. Tokens create a market for attention where eyeballs are converted into tokens.

Some tokens are derivatives of other tokens. The functionality of smart contracts is used to create these derivative tokens. Augur, a market-prediction platform, and Golem, a distributed supercomputer, are both built on top of the Ethereum Blockchain platform and create their own token derivatives. Augur users who correctly predict events are rewarded with REP (reputation) coins. Golem users that contribute processing

to the Golem distributed supercomputing platform are rewarded with
Golem Network Tokens (GNT).

Tokens incentivize behavior. They remove the need for a centralized management structure and replace it by using tokens to align the
incentives of the platforms' contributors and users. The details of these
incentives define the governance of the Blockchain. A Blockchain-based
supply-chain platform might reward manufacturers, shipping companies,
distribution centers, logistics companies, and retailers to scan products
as they flow through the supply chain and contribute that data to the
platform. Companies are thus incentivized to install and maintain scanners and other sensors that contribute data. Brands using the supply
chain could use tokens to incentivize compliance with contracted practices. For example, a seafood company might reward a logistics company
for contributing temperature data from its refrigerated trucks. This cold-
chain compliance enables the seafood company to have confidence that
their product was properly handled during its journey to market.

Key Applications for Blockchain Technology

Blockchain technology speeds transactions, decentralizes operations, reshapes market incentives, changes behaviors, boosts security, ensures privacy, enables new collaboration models, creates new securities, tokenizes
assets, and increases transparency and traceability. Let's review some of
the main applications (dApps) of Blockchain technology.

Payments, E-Commerce, and Contracts

Blockchain technology speeds and reduces the cost of transactions. By
establishing trust digitally, Blockchains enable strangers to do business
without needing third parties to mitigate for any lack of trust.

Banks and credit card companies have embraced Blockchains to improve the speed, security, and functionality of their payment networks.
MasterCard, Visa, and American Express have all filed patents in this
space. Many central banks are either investigating or experimenting with
Blockchains to improve the safety and efficiency of systems.

Major banks, including JPMorgan and Bank of America, are investing heavily in Blockchain research and deployments. JPMorgan's "JPM Coin" cryptocurrency is used to settle payments between the bank's main clients. JPMorgan announced the project in February 2019. JPM Coins are pegged against the U.S. dollar, so one JPM Coin is worth one dollar. JPMorgan designed the new currency to make instantaneous transfers between institutional accounts. It is not designed for consumer use, at least not anytime soon. Bank of America has filed more than 80 Blockchain-related patents since 2014, including everything from a Blockchain-powered ATM to a cryptocurrency wallet.

In many parts of the world, smartphone-based digital payments are the best way for people to make and receive payments and build savings. Traditional payment platforms have high settlement fees that make them impractical for small payments, known as micro-payments. Micro-payment platforms use Blockchains to handle transactions at very low cost, making tiny payments practical. Wala is a zero-fee money and payment app aimed at the African market. Wala's goal is to enable the unbanked to receive and make payments, to save up money, and take steps toward financial prosperity. Payments are made using Wala's digital currency, Dala. People make payments to friends, pay bills for electricity, water, TV, and phone airtime, all with no fees, even for payments made to people in other countries. By using a decentralized platform, Wala keeps costs low. Any costs are covered via partnerships with service providers. Eventually, Wala hopes to offer small loans through their app. Wala is currently available in Zimbabwe, South Africa, and Uganda and has future plans to expand into Botswana, Ghana, Kenya, Mozambique, Nigeria, Tanzania, Zambia, and the UK.

Micro-payments enable newspapers and bloggers to charge readers a fraction of a cent to read their online articles, offering an alternative funding model to subscription and advertising. Coinetize creates an online paywall so writers can charge small fees in Bitcoin to access articles.

The Brave Web Browser is a collaboration between the inventor of JavaScript and the co-founder of Mozilla. The browser blocks ads, pop-ups, and trackers to maximize user privacy and boost speed. Brave claims their browsers run up to seven times faster than their competition because they don't handle ads or track users. This approach might seem counterproductive: If we starve our favorite websites of ad revenue, they will eventually have to shutter their operations. The Brave browser addresses this in a novel way. Users reward their favorite websites with tokens. Users set a weekly spending budget and tokens are allotted to sites based on the amount of time users spend browsing them. Rewards are sent anonymously, protecting user privacy. Users can opt in to receive limited ads as a way to support publishers, too.

Philanthropists want to know that their money is used as intended and reaches the people who need it, without being diverted or lost to corrupt officials. BitGive Foundation's GiveTrack project brings transparency and accountability to philanthropy. GiveTrack tracks charitable donations and ties them to results on the ground. Funds are transferred safely over a Blockchain network and payments are made using Bitcoin. Donors can view the financial results of projects they fund. BitGive has partnerships with nonprofits that include Save the Children, Medic Mobile, and The Water Project.

E-commerce sites like Amazon, eBay, and Alibaba charge sellers a fee to operate within their markets. Fees vary but can be 10–50% of the sale price. Blockchains connect buyers and sellers without the need for intermediaries or listing fees. Distributed e-commerce markets like OpenBazaar and Haven enable low-cost, trusted transactions between buyers and sellers. OpenBazaar charges no fees and accepts payments in more than 50 cryptocurrencies. These platforms have built-in reputation management so buyers and sellers can build a track record of timely payment and high-quality service. Elysian makes a Blockchain platform designed specifically for people to build decentralized e-commerce websites.

Energy Trading

Energy is traded just like anything else. Blockchain-based platforms exist to trade energy between a variety of different entities: generators, consumers, and energy storage facilities. When generators produce renewable energy, they are issued carbon credits. Electricity grids are a giant, interconnected web of power lines and substations that link consumers to power generation, so there's no way to guarantee that the electrons you bought came from renewables. Credits are used to track how much power was generated from renewable sources and who paid for that power. These credits—known as certificates of origin or Renewable Energy Certificates (RECs) in the United States, Guarantees of Origin (GO) in Europe, I-RECs in emerging markets, and the low-carbon fuel standard (LCFS) in California—are tracked and traded on Blockchains.

Grid+ offers an energy-management service to prosumers—both producers and consumers of energy. A prosumer with solar panels and a home energy storage battery might generate more power than they can use during the day but need to buy power from the local utility at night. The Grid+ system negotiates energy pricing every 15 minutes and intelligently buys and sells energy to take advantage of constantly fluctuating prices. It charges the battery when prices are low and sells energy back to the grid when prices are higher.

Blockchains handle secure metering and payment at electric vehicle charging stations. The same way that Grid+ makes money buying and selling power, future electric vehicles (which are essentially a giant battery on wheels) will make their owners money buying and selling energy whenever they are connected to the charging network.

Peer-to-peer energy-trading platforms let prosumers trade energy directly with each other. PowerLedger makes a variety of systems for peer-to-peer energy trading, demand management, and carbon credit tracking. Their Power Port product is a Blockchain-based platform for electric charging stations.

Other Blockchain-based energy companies include Leapfrog Power (aka Leap), which incentivizes consumers to shift the timing of their energy usage, OMEGAGrid, which incentivizes clean energy usage, and LO3energy, which uses their Exergy platform to optimize operations on energy grids and microgrids. LO3energy was the first company to build a Blockchain-based microgrid. The grid enables peer-to-peer energy transactions between residents in an area of Brooklyn, New York, using Ethereum and PayPal.

Sharing Economy Apps

La'Zooz and Arcade City are Blockchain-based ride-sharing platforms. Rather than trying to compete with Lyft and Uber, La'Zooz aims to increase the carrying capacity of the existing road infrastructure by matching passengers with drivers who are already heading the same way. Both driver and passengers are rewarded with Zooz tokens for their good behavior. Arcade City hopes to disrupt every corner of the global sharing economy. Arcade City claims their initial foray into ride-sharing delivered industry-leading driver earnings, driver retention, and cost efficiency. They plan to expand into home-sharing, deliveries, caregiving, contracting, and consulting. Companies like AirBNB, VRBO, Lyft, Uber, and DoorDash should pay close attention.

Media Rights

British singer and songwriter Imogen Heap is a talented and innovative musical artist. Heap uses leading-edge technology to make her music. Her music is widely sampled by other music artists. For example, Jason Derulo used a sample from Heap's "Hide and Seek" single on his track "Whatcha Say."

Mycelia, Heap's fair-trade music platform, makes it easier for artists to share their work with fans, protect copyright, and receive direct payment for their music. The platform holds information on each artist in a "Creative Passport." This lists their works, their business partners, payment mechanisms, acknowledgments, and other relevant meta data. Acknowledgments describe how artists wish to be compensated when their music is sampled and used in other works. Heap's subtle hint is that she'd like compensation for all that sampling.

Blockchain platforms enable fans to buy music direct from artists without paying platforms, distributors, or record companies. Ujo and Musicoin use Blockchains to simplify digital-rights management, remove intermediaries (including streaming services), and enable micropayments from fans.

Supply Chain

Blockchains will ensure the provenance of goods, certify authenticity, and reduce counterfeiting, theft, and fraud in supply chains. They will empower consumers to make better-informed purchase decisions that consider the sustainability and origin of products. Supply chains of the future will track the amount of energy, water, and other resources used to make products. They will also track carbon emissions, waste, and the fair-trade status of goods. We will discuss this further in Chapter 13.

Forecasting and Hedging

Time to get out your crystal ball. Blockchains underpin global, decentralized prediction markets that harness the wisdom of crowds to make predictions about the world. Leaders in the field—Augur, Stox, and Gnosis—let people predict anything they want: election results, the weather, stocks, sports scores, currency values, Oscar winners, technology launches . . . anything. Augur defines their platform as a decentralized oracle. It is used to create specific prediction markets. Users of these markets essentially bet on a forecasted outcome. They place bets using the platform's Reputation (REP) cryptocurrency. It's like buying shares in an outcome. All of the REP tokens staked on an outcome go into a pot. If a user incorrectly forecasts an outcome, they lose their stake. If they correctly forecast an outcome, they receive a proportionate share of the pot. People build their reputations on their ability to accurately predict outcomes, a reputation expressed in terms of the number of REP tokens that they hold. It's a fun notion: users programmatically stake their reputation on their predictions.

Prediction markets are used to hedge against risk. For example, you might place a small bet against a low-probability event that you hope won't occur. If it does happen, you have the upside of having correctly forecast the (undesired) event and can offset losses. Airlines might hedge against a rise in the market price of fuel. Currency traders might hedge against currency fluctuations. Winemakers might hedge against poor weather and growing conditions that reduce grape yield and quality.

Insurance

Many insurance companies operate in the technological dark ages. Policies are processed on paper, claim details are gathered by phone, settlement times are slow, and the system is open to fraud. The annual cost of insurance fraud in the United States is $40 billion (Source: FBI), which costs the average American family about $700 per year in increased premiums. Criminals make multiple claims against a single loss, and brokers sell policies they never file and pocket the premiums, a practice known as diversion.

Blockchain-based shared claims databases coordinate insurance companies' efforts to find suspicious patterns and claims. Policies written on Blockchains can't be forged by a broker, eliminating diversion. Blockchains speed claims processing by simplifying the flow of information. Etherisc uses smart contracts to write flight insurance policies and has plans to expand into hurricane and crop insurance next. InsureX brings together insurers, reinsurers, and brokers in an alternative insurance marketplace that removes layers of intermediaries found in existing models. Insurwave is a Blockchain-based marine hull insurance program launched in 2018. A collaboration between shipping giant A.P. Møller-Maersk, Microsoft, Willis Towers Watson, EY, and others, Insurwave underwrites ships and cargo. It gathers real-time information on ship location, condition, and safety conditions. When ships enter high-risk areas, such as war zones, the platform automatically factors it into underwriting and pricing calculations. Insurwave handled more than 1,000 commercial vessels and 500,000 automated transactions in its first 12 months of operation.

Decentralized Platforms

The decentralized nature of Blockchain networks has led to the creation of a range of applications that offer decentralized technology services—storage, and computing—at a fraction of the price of traditional, centralized cloud services.

Decentralized Storage

Customers trust cloud-based storage services—Microsoft Azure, Amazon Web Services, Dropbox—to store data in secure, centralized locations. Decentralized cloud storage services—Filecoin, MaidSafe, Sia, Internxt, IPFS, Fortknoxster, and Storj—use the distributed nature of Blockchain networks to reinvent cloud storage. AirBNB lets you rent out your spare room; decentralized storage companies let you rent out spare space on your hard drive in return for crypto-currency. Distributed storage is consolidated into a high availability, secure cloud storage service. Data is encrypted on a Blockchain and stored over many computers. Sia stores three copies of their data, spread across 50 host computers. This ensures customer data is always available and cannot be compromised. Decentralized storage costs far less than traditional cloud storage services, often half the price, sometimes significantly less than that.

Decentralized Computing

Golem, Sparc, Gridcoin, SONM, and iExec offer decentralized computing resources that are aggregated to create powerful virtual supercomputers. Host computers are paid with cryptocurrency to contribute processing power. Golem, based in Poland, is optimized for computer-generated image (CGI) rendering, mathematical calculations, DNA analysis, medical research, and machine learning. SONM is focused on docker containers for supercomputing applications. Gridcoin is an open-source project built at the University of California, Berkeley. It decodes signals from the SETI institute (Search for Extra-Terrestrial Intelligence). iExec focuses on scientific research, cryptography, 3-D rendering, finance, and machine learning. Sparc runs physics simulations using a novel approach. Sparc has browser compatibility so that websites can generate revenue through micro-computations performed on their users' computers rather than showing ads.

Social Media

Steemit, Diaspora, Kik, Minds, Props, and Sapien offer Blockchain-based social media platforms. These networks allow people to share information while retaining control over their personal data. Rather than monetize users with targeted advertising (as Facebook does), Steemit pays its users to curate high-quality content on their network, rewarding users who post popular content or who share it early on. DTube, Flixxo, and Synereo use a similar approach to distribute video content.

Digital Voting

Blockchains help to establish voter identity, reduce voter fraud, eliminate voter suppression, and increase access to democracy. Voting becomes transparent and easy for voters. Elections become easy to audit and hard to manipulate. Votes are counted without compromising privacy or security. Democracy.earth and followmyvote.com advocate Blockchain to shore up democracy, improve governance, and fight corruption. Follow myvote promotes secure online voting that removes the need for voters to attend a physical polling station. Democracy.earth promotes direct democracy and platforms that enable vote delegation to a friend, colleague, or other person you trust as an expert on a topic.

Government Services

Governments are known for their titanic bureaucracies. Access to government services often involves reams of paperwork and waiting in lines. Blockchains will improve the efficiency and transparency of government operations. Digitized information is shared securely between government departments, reducing bureaucracy and paperwork.

Estonia, perhaps the most advanced digital society in the world, stores national data registries related to health, judicial, legislative, security, and commercial code systems on Blockchains. The Estonian government plans to expand the use of Blockchains to store health records, boost cybersecurity, and create data embassies. Data embassies are secure copies of government data located in other countries to increase data resilience and digital continuity. Estonia's first data embassy opened in Luxembourg in 2019. The Dubai government plans to move all its documents and conduct all major transactions on Blockchain by 2020.

Healthcare

Healthcare records hold sensitive, highly regulated, personal information that must be stored securely. How many times have you filled in the same information on forms when you visit the doctor's office? Blockchains provide a secure foundation to store electronic healthcare records and make them easy to share between providers while maintaining high levels of privacy. A single, portable, accurate healthcare record will improve the speed and accuracy of diagnosis and make it easier for data to be shared between patients and clinicians. Blockchains make patient and hospital data harder to hack, reducing the threat of ransomware attacks.

Journalism

Blendle, based in the Netherlands, is a Blockchain platform designed to be "the Spotify of journalism", a one-stop shop to browse premium articles from leading newspapers and magazines. Blendle signed deals with the *New York Times*, *The Economist*, *Time*, the *Financial Times*, *Vanity Fair*, the *Wall Street Journal*, and many other premium publishers that typically keep their content behind a pay wall. Blendle wants to make it easy to support quality journalism without committing to many expensive subscriptions. Blendle has more than a million users, half of whom are under the age of 35, people who might not otherwise pay for journalism. Blendle editors curate the best articles that are available via the web and a daily email. Algorithms personalize the selection based on a user's reading history. Users receive a steady diet of analysis, investigative reporting, backgrounders, and interviews. To view each article, readers pay just a few pennies. Each article comes with a full money-back guarantee. If you don't think an article was worth it, you can request your money back.

Civil is a blockchain-based community platform for independent journalism. Newsrooms that participate in the Civil platform have pledged to abide by high ethical standards. To verify that journalists keep their pledge, Civil holds them accountable to the "Civil Constitution," a document that attempts to define standards for ethical journalism. Civil operates a token economy based on the CVL token. Token ownership represents a stake in the governance of the platform. Members (readers) can buy tokens as a way to support Civil's efforts and to unlock access to content. Articles are stored on the Civil Blockchain to make them indelible and thus resistant to censorship. Members can vote to challenge unethical newsrooms and throw them off the network. The Civil platform self-governs, and decisions are distributed across members. The more tokens a member holds, the greater their say. No single entity or ideology can wrest control of the governance of the site since governance decisions are so highly distributed. There is a process of appeal available to a body of journalists, academics, and free speech experts known as the Civil Council, but ultimately the crowd determines how the platform is run.

One major modern challenge to journalism is the rise of fake news. In the future, Blockchain technology might help to combat the scourge of misinformation and disinformation. Blockchains allow information to be time-stamped and certified. An immutable database of facts could be created, each linked to its certified source. Articles could be certified as being built around certified facts and information. Consumers could then trace any information cited in a news article back to trusted sources and evaluate the article based on verifiable merits.

Gift Cards and Loyalty Schemes

Gift cards have been a wild success for retailers. But about $1 billion of gift card value goes unused each year (Source: *Marketwatch*), a liability that retailers must carry on their balance sheets. Some retailers are exploring Blockchains to underpin new e-gift cards. E-gift card transactions cost less to process, and the use of cryptography reduces opportunities for fraud and money laundering. By shifting from dollar-value cards to electronic prepaid vouchers—one token equals one dollar—retailers may also be able to avoid having to carry unused vouchers on their balance sheet as a liability. Loyyal uses Blockchains to make it easier for loyalty rewards to be exchanged across sectors, for example, spanning airlines, hotels, ride-sharing, and car rental companies. Retailers use Loyyal to build digital rewards programs and connect them into a partner network. This makes loyalty points more liquid for customers, increasing their perceived value.

The Future of Blockchain

Older Blockchains can't scale to handle the demands of modern, distributed applications. They consume far too much energy, and they aren't designed to work in conjunction with other Blockchain platforms. This has been a significant reason for Blockchain's slow adoption to date. Let's review how third-generation Blockchains improve over the past.

Scalability and Speed to Meet the Needs of the 2020s

The original Bitcoin Blockchain handles about four transactions per second (tps). Ethereum, a second-generation Blockchain, operates at about 15 tps, though architectural tricks may improve that significantly in the future. By comparison, PayPal handles about 400 tps, and the Visa network handles up to 60,000 tps at its Christmas peak. Some companies propose applications that require support for millions of transactions per second. For example, a system that tracks millions of products as they move through a complex supply chain would need to record data each time an item moved through a step in the logistics process. Third-generation Blockchains can store enormous amounts of distributed data and can handle tens or hundreds of thousands of transactions per second. Some are aiming for 1 million tps or more. These Blockchains implement different data mechanisms than traditional Blockchains; third-generation Blockchains look less like chains and more like highly interconnected spiderwebs.

Interoperability Enables Rapid Value Creation

Third-generation Blockchains can talk to each other and securely share data. For example, a Blockchain that underpins a mortgage loan platform could interact with another Blockchain that stores a borrower's financial and identity information and yet another Blockchain that stores property information such as the title, liens, planning permission, property tax, and sales history.

Sustainability: Data Integrity without Killing the Planet

One of the major shortcomings of early Blockchains is their energy consumption: Brute-force cryptographic problem solving keeps powerful computers whirring 24/7 and sucks shocking amounts of electricity from the grid. It's been estimated that one Bitcoin transaction consumes the same energy as four average American homes in a day. Third-generation Blockchains employ new approaches that do away with mining and significantly reduce the computational power needed to operate.

Beyond Blockchains

Some new Blockchains aren't really chains anymore. To speed transactions and reduce energy consumption, new distributed ledger technology (DLT) has been developed that goes beyond traditional Blockchains. These DLTs use new topologies including a structure known as a directed acyclic graph (DAG). The details of these approaches are beyond the scope of this book, but you can think of DAGs as being multidimensional networks versus Blockchain's one-dimensional chain. These new structures speed operations and improve security. Examples of these new "DAGchain" platforms include Hedera Hashgraph, IOTA, Nano, ByteBall, and Dexon. IOTA can handle about 1,000 transactions per second. Hedera Hashgraph claims their platform can deliver "hundreds of thousands" of transactions per second.

Strategies to Get You Started with Blockchain

Technologies are not all created equal. Some have far greater potential than others. As a strategic planner and futurist, I've learned to watch out for these mega-technologies. The web, mobile, artificial intelligence, and Blockchain are all examples of mega-technologies. Blockchain has significant strategic implications for almost every marketplace, and thus every business.

Blockchain technology will change how you pay people, how you track your operations, how you manage your supply chain, how you raise capital, and the way you collaborate with others. Blockchains will help you to reduce risk and secure your assets and data. Blockchains will give competitors a new launching pad from which to mount attacks upon you but also may provide you with the capabilities you need to overwhelm your competition.

Collaborate in New Ways: Build Open Teams and Reward Up-Front Investment with Tokens

Blockchain provides a new way for people to share in the profits of collaboration. Last year, I met a guy who was building a new global payment system. He had only seven full-time employees but more than 100 virtual employees. He and his seven employees drew a traditional salary. He had never met any of his virtual workers. These workers contributed their time and toil for the promise of tokens, which are awarded based on contribution. The more quality code virtual workers write that ends up in the final product, the more tokens they receive. They are motivated to build a strong platform (and not just write lots of terrible code) because the future value of tokens is proportionate to the ultimate success and value of the platform. Token economics enable entrepreneurs to attract workers from the global labor pool and coordinate their efforts using tokens as incentives. Good ideas will attract talent that believe in a project and wish to share in the rewards of future success. Tokens are used to create "crypto-shareholder virtual employees" that work "for free" in return for potential future profit. This opens up a new collaboration and development model that every business should consider.

Understand the Threat to Centralized Power in a Decentralized World

If your business is a large centralized authority that exerts strong control over a marketplace, be on the lookout for ways competitors might build a decentralized capability that threatens your unique value and the market that you have created. If seven guys and a virtual, distributed workforce can build a platform with ambitions to compete with Visa, what might a small startup be able to do to you? Conversely, what might you be able to do to the 800-pound gorilla in your industry?

Create Digital Provenance to Speed Audits, Add Traceability, and Establish Chain of Custody

Blockchains makes business operations more transparent, aid traceability, and speed audits. They make it easy to track and prove the provenance of products so we can answer important questions like "Where did it come from?," "Who made it?," "Is it safe?," "Was this properly transported and stored?," "Is this the product I am paying for?," and "What's the story behind this thing?" Consumers will demand answers to these questions, and every business should be ready to answer them *and prove it.*

Reduce Transaction Friction, Remove Intermediaries, and Offer Competitive Payments

Blockchain technology will create winners and losers. Blockchains can establish trust between strangers and remove the need for third-party validators like clearing houses, brokers, and title companies. Companies that add friction to transactions in the name of added security and trust will ultimately be losers. Companies that charge high fees for access to marketplaces may also be losers. Distributed e-commerce and sharing economy platforms will challenge current industry titans. Companies that hoard data and exert centralized control over markets may also be challenged by decentralized alternatives that don't need to generate revenue by selling customer data.

The winners will be companies that use Blockchain technology to streamline the flow of data inside and between organizations and remove intermediaries from value chains. Companies will use Blockchains to speed operations, reduce costs, and become more competitive. The ultimate winners will be consumers who will experience more secure, easy-to-use, speedy transactions and services that cost less.

5 Virtual, Augmented, and Mixed Reality

What Are They and Why Are They Important?

Virtual, augmented, and mixed reality (VR, AR, and MR) offer exciting new ways for us to interact with digital information, services, and each other. In virtual reality, we can dive into digital worlds that transport us somewhere new. With augmented and mixed reality, we invite digital objects, information, and services to inhabit our physical spaces. These technologies build bridges between the physical and digital worlds and allow us to pass back and forth across these bridges at will. They offer us new ways to connect with digital content, and the ability to edit our own visual perception. At maturity, these technologies will have a profound impact on the world, perhaps outstripping that of the smartphone.

Understand the Reality Spectrum: Virtual, Augmented, and Mixed

Virtual, augmented, and mixed reality exist on a spectrum with physical reality on one end and virtual reality on the other. A VR headset immerses us in a 100% digital world. Users are isolated from the physical world and feel transported to another place. Augmented and mixed reality experiences sit in the middle of the spectrum, halfway between physical and virtual reality. In augmented reality, digital information and content is overlaid on top of a user's view of the physical world. Users remain connected to the physical world, which makes AR far more useful in real-world applications. Mixed reality—sometimes referred to as blended or hybrid reality—is a more sophisticated version of augmented reality. Here, digital content interacts with the physical world. For example, a digital character walking across a coffee table might appear to step behind a glass placed on the table. To display that scene convincingly, a computer must build a complex understanding of the physical world that includes the shape and location of objects and lighting conditions in the room. This is a hard problem to solve and explains why mixed reality is taking time to come to market. When perfected, MR will change how we think about the digital world forever.

While MR is distinct as a more sophisticated form of AR, the term "augmented reality" is increasingly being used as a catch-all term that includes mixed reality experiences. For the sake of simplicity, I will use that shorthand for the remainder of the book, referring to both AR and MR experiences simply as AR.

Augmented Reality Is the New Display

If artificial intelligence is the new computer and Blockchain is the new network, then augmented reality will become the new display. With AR, digital information is no longer trapped inside rectangular screens on our desks and walls. The breakthrough display of the twenty-first century will be the physical world itself, a canvas on which we will blend digital information, objects, and scenes that augment our perception of the world. With AR, we will customize our visual perception and see the world the way we want to see it. We may eventually persuade others to allow us to augment their perception of us, so they see us the way we want them to see us.

Displays as we have understood them in the past will become virtual. Some virtual displays will be personal, only visible to one person, while others will be public and shared. Over time, virtual displays, rendered in the physical world, may reduce the need for physical displays. Your next 150″ TV might be a 99-cent app sourced from an app store. AR will let you place a TV on any surface in your home, including the ceiling above your bed, scaled to any size that you'd like with a simple gesture. Floating displays in the kitchen will show recipes while you cook. Of course, this vision of TV-like virtual displays demonstrates old-paradigm thinking. Early TV shows were nothing more than a televised radio broadcast of people talking into microphones in a studio. It took time to jettison old thinking and create the new paradigm of TV shows. The same will be true of AR media. With time, content creators will use AR holograms to escape the constraints of flat, rectangular displays and make full use of the medium.

Gesture and Voice Are the New Keyboard and Mouse

With a new class of computing comes a new interface. AR platforms are designed to be used while interacting with the physical world. This is hands-free computing. A keyboard, mouse, or even a touch interface is not appropriate. AR systems primarily use gesture and voice interfaces to control interaction. This makes AR useful to a whole class of workers for which previous generations of computing technology were just not relevant.

Hands-Free, Click-Free Computing: Computing for the Other 80%

Roughly 80% of workers neither work in traditional office environments, nor in roles where they can make use of traditional computing devices like laptops, tablets, or smartphones. These people often work with their hands or operate in fast-moving, mobile environments: think retail sales assistants, construction workers, and surgeons. These people have not benefited from the productivity and efficiency improvements that digital technology has brought to others. AR headsets keep users connected to their physical environment, with their hands free, while still accessing digital value. These devices have huge market potential. They offer "computing for the rest of us," platforms that provide value to all workers.

What Can You Do with Them?

Virtual and augmented reality will quickly move beyond novelty applications, gaming, and porn to become vital work tools that boost productivity and transform work. Experiences will continue to improve. Advances in optics, displays, software, graphics hardware, sensors, and wireless networks will make experiences more realistic, improve image fidelity, increase scene detail, and reduce prices.

Virtual Reality: Beyond Games and Porn

VR gaming offers immersive experiences. If you've ever seen somebody playing a game like Beat Saber (find a video on YouTube if you haven't), you know how physical they can get, too. VR applications from Netflix, Hulu, HBO, and other content providers seat you in a virtual home theater to enjoy content on a giant virtual screen. No popcorn, but the experience is a decent substitute for a big screen while sitting in a cramped airplane seat. VR is inevitably used as a content platform by the porn industry, too. No surprise given that porn has driven the adoption of many previous technologies, including VHS, multimedia, CD-ROM, and DVD. Beyond games and porn, VR has many valuable applications in training, design, simulation, medical therapy, communication, and education.

A good VR experience makes the viewer feel totally immersed in the scene that they are experiencing. This feeling, known as "immersion," is what makes VR so compelling. You feel like your consciousness has been teleported to a different reality, sometimes to an entirely new universe. VR allows you to travel through time and space and explore new realities that only exist inside the mind of a computer. It is this quality of immersion that is being used to deliver digital therapeutics and experiential education.

Digital Therapeutics: PTSD, Pain Management, Autism, Paraplegics, and Spiders

VR is used to treat patients with posttraumatic stress disorder (PTSD). Patients are reintroduced to simulated scenes of war in a controlled and safe environment, under the guidance of counselors. Difficult, buried memories are unlocked and accessed. Trained clinicians offer support and help patients to cope with these painful memories.

VR exposure therapies help people overcome a range of chronic fears: heights, crowds, flying, spiders, maybe even the ultimate . . . flying spiders! VR is used to calm patients in dentist's chair, to treat anxiety, and to guide relaxation. Clinicians at Cedars-Sinai Medical Center partnered with AppliedVR to build digital therapeutics that divert a patient's attention to alleviate pain. In studies at Duke University and the University of São Paulo, patients with chronic spinal cord injuries were immersed in a therapeutic VR simulation designed to improve the mobility of their lower limbs. Patients wore a brain-machine interface (BMI), an exoskeleton, and a VR headset, which showed them images of a simulated pair of legs. Thoughts sensed by the BMI controlled the exoskeleton. When patients move the exoskeleton legs with their thoughts, they see their virtual legs moving inside VR. Patients quickly learned to control the exoskeleton with the BMI. Remarkably, in the process of seeing their virtual legs move in VR, new pathways were formed between the brain cortex and undamaged nerves in the spinal column. After extensive training, once the BMI and exoskeleton were removed, some patients regained limited control and sensation in their legs.

Experiential Education That Escapes the Classroom

With its ability to "teleport" users through time and space, VR is a great tool for education, simulation, and experiential training. Verizon, Chipotle, Tyson Foods, JetBlue, and Fidelity Investments all use VR training. Walmart uses VR to train customer service, checkout, and warehouse employees. Walmart trains new employees in a simulated environment before letting them loose on real customers, leading to a consistent customer service experience across all their stores. Employees credited the training they received in VR for their ability to quickly and calmly respond to the tragic 2019 shooting incident at Walmart's Dayton store. The VR training they received probably saved lives.

Talespin sells a VR simulator to coach leaders on difficult work situations, including how to fire employees. Managers practice on an AI-powered virtual human that reacts realistically to the conversation and displays emotion. The simulation is designed to develop a leader's emotional intelligence and empathy, and to help them avoid common pitfalls.

Some football teams, including the New York Jets and Arizona Cardinals, complement traditional training with VR. VR is especially helpful for injured players who need to rest up and stay off the field for a while. STRIVR builds VR software to help teams plan their plays and practice repetitions before the game. This mental practice improves response times on the field when players are under pressure.

OramaVR creates experiential training for surgeons. OramaVR claim their VR training improves patient outcomes, reduces errors, and decreases training time by allowing surgeons to practice new surgeries inside detailed simulations.

The True Breakthrough Is Augmented Reality

While VR is useful, it has a major limitation: Users are disconnected from the physical world while they use it. Augmented reality has far greater utility because it keeps users connected to the physical world and blends in digital value. AR is far better suited to enterprise work environments than VR.

3-D Computing for a 3-D World

For decades, two-dimensional computer displays have shown us two-dimensional information with two-dimensional applications. Even three-dimensional models are displayed on flat screens. Augmented reality changes that. AR applications display information in the most natural format for human consumption: glorious three-dimensional space. Complex project plans, data, and other information can be visualized and manipulated in 3-D. Plans for electrical and plumbing systems are overlaid on a building so construction workers no longer spend time trying to decipher 2-D plans and map them onto 3-D space. Product designers and engineers can instantly review their latest creations, right in front of their eyes. AR is truly a breakthrough technology that will boost productivity across many industries.

Augmented Reality Workers

Augmented reality workers will transform the workplace in the next decade. With the advent of AR, we will create "hybrid workers," a hybrid of digital intelligence, human intelligence, and human physicality. AR systems will display relevant information in the worker's field of view: production line performance statistics for a factory line worker, or x-rays and CT scan images overlaid on a patient for a surgeon. Sophisticated AR systems will monitor worker activity and guide them step-by-step, essentially providing training in real time.

Bell's Law Goes through the Looking Glass

For more than 50 years, Moore's Law successfully predicted the exponential evolution in the capabilities of silicon chips: twice as many transistors roughly every two years, which translated into faster, cheaper, more energy-efficient computing.

A lesser-known law from the world of computing is Bell's Law, formulated in 1972 by Gordon Bell. This law observes that roughly every decade, computers shrink in both price and physical size to create an entirely new class of computing. Bell's Law and Moore's Law (both of which are observations and not laws at all) are highly interconnected. Room-sized mainframes from the 1960s gave way to refrigerator-sized mini-computers in the '70s, which in turn were succeeded by PCs in the '80s. PCs shrank to become laptops in the '90s. Tablets and smartphones followed laptops in the 2000s. One could argue that the Internet of Things (IoT) continues the trend. Typically, each new class of computing is roughly 10% of the physical size and weight of the previous generation.

Bell argues that each successive new class of computing brings with it a new programming platform, network, and interface. Windows PCs with keyboard and mouse were succeeded by iOS and Android-based smartphones that primarily use touch and voice control.

Do AR and VR fit Bell's Law? They check most of the boxes: a new user interface, a new operating system, new development paradigm, and they will connect to the new 5G network. But the size and weight of a VR or AR headset is not 10% that of a smartphone, at least not anytime soon. Perhaps the future of Bell's law isn't to asymptotically approach a zero-sized computing device, but instead to shoot straight through physical limitations and out the other side into the virtual world. A bit like passing through an event horizon, or through the looking glass (see Figure 5.1).

Early augmented reality devices are powerful enough to place one or more virtual objects into the user's field of view. Over time, improvements in computing will make those objects appear more realistic and they will interact with the physical world in more realistic ways.

The next breakthrough milestone for AR experiences will be headsets capable of augmenting an entire scene. With this capability, people can edit their perception and choose what they want to see. The view from the windows of our homes could be an alpine vista, a sandy beach, a coral reef, or even outer space. Imagine the implications for real estate

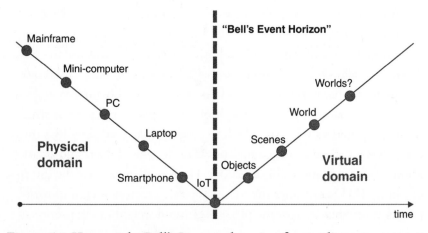

Figure 5.1 How might Bell's Law apply going forward?

prices if location and views matter less. Walking down the street, the sky could always look blue no matter the weather, trip hazards on the sidewalk could be highlighted, advertising images could be blocked and replaced with personal photographs. Full-scene AR is still likely a decade away, so this next jump in capability seems consistent with the timescales of Bell's Law. The next step beyond full augmented scenes would be an entirely augmented world. I offer this idea as a new way to think about how continued advances in computing might show up in our lives. Instead of ever-smaller, ever-cheaper physical computers, maybe the future of computing is virtual infrastructure that becomes ever more detailed, realistic, and delivered on an ever-grander scale.

Strategies for Success

VR and AR technology are still maturing, and AR is not yet ready for prime time. That said, these technologies will have such a profound impact on the future of work that it's important to run pilots, gain feedback, and build strategies to transform business operations starting today. Imagine how valuable it would have been to get a multiyear advanced start on the deployment of mobile technology. Use today's fledgling VR and AR technology to get ready for the profound impact AR will have by the mid-2020s.

Create Hybrid AR Workers That Blend Human and Machine Intelligence

Any automation plan should include an augmentation plan, a plan not to replace human labor with technology but instead to augment and support the effort of humans with technology. Every organization will need a labor augmentation strategy. Find ways to use AI and data analytics to support decision-making, leverage the vast knowledge repository of the cloud to supplement the knowledge of workers, and consider AR interfaces as the most natural way to communicate contextual information, guidance, or instructions to workers. Elevate your workers by augmenting them with superpowers.

A major challenge for many businesses is to find, hire, and train workers to reliably perform work. For industries with labor shortages or high turnover rates, a shift toward real-time AR training is attractive. Clear, visual directions are overlaid in the worker's field of view to show them what to do next. Machine vision capabilities in the AR headset track the worker's progress. As the worker performs each task, the system tracks whether work has been done correctly. The system then shows the worker the next task. In this way, a worker can learn a new job starting on their first day, maybe in their first hour of work. Over time, the worker needs less and less guidance from the AR system, only using it for unfamiliar scenarios. Imagine a robot repair worker that dons a 5G-connected AR headset to learn how to diagnose and repair a malfunctioning robot in the field. By recording the repair process, the headset aids compliance and reduces liability. Should a repaired robot later exhibit an issue, a supervisor can review the work for errors. If errors were made, additional training can be given. The AR software might also be updated to improve the quality of instruction. If no error was made, the recording can be used to absolve the repair company of liability with the client.

Build Enterprise Applications That Aid Collaboration and Speed Decisions

Augmented reality systems give workers superpowers. Workers gain the ability to connect and collaborate with colleagues in new ways. AR puts vast troves of information at workers' fingertips, displayed in easy-to-consume and natural ways that speed comprehension and decision-making.

Aid the Visualization of Complex Plans or Data

Augmented reality overlays information and visualizations on the physical world. For example, thermal camera information is overlaid on a firefighter's view as they navigate a burning building. Building plans, rendered on the firefighter's display, show where they are inside the structure with a "you are here" dot. A project manager views a complex project plan not as a flat, 2-D Gantt chart but as a sprawling, color-coded 3-D model they can walk around, manipulate, and explore. A farmer walking through their fields sees color-coded drone survey data overlaid on their crops, making it easy for them to locate areas flagged with potential blight. An engineer reviews a complex 3-D model of a design and reviews comments left by coworkers located thousands of miles away, each linked to specific locations on the model. These comments are a mix of text, video, and animated demonstrations of suggested design changes. Augmented reality fully embraces the innate visual abilities of human beings.

Bring in Remote Experts to Solve Problems Quickly

We don't always have the answers. Sometimes we need help from experienced coworkers with specialized knowledge. AR systems enable experts to support workers remotely, whether that worker is maintaining a turbine or performing surgery on a patient. A floating video window enables the worker to see the expert. The expert sees what the worker sees and can annotate the scene to illustrate suggestions: "Apply pressure here," "Undo these three screws and release this wiring harness." AR headsets go beyond traditional voice or video calls and allow a remote expert to visually assess the situation and communicate visually, too.

British developer Black Marble piloted an AR system designed for use at crime scenes. The system was evaluated by the Bedfordshire police department. The proof-of-concept should eventually become part of Black Marble's tuServ collaboration platform. The application runs on Microsoft's HoloLens platform and maps crime scenes in three dimensions. Police officers use the AR headset to capture digital evidence without contaminating the scene. Holographic evidence markers record the location of evidence in 3-D, preserving important spatial information. Digital photos and audio notes can be recorded to annotate the scene. Senior officers back at police headquarters use a HoloLens-based command and control application to review crime scenes remotely, track officer locations, and review incident progress. This allows them to make informed decisions and direct activity using the latest information available. While this capability is still a proof of concept at the time of writing, it demonstrates the possibilities of the augmented 3-D workflows of the future. Once a crime scene has been cleared, investigators can return to the scene of the crime virtually to review visual evidence and markers. Prosecutors and defense lawyers also get a much better understanding of the crime scene, which is preserved in three dimensions.

Context-Sensitive AR: Avoid Turning Our World into a Vegas-Like Assault of the Senses

What's better than information served up directly in your field of view? Even more information in your field of view! Said nobody, ever. If AR glasses become the next smartphone, we may surrender our visual perception to app developers and marketers. Pop-up ads could become personalized virtual billboards everywhere we look. An uncontrolled visual computing platform would be filled with attention-grabbing animations, content, and other distractions. Our field of view would look like the Las Vegas Strip at night wherever we look. That's not a world that consumers will readily accept.

AR interfaces will need to understand a user's context and show only the digital information and layers that are currently relevant. A breaking news alert may be appropriate while you're heading home on the bus, but not while you're talking to your boss or reading your kids a bedtime story. AR glasses won't find broad success until they understand and respect the current context of users. Enterprise applications will be no different. AR app developers will need to be mindful of visual overload and show appropriate respect for the power of the platform.

6 Connecting Everything and Everyone

5G Networks and Satellite Constellations

In the last decade or so, we have come to understand the benefits of being connected. Our phones lose most of their utility when we switch them into airplane mode. Being connected allows us to access incredible troves of information, to connect with the people we care about, and to use the amazing capability of the cloud.

Not being connected is a major disadvantage. While over half of the world's population is now online, billions of people still have no access to the services that many of us take for granted, including financial services. The ability to save, make payments, and gain access to credit is fundamental to enabling a billion people to lift themselves out of poverty. Connectivity matters.

For farmers in southeast Asia, internet access means access to information, and information is power. Farmers need to know which crops to plant, when to plant them, and how to improve crop yields. Most importantly, farmers need to know the fair market price for their crops. Internet connectivity empowers them to negotiate from a position of strength when selling to intermediaries who might otherwise try to rip them off. Internet access enables people to learn more about the world, about other cultures, and to raise their level of education. Sites like YouTube hold a remarkable mount of high-quality educational material, all available for free. Whether you're trying to brush up on machine learning, learn how to become an entrepreneur, or understand how to build a wind generator that brings electricity to your village, internet access is empowering.

Connecting people to the internet is just part of the story, though. As we saw in Chapter 2, huge benefits come from connecting objects, infrastructure, vehicles, and other things to the internet. The more things that we can connect, and the faster the speeds we can connect those things at, the more value we can create for people. We are on a path to connect everyone and everything, at blistering speeds, within a decade.

5G—A Lot More Than Just Faster Phones

The latest in connectivity is a set of networking capabilities collectively known as 5G. These fifth-generation cellular networks are a big deal. They offer far more than faster data rates. 5G networks will enable important new applications and make digital communication more reliable, especially in congested urban areas.

One More G!

As you might expect, 5G networks are faster than 4G LTE networks. In turn, 4G networks were faster than the 3G networks before them. How much faster will 5G networks be? Your mileage may vary, and speeds will increase with time, but carriers promise 5G networks will have data rates that are 10 to 100 times faster than 4G LTE networks. Theoretically, 4G

LTE networks have top data rates of 300 Mbps, though typical download speeds are more likely 10–30 Mbps, which are significantly lower during times of heavy network traffic. Future 5G networks could have cellular data transfer speeds of between 1 Gbps and 10 Gbps, maybe more. Typical download speeds are likely to be in the 2–3 Gbps range, fast enough to download an entire HD movie in a few seconds. This represents a substantial speed increase over both 4G LTE and existing wired broadband networks. 5G networks will be more responsive, more reliable, more scalable, more secure, and in some cases will consume less power than previous networks.

Low Latency Enables New Applications

One of the main new advantages of 5G networks is their low latency. Many compelling applications benefit from, or require, a low-latency network connection. Examples include telemedicine, next-generation manufacturing, and streaming virtual and augmented reality.

Latency is the time that elapses between when a device, like a smartphone, requests data from the network, say a Google search inquiry, and the moment that data, the search result, starts being received by the device. There are several components to overall latency: the time for your request to go from your device to the cellular base station over your wireless connection, the time for the request to travel from the base station to the Google server, the time for the server to act on your request and respond with data, and then the time for the data to head all the way back to you via the base station. Network latency is just a part of overall latency.

While the overall latency depends on how fast and responsive the server is, and how quickly the data moves between the server and the base station over the wired internet backbone, it's often the latency between the device and the base station that is the largest component of overall latency. By significantly reducing latency to the base station and back, overall latency tumbles. Network latency on 4G LTE varies with your location and network carrier. Average latencies are 40–60 milliseconds, but sometimes more than 100 milliseconds, and specific maximum latencies are not guaranteed. Applications that require low latency cannot run reliably on 4G LTE networks. On 5G networks, latency can be as low as 1 or 2 milliseconds, guaranteed. This is a game changer and enables many exciting new applications.

The low latency and high data rates offered by 5G networks make it possible to build connected devices that are cheaper, lighter, and have a longer battery life than before. This is achieved by moving much of a device's computing capability to the cloud, or to the edge of the network.

Consider a connected delivery drone with an onboard machine vision system to avoid collisions, navigate to destinations, and safely land in a customer's front yard. The computer that runs the vision, navigation, and control systems is typically located on the drone. A 4G LTE connection is neither fast nor reliable enough to safely offload that computing to the cloud. The computer adds to the cost and weight of the drone. The computer also requires a heavy battery to power it.

5G networks change the cost equation for products like this. Fast, reliable 5G connections will enable safe, remote control of cloud-connected drones. Video is streamed to the cloud from the drone's camera where machine vision algorithms process the video, make split-second decisions, and return flight instructions. Cloud-connected drones will use simple onboard computers that consume less power. Battery energy is focused on the flight rotors to extend the range and flight time of the drone. The drone is cheaper to make, too. The cost of cloud computing to support 100 drones is far less than the cost of building powerful computers into each of those drones.

Cloud offload over 5G will allow engineers to add "smart" functions to nearly any device at very low cost, changing the economics of smart devices from robots to smart washing machines. This shift to simpler, cheaper devices has potential security implications. Lower-cost computing devices have traditionally come with lightweight security capabilities, increasing the risk of compromise. Engineers will need to push suppliers to deliver end-to-end security solutions even for low-end components.

Dropped calls are annoying but dropping a mission-critical data connection can be disastrous. Next-generation robots, autonomous vehicles, and smart objects need a constant connection to maintain full product capability. 5G networks are designed for high resilience and availability, making it possible to use them for mission-critical applications. Fewer dropped calls will be nice, too.

Connected Factories, Hospitals, Cities, Vehicles, and People

Screaming fast 5G networks will enable new capabilities and bring new economic models to many industries. Let's review a few examples.

Flexible Factories

Rather than connecting production line machinery with a tangle of cables, production engineers will be able to link equipment using high-speed, reliable, low-latency 5G networks. Factories will be far more flexible: It's far easier to retool and reorganize the flow of a production line or to switch a line over to a new product if you don't have to worry about network cabling. Machinery still needs power, but at least one set of cables is gone. In an Industry 4.0 manufacturing world, where everything is connected and factories need to be flexible, this is a big deal.

Telemedicine and Telesurgery

The internet allows businesses to break the barriers of time and place. For example, streaming media lets us watch what we want, when we want, where we want. The responsiveness of 5G networks should make telemedicine a common reality, allowing clinicians to work with patients who are hundreds or even thousands of miles away. Telemedicine isn't new but has been limited by infrastructure. A remote 5G-connected clinic might deliver a range of services to patients including robotic procedures performed by remote surgeons. My wife is a physician assistant. Her surgeons regularly use a da Vinci robot for specialist procedures. The surgeon stands on one side of the operating theater at a control console; my wife, the robot, and the patient are on the other side of the room.

5G networks simply widen the potential distance between the surgeon and patient.

Connected Vehicles

This next one is still up for debate: 5G networks might play some kind of future role in vehicle-to-vehicle (V2V) communications. Standards discussions are ongoing, and some argue V2V over 5G will never work because cars will always find themselves in regions with poor network coverage. That said, many companies are proposing that 5G networking be used as a way for cars to gossip about traffic conditions. When a child chases an errant Frisbee into the street and causes a connected car to screech to a halt, all the cars immediately behind would receive rapid notification so they can take apply the brakes and avoid a pile up.

Streaming Media: Games and Augmented Reality Headsets

The low latency of 5G networks will enable a new generation of streaming video game services. The latest multiplayer twitch video games require split-second response times. A slow network connection can be the difference between victory and defeat. Mobile gamers will love the responsiveness of 5G network connections. Early game streaming platforms include Sony Playstation Now and Google Stadia. Apple took a more conservative approach with Apple Arcade and downloads games rather than streaming them. 5G could ultimately be the end of consoles as we know them. More likely, 5G will fuel a new generation of gaming consoles that fuse high-performance computing power in the console with additional computing oomph in the cloud.

Augmented reality represents the future of human–computing interfaces, both at home and in the workplace. Early AR headsets are impressive, but to reach mass adoption they need to improve the experience and reach mainstream price points. 5G networks will help with both.

Early augmented reality headsets were unwieldy and had limited capabilities. So far, most AR headset companies have not been able to miniaturize enough high-performance computing to fit it within the headset itself. The result is clunky designs with wires leading from the headset to computing packs worn on the hip or back. These limitations have kept augmented reality on the fringe.

Each time you move your head while wearing an augmented reality headset, it's important that the headset quickly senses that movement and updates the display. If it doesn't, digital objects shudder and slide around as you move your head. This not only breaks the illusion but causes nausea. If the frame rate of the image update falls below about 90 frames per second, users quickly experience motion sickness. Putting enough computing power in a pair of glasses so they can render two high-resolution images (one for each eye) at more than 90 frames per second is a serious design challenge.

Using the same approach as for the delivery drone, AR headset designers will use the low latency of 5G networks to offload computing power to the cloud, reducing cost, boosting battery life, and improving performance. Major US carrier *AT&T* has already announced plans to build high-performance graphics processing capabilities into its 5G base stations. This kind of edge computing capability may hold the key to building the low-cost, lightweight AR headsets of the future.

The Structure of 5G Networks

New 5G networks have a different topology than old 4G LTE networks. To reach such incredible speeds, 5G networks use a dense network of many small cells. This approach makes 5G networks more scalable than 4G networks. The performance of 4G LTE networks often drop significantly in populated areas where they simply can't handle demand. Deploying many small cells in densely populated areas enables 5G network operators to scale their network capacity and match it against population density. While there is provision for small cells in the 4G LTE spec, 5G is inherently designed to be more scalable, which should lead to a strong signal and high data rates even in busy locations.

5G networks hold great promise and seem too good to be true. How do they achieve rapid data rates, low latency, high scalability, high reliability, better security, and lower power? The simple answer is that they don't. A single network can't do all of these things at the same time; some of these goals are at odds. For example, screaming-fast data rates and ultralow power data transmission are incompatible goals. So, 5G networks cheat.

Three Networks in One

A 5G network isn't a single network. A 5G network is actually several physical networks, each running on different spectrum, using different protocols, and having characteristics that are optimized for specific goals. They work together under the umbrella of the 5G moniker. Here are the three main components:

1. **Enhanced Mobile broadband (eMBB)** is designed to meet the high-data-rate and high-traffic needs of devices like smartphones, laptops, set-top boxes, game consoles, UltraHD TVs, and Streaming VR/AR, where 4K, 8K, 16K, and 360-degree streaming video are the norm. eMBB is optimized to deliver blistering fast data transfers up to 10 Gbps.

2. **Ultra-Reliable Low-Latency Communications (URLLC)** is designed to provide ultra-responsive connections with low end-to-end latency across the network for mission-critical latency-sensitive applications. Such applications include factory automation, smart energy grids, and remote surgery where surgeons need to be able to "feel" remote objects using haptics. URLLC is optimized to deliver a latency

of just 5 milliseconds or less and high reliability with an availability of 99.9999%.

3. **Massive Machine Type Communications (mMTC)** is designed for low-power, embedded applications like connected parking meters, smart agriculture, and connected healthcare monitors where data rates aren't as important, but low-power connections are vital. mMTC incorporates two different approaches known as Low Power Wide Area (LPWA) and Narrow Band for Internet of Things (NB-IoT). mMTC sacrifices data rate, which is reduced to a maximum of 100 Kbps, to optimize its support for a high density of devices, long-range communications, and extreme battery life.

Between them, this alphabet soup of eMBB, URLLC, and mMTC should offer people most of the feature combinations needed to cover the demands of any given application. 5G has an additional trick up its sleeve that enables developers to further tailor their network experience for each application. This is the concept of "network slicing."

Network Slicing

Slicing allows network operators to divide their network up into multiple virtual slices, with the functionality of each slice being optimized around the needs of a particular client or set of users. Operators lease access to these slices to customers, known as tenants.

Leases can be short-, medium-, or long-term arrangements. A city might enter a long-term lease for a network slice to securely connect all of its infrastructure—traffic signals, garbage cans, parking meters, and so on. A stadium might enter a short-term lease for a network slice optimized for streaming high-definition video and to handle in-stadium, geo-fenced media. The contract might only cover a few hours during each event. A police department might want a highly secure network slice to share location data for cars and officers, to stream video from body cameras, and so forth. A hospital network might lease a secure network slice over which it can share HIPAA-regulated data so it can comply with privacy laws.

When Will We Experience 5G?

Network infrastructure upgrades require major investment and the global buildout of 5G networks will take years. When you get first access will depend on where you live. Most people should have coverage by 2025, much sooner if you live in major cities in the United States, Europe, and Asia. To access 5G networks, new phones, routers, and connected devices—5G-connected cars, washing machines, and parking meters—will be required. 5G coverage in rural areas will come later than for urban centers, but there is good news for rural communities coming in the very next section.

Connected Planet: Reaching the Next 4 Billion People

While over half of the world's population is now online, billions of people have intermittent and low-bandwidth connections, or are not connected at all. Several companies are working to solve this problem with constellations of satellites. Their goal is to make high-speed communications available anywhere on the planet.

Satellite Constellations

Satellites have been used for communication since the 1960s. More communication satellites will be launched into orbit in the 2020s than all satellites launched ever. Low orbit satellites reduce the latency of communications by reducing the distance that signals have to travel up from earth and back. But, there is a compromise. The closer a satellite is to earth, the smaller the area it covers on the surface and the faster it must travel to stay in orbit.

A new set of entrepreneurs are competing to build satellite constellations that use thousands of small satellites, organized in an ever-shifting patchwork network, to move data from one point on earth to another. These networks will be used to connect planes, cruise ships, and cars to the internet. Perhaps more importantly they will bring low-cost, broadband internet to billions of people who are currently offline. Network speeds will be impressive. Think 4.5G.

OneWeb—in collaboration with SoftBank, Qualcomm, Airbus, Richard Branson, the government of Rwanda, and others—plans to launch a network of 648 satellites, rising to perhaps 2,000 by the mid-2020s. Modular design and a mass-production assembly line allow One-Web to build two satellites per day and keep costs down. Satellites will orbit at 1,200km and connect users with a set of ground-based gateways. OneWeb will offer initial download speeds of 500 Mbps and 30 ms latency. OneWeb has a stated goal to connect every unconnected school by 2022, and to bridge the so-called digital divide by 2027.

Elon Musk's SpaceX will compete against OneWeb with their Starlink program. Ultimately, SpaceX plans to build a constellation of perhaps as many as 30,000 low-earth-orbit satellites, each the size of a mini-fridge. An antenna the size of a pizza box is needed to receive a signal on the ground. Satellites will orbit in shells at altitudes of between 335km and 1,325km to deliver global network coverage at gigabit speeds. Satellites operate in a mesh network, passing data from one to another using lasers to communicate. Light moves much faster through the vacuum of space than it does inside glass fibers, so Starlink may be able to offer faster point-to-point communication than traditional ground-based fiber optics. Trading desks in major financial centers like New York, London, Tokyo, and Shanghai will likely have strong interest. In high-velocity automated trading markets, every millisecond counts. SpaceX is betting that financial giants will pay billions to speed the links between their data centers and trading desks by 10 milliseconds or more. SpaceX should have their initial network up and running in the early 2020s.

Amazon plans to build a satellite constellation consisting of 3,236 low-earth-orbit satellites with an effort known as Project Kuiper. Launches will presumably be made by Jeff Bezos's Blue Origin space company.

SES networks will partner with Boeing to create the O3B mPOW-ER network of satellites, which will orbit in medium-earth orbit at 8,000km. O3B stands for "other 3 billion," which speaks to the target audience for this network. An initial network of 16 satellites already brings connectivity to small island nations and countries with poor communications infrastructure. In 2021, the existing O3B network will be upgraded with seven new satellites to form the O3B mPOWER network designed to bring increased speed and flexibility, including multi-terabit data rates.

Other satellite constellation efforts are planned by Telesat and LeoSat, which are focused on the enterprise market and plan to deliver 10 Gbps connectivity. With plenty of competition between well-funded players, high-bandwidth, low-cost global communications will become widely available within the decade.

Balloons

Firing satellites into orbit is not a cheap endeavor. Loon, an Alphabet company (formerly known as Google's Project Loon), takes a different approach. Loon plans a network of stratospheric balloons to reach underserved communities with internet connections.

Giant, solar-powered balloons, measuring 15 by 12 meters, float about 20km (12 miles) above the ground. This vantage point allows them to deliver a 4G LTE connection of 10 Mbps to an area of 5,000 square miles. The balloons, spaced up to 100km apart, connect to each other in a mesh network. A highly automated, sophisticated navigation system uses machine learning and solar-powered pumps that add or release air from the balloon. This moves the balloon up and down so it can catch air currents that move it in the desired direction.

Loon has conducted several successful tests of its technology in real-world conditions. The communications and power infrastructure of Puerto Rico was devastated by Hurricane Maria in September 2017. Loon launched five balloons and partnered with AT&T and T-Mobile to bring basic text messaging and internet access to more than 200,000

Puerto Ricans. Loon also deployed their balloons to bring emergency connectivity to Peru after their communications infrastructure was destroyed by a series of floods and landslides. Until global satellite networks bring high-speed, always-available connections to every corner of the earth, the Loon balloons will play an important role in connecting the unconnected.

Connectivity is vital to future innovation, economic development, and a host of important services. Between 5G networks, satellite constellations, and balloons, the 2020s will see a major advance in global connectivity. Blazing fast speeds, exciting new applications, and billions more minds are being connected together. It will be an exciting decade.

Part II

Key Concepts to Help Your Business Adapt and Thrive

7 Align Your Automation Strategy with Your Corporate Purpose

The digital revolution has transformed every industrial sector. Over the last 40 years, businesses deployed computers to improve productivity, boost operational efficiency, reduce cost, and connect with customers in new ways. To remain competitive, businesses embraced wave after wave of computing innovation: mainframes, minicomputers, PCs, multimedia PCs, the internet, mobile devices, and cloud computing. Offices deployed spreadsheets, word processing, email, CRMs, ERP, and all manner of enterprise software. Manufacturers installed computer-controlled equipment, computer-aided design, and robotics. Adoption was more limited in other sectors—farming, retail, hospitality, construction, and to some extent healthcare—where much of the work remained physical in nature.

In the 2020s, *every* business in *every* industry will have to embrace new technology to stay ahead of the game. No exceptions, including former slow adopters. Every industry will reimagine how they operate, how they serve customers, and how they create value. Every business, including yours, will need to build new strategies that trample the old playbook and challenge long-held maxims.

Automation Is Inevitable: Make Sure You Get It Right

AI and advanced robotics will automate more physical work and some knowledge work, too. To remain competitive, every organization will automate or semi-automate every business process. Technology will augment and extend the capabilities of employees and elevate human work.

A tsunami of automation is coming. Winning companies will take the time to understand, acknowledge, and retain the core business elements that define their brand as they embrace new ways of doing business. This is as much about understanding what you stand for as it is about anything else. Companies will be so utterly remade by the next wave of digital transformation that they will need to know what to cling on to and what to let go of in the name of progress. The best digital transformation strategies will be driven to a deep understanding of a company's humanistic purpose. The question for every business will be how to use automation to boost the customer-facing humanity of the organization. A fancy restaurant might automate some of the back kitchen, but won't replace the high-end service provided by serving staff.

Every company needs a clear automation philosophy. It's vital to understand and agree on high-level goals before you start the difficult work of deploying new technology. Who are you as a brand? What are you ultimately trying to achieve? And how can technology help you achieve that more effectively?

Most of the top companies on the planet have a clearly stated humanistic purpose that focuses and guides their efforts. Coca-Cola seeks "to refresh people." Disney's purpose is "to make people happy." For Southwest Airlines, it's "to democratize flying." For Nike, it's "to bring innovation and inspiration to every athlete in the world." These companies align their business processes, their corporate culture, and their management focus to execute flawlessly against their core purpose. Their purpose guides their strategic plan and informs their corporate values.

Purpose and Profit

The leaders of these companies focus on delighting customers and executing against their core purpose, not on financial results. The purpose of a company is *not* to make money. As the great Simon Sinek points out, strong financial results are the *result* of excellent execution against your core, humanistic purpose. This can be hard for some business people to accept, particularly those working in finance, so I'll say it again. Profit is not the reason that your organization exists. If making money was truly your company's only purpose, you would be a drug cartel. But you're not a drug cartel, which means you have some other, higher purpose that your organization seeks to fulfill. A clear corporate purpose, combined with strong business process execution, leads to stellar business results.

Clear Purpose + Strong Execution = Results (Profit)

This goes against the orthodoxy of Nobel economist Milton Friedman, who stated that the only social responsibility of business was to "engage in activities designed to increase its profits." Yet purpose-oriented businesses consistently outperform those that focus purely on profit. The book *Firms of Endearment* notes that 30 companies driven by a sense of purpose and humanistic principles, that put their customers and employees first, ahead of shareholder considerations, saw a stock market performance eight times the average company. They also saw higher productivity and lower turnover.

Major businesses have taken note, realizing that naked capitalism needs to be balanced with a concern for sustainable operations and a focus on stakeholders beyond shareholders. In August 2019, the Business Roundtable, chaired by JPMorgan Chase's Jamie Dimon, released a statement that updated its view on the purpose of business. The statement seems to recognize the many calls to update capitalism to create what has variously been described as "conscious," "compassionate," "sustaining," "inclusive," or "shared values" capitalism. Signed by the CEOs of 181 major companies, the statement commits to deliver value to customers, invest in employees, deal fairly and ethically with suppliers, support communities, and generate long-term value for shareholders. This rebalancing of purpose and profit is a big deal and recognizes consumer angst over rising inequality. The general public seems aligned, with 64% of Americans saying the primary purpose of a business should be to "make the world better" (Source: *Fortune*).

Beyond a clear corporate purpose, every company should have a clearly stated vision and mission. Mission states what the company does on a day-to-day basis in an effort to fulfill its purpose. Vision explains what the world will look like if the company successfully executes their mission and fulfills their purpose.

As businesses deploy AI, leaders will need to stay laser-focused on their core, humanistic purpose and communicate it clearly and relentlessly to every employee. Purpose statements act as employees' North Star as they train, deploy, and work alongside AI. AIs learn from historical data and from historical behaviors and thus reflect human biases and values. If your employees aren't fully aligned with your purpose, mission, vision, and values, your AIs won't be either. Watch for unintended bias. Reinforce vision and values at every opportunity. Explain how automation will help employees to achieve your purpose and accelerate your ability to reach your vision. If you articulate that story successfully, employees will embrace automation and help you to deploy it throughout the organization.

In the 2020s, automation will be used extensively to optimize business processes execution. Automation technologies—artificial intelligence, autonomous machines, augmented reality, and the Internet of Things, underpinned by Blockchain-based platforms and 5G networks—are vital to every company that wishes to execute flawlessly against their corporate purpose.

The Recipe for Success

The unbeatable recipe for business success in the next two decades is this:

> A clearly articulated core purpose, executed flawlessly by well-trained, highly motivated, passionate employees who believe in the mission, feel valued for their contributions, and who are supported by thoughtfully deployed automation and augmentation technology.

High-functioning teams will be formed by a strong partnership of automation technology and human talent. The strongest teams of the future will use automation to augment human talent, to elevate human work, to maximize the human impact of labor, and thus maximize the humanity inherent in the company's brand.

Business leaders who invest the time to set and communicate clear humanistic purpose for their organization, and managers who can translate that purpose into well-implemented, semi-automated business processes, will win in the marketplace.

Examples

Let's consider a few examples of how companies could use automation to up-level their offerings and rally their organizations around a higher-level purpose. Some of these examples are outlined in more detail elsewhere in this book.

- **From selling clothes to selling confidence.** An apparel store goes beyond selling clothes and focuses on the purpose of styling customers for success. They deploy IoT and analytics tools to offer an automated styling service in their fitting rooms.

- **From daycare to relationships and transformations.** A doggy daycare company focuses on a purpose of supporting pet owners to maintain strong relationships with healthy, happy pets. They offer more than a safe place for owners to leave their pets. They treat your dog like it's family, keep you connected through the day, and help you to maintain or improve your pet's health and habits. IoT technology, cameras, and digital devices let owners check in on their pup and help them maintain a sense of connectedness. A comprehensive digital dashboard tells the story of the dog's day: the dogs they socialized with and how much they ate, drank, played, and slept. The company offers semi-automated interventions to help dogs become more social, more active, or to lose weight.

- **Safety and mass customization.** A manufacturing company uses automation to ensure worker safety and delight every customer with tailored products that exactly meet their needs. Sensors turn off dangerous machinery or divert robots when workers get too close. "Industry 4.0" mass-customization capabilities enable them to build one-of-a-kind products at mass-production prices.

Raise Your Aim: Solve a Higher Class of Business Problems with the Intimacy of IoT

In the coming decade, business leaders will need to make tough choices. Advances in robotics, AI, and other technologies will enable many tasks to be automated. The natural temptation will be to use technology as we always have: to increase efficiency, boost productivity, and reduce cost. Those goals remain valid, but a limited focus will not serve businesses well. The intimate cyber-physical connections made possible by the next wave of digital technology offers businesses the ability to reach far beyond these traditional goals. Organizations can and must aim higher than operational efficiency.

The potent combination of AI, sensors, IoT, AR, and autonomous machines solves previously impossible problems. The enormous capability of next-generation automation technologies can be overwhelming, and when overwhelmed, people retreat to their comfort zones. Companies that plow familiar territory will leave value on the table and expose themselves to more progressive competitors. Using automation to optimize for the right goals is crucial to remaining competitive. For every automation effort, leaders should step back, take a breath, and ask one simple question: What are we *really* trying to optimize for? We need to get philosophical before we get practical.

Hierarchy of Goals

Automation philosophy can be expressed in terms of a hierarchy of goals, as shown in Figure 7.1. Each level in the hierarchy represents a loftier set of goals around which to optimize an automation project.

As you review this hierarchy you might choose to group these optimization points in slightly differently ways than I have. That's okay, this is not an exhaustive list, and you may have a way to organize goals that makes better sense for your business. This hierarchy is provided as a generalized guide to help you up-level your thinking. A few comments on each of the layers in the model follow:

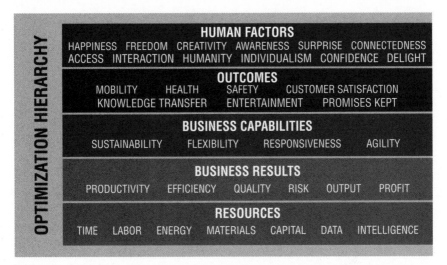

Figure 7.1 A hierarchy of business goals for automation projects.

Resources

Most automation implementations seek to minimize resource usage as a way to reach higher-level goals. For example, labor utilization is optimized to improve productivity and profitability. The term "materials" is intended to capture everything from fabric and steel to water and fertilizer. Artificial intelligence falls into a curious middle ground where it can almost be thought of as both labor and capital at the same time. As AI becomes a vital resource in every business, its use will be optimized, alongside labor and capital.

Business Results

Every successful business keeps a close eye on key business metrics and seeks to optimize revenue and profit. Top line results are optimized by improving labor productivity, production efficiency, product quality, and production output. No business likes surprises, and so they also try to minimize their risk and limit uncertainty. Note: By optimizing for higher-order goals and carefully managing the use of resources, business results often take care of themselves.

Business Capabilities

Automation will build stronger business capabilities. Stronger capabilities come from improvements to business processes, strengthening corporate culture, and strong governance. Blockchain technology may offer assistance in semi-automating and assuring strong governance. Businesses should use technology to anticipate customer needs and meet them before the customer is even aware of them. Building sustainable operations meets customer expectations for sustainability, but also helps to control costs and ensure the long-term viability of a business. In fast-moving markets, agility and flexibility are key to success. Businesses will need to shift their focus and move into new markets with speed and ease.

Outcomes

Outcomes are higher-order goals; a distillation of corporate purpose, not to be confused with business results, which are a *result* of executing well against the corporate purpose. Healthcare organizations optimize for positive health outcomes. Factories optimize for worker safety and customer satisfaction. Transportation planners strive to improve human mobility and increase the velocity of goods, services, and waste through a city. Universities want their students to be better informed. A theater group optimizes productions for entertainment value. A logistics company strives to keep its delivery promises.

Human Elements

Sitting above outcomes is a more rarified but important set of business optimization goals. These goals relate to improving the human condition. Disney uses automation to tune their operations with the goal of boosting human happiness. This, after all, is their stated mission as a company. Adobe and Autodesk embrace automation to unleash human creativity. Nonprofit organizations might set the goal of increasing human access to key resources or services such as water, education, and healthcare. Social networking companies and fan clubs might try to optimize human connection. An event company could use automation to boost interpersonal networking. For example, a smart ID badge at a conference might glow a certain color to indicate you are in the proximity of someone with a common interest.

In my experience, the higher up the optimization hierarchy that you can start, the greater the impact you will have and the stronger the business results that you will achieve. Bold, inspiring visions communicated clearly to employees, customers, suppliers, and shareholders give organizations the best chance of eventually achieving those visions.

Get Quick Wins but Keep Your Aim High

There is a lot to be said for getting quick wins and early impact, especially if you're trying to secure future funding. Implement a few small, lower-order projects to give you short-term wins and generate momentum. Once you've proven your team's ability to execute, raise your aim and rapidly shift to tackling higher-order goals that boost your impact. The higher up the hierarchy that you can operate, the more value you will create, the stronger your brand will become, and the more competitive advantage you will enjoy.

To illustrate this thinking, let's consider agricultural automation. Fields are a dynamic environment—some parts of the field will be too dry, others too moist; some will need fertilizer, some will not. With a focus on resource management, a farmer uses drones to survey fields and build digital maps of soil and crop health. The farmer spot-sprays or waters specific areas of the field based on guidance from the drone. This reduces water and chemical usage. Moving up the optimization hierarchy, the farmer looks to IoT, AI, and autonomous machines to boost overall farm productivity (a business result), to make their operation more sustainable (a business capability), to increase the health of livestock (an outcome), and to delight customers by providing fresh, safe produce that they can purchase with confidence. To achieve this top-level goal, sensor data, secured on a Blockchain, is used to tell a story of how produce was grown, processed, packed, and transported from farm to fork. Food provenance information boosts consumer confidence, minimizes food safety issues, and improves public health.

It's easy to drift from the core mission when leaders don't communicate it regularly and clearly. As a friend once told me, the *Deepwater Horizon* disaster didn't happen because a group of oil execs got together and thought, "Screw it, let's risk everything to make a buck." BP focused on optimizing for the wrong business metric: They did everything they could to reduce the time it took to drill through 10,000 feet. This focus improved operational efficiency and reduced time to money, but it also cost BP $20 billion and created an ecological disaster on the Gulf Coast of the United States. What we optimize for, and what we aim for, matters.

Build Human/Machine Partnerships to Boost Productivity, Improve Quality, and Increase Employee Engagement

Workforces of the future will blend human and digital intelligence. AIs, robots, and other autonomous machines will become teammates. Winning businesses will create high-functioning teams that build strong partnerships between human and nonhuman workers as a way to elevate human work, boost employee engagement, and improve quality, efficiency, and customer service.

The New Diversity: Teams of Humans and Nonhumans Working Together

Workplace diversity is vital to a high-functioning organization. Diverse perspectives, a broad spectrum of life experience, and a range of cultural backgrounds make an organization stronger. Diversity limits the possibility of "group think" and maximizes your chances of matching the diversity of your customers. It's easier to understand customers' needs when your organization has a similar demographic. It's good business sense to build teams with a diversity of age, gender, race, culture, and experience, quite aside from the need to meet any government-mandated diversity targets.

In the near future, teams will need to add a new dimension of diversity, a mix of humans and nonhumans working together.

High-functioning teams of the future will blend human intelligence and human dexterity with machine intelligence and robotic strength. Some team members will be pure human. Some will be pure machine. Many team members will be augmented, a hybrid of human and machine intelligence. All need to come together in a high-performance team that delivers stellar results.

Most businesses tend to have three to five major business processes (a sales process, a manufacturing process etc), though your organization may be different. For each business process in your organization, map out all the individual tasks that need to occur in sequence. Get as granular as you can. Plot how information and data are generated and passed from task to task. Identify the handoffs and the triggers that determine how and when one task hands off to the next. Sensors may play an important role here. Now ask the tough question: Given the latest capabilities of technology, which tasks are best done by humans, which best done by robots, and which best done by software algorithms and AI?

Know When to Use Each of Your Resource Pools: People, Robots, and Artificial Intelligence

To decide which tasks should be offloaded to AI and robots, we must understand the relative strengths and weakness of people, robots, and AIs. In a landscape of rapidly improving tech capabilities, this is a moving target. Let's consider the strengths of each of these three.

1. **People** have strong problem-solving skills that involve imagination, planning, and creativity. Humans are capable of complex critical thinking. They can generate and test new ideas and think about projects and situations holistically, exhibiting systems-level thinking. Some have entrepreneurial skills. Many have well-developed emotional intelligence and social skills, including leadership skills (the ability to inspire others) and influencing skills (the ability to persuade others). Other vital social skills include interpersonal communication, teaming, and empathy. Human curiosity and adaptability round out some of the many qualities that will continue to separate

us from the machines. There are many tasks that only humans can do. We aren't all out of jobs just yet.

2. **Robots** (and their drone cousins) are best used to perform repetitive physical tasks that require strength and endurance. Robots work long hours, often operate faster than humans, don't call in sick, work at night, and don't generate worker's compensation claims. Robots are a natural fit for noisy, uncomfortable, and dangerous environments.

3. **Artificial intelligence and other algorithms.** Digital voice agents may be suitable for simple interactions, for example, to take orders by phone, and as the technology improves to handling other customer interactions including customer support. Artificial intelligence is highly suited to tasks that involve finding patterns and insights, including diagnostic or predictive tasks. AIs usually handle complexity and complex data better than humans too. Software algorithms should also be considered for tasks where accuracy or a split-second response is important to a business process. Computers can calculate accurate results and respond far more quickly than humans. Human judgment may be a welcome and integral component of some tasks, while data-driven decision-making that eliminates human bias may be desirable for others. Software, often based on AI, can be a good choice for tasks where human bias must be removed. AI may also provide a valuable boost to human creativity, exploring thousands of design options that help workers to push creative boundaries in an efficient co-creation process.

Once a business process has been parsed into tasks and those tasks have been assigned to humans, algorithms, and robots, the next challenge is to build a plan that enables digital intelligence to understand what is happening in the physical environment. This requires sensors to be installed throughout the business process so that physical activity can be mirrored in the digital world, creating a cyber-physical system. This allows the efforts of the humans, AIs, and robots to be properly coordinated.

Retail Example: The Semi-Automated Changing Room

To illustrate the concept of building human-machine partnerships, let's consider an example from the world of retail. Most of us shop, and many people either work in retail today, or once did, so the example should be familiar to most readers.

In this scenario, human labor and simple machine intelligence work together. Sensors gather information from the physical world so that tasks can be handed off to the digital world. A mobile or wearable device provides the interface to the human worker.

First, let's review the baseline, nonautomated experience. Imagine you visit a high-end clothing store. You peruse the displays, find items you'd like to try on, and head toward the fitting room. A sales associate intercepts you, takes the items, guides you to an open room, and carefully lays the clothes out for you to try on. "What great service!" you think. As the associate arranges the items, he quietly notes the size and colors of your selections and attempts to get a feel for your personal style. Once you are safely installed in the fitting room, the associate runs back into the store and gathers additional items for you to try, and hopefully buy. In retail, this effort is referred to as increasing both "basket" (more items) and "conversion" (getting you to buy). To you, this feels like a value-added "styling service." To the store, it's an opportunity to sell more product.

To perform well, the sales associate must (a) have a good sense of style, (b) accurately remember your size and which garments you picked, and (c) know the inventory of the store, including which products are in stock and where they are located. This presents a challenge for retailers. Few people have the ability to recognize and cater to another person's sense of style. In a large, fast-moving store, store associates inevitably make mistakes. It's tough for them to know what's in stock and it takes time to locate items. You may have already left the fitting room before they return. Opportunity blown.

Semi-automation of the process would help the sales associate to deliver a high-quality, efficient, and consistent service that results in increased basket and conversion. A well-executed implementation should achieve this without compromising the vital human connection between the store associate and the shopper.

Many manufacturers add RFID (Radio Frequency Identity) tags to their products to monitor the flow of goods through their supply chain. In our semi-automated fitting room, an RFID sensor reads the RFID tags on each of your garments to determine their sizes, colors, and styles. The store's digital intelligence now knows exactly which items you took into the fitting room. A Wi-Fi sniffer reads the unique physical address of your phone, known as a MAC address. The sniffer can't tell who you are from this information, just the address of your phone. By checking a list of known MAC addresses, it's possible for the retailer to determine if you have (or more accurately if your phone has) visited the store before. The retailer may cross-reference previous purchases associated with that phone to understand your purchase history and build a better picture of your personal style. If you have previously loaded the store's app onto your phone and linked it to an account at the store (which opts into their privacy policy) the retailer would also be able to identify who you are. This would allow them to consider any previously expressed preferences. Perhaps you are allergic to natural fibers, don't like to wear stripes, or really love the colors green and black.

The store intelligence now understands which items are in the fitting room and something about you as a customer. Analytics software references a "goes with" database created by the store's fashion designer to get recommendations for items—clothing, shoes, accessories, and so on—that would create a snazzy-looking outfit when combined with the items in your fitting room. The software checks inventory to eliminate out-of-stock items and consults the store planogram (a map of which products go where) to locate the items in the store. The software determines the shortest path between these locations and sends a picking map to the store associate's mobile or wearable device. The associate, guided by the map, whizzes around the store, grabs the items, and brings them to you. The associate's dexterity and visual capabilities mean that the task of picking the items and bringing them to the fitting room is still best done by a human, not a robot. For an enhanced experience, a retailer might display suggested products on a screen located in the fitting room. Photographs or computer-generated images of suggested outfits, built around selected items, might provide value to the fashion-impaired among us.

In our semi-automated process, the choice of sell-up items, the inventory check, and the planogram search have been shifted to digital intelligence. The store associate still performs the important human tasks: connecting with the customer and providing encouraging feedback on how clothing looks. The result of this human–machine partnership is a high-quality service for the customer. The implementation maximizes sales for the retailer and enables the associate to serve more customers per hour, boosting the pay of commissioned sales associates. The automation results in a win for the customer, a win for the associate, and a win for the retailer. Even associates with poor fashion sense can now deliver terrific service. The style instincts of the store's fashion designer are essentially coded into software and made available to every single customer, channeled through a consistent experience that can be delivered by any associate. This consistency makes it easier to deliver against a strong brand promise.

Some readers may have privacy concerns in the scenario described earlier. These are valid concerns and privacy should always be respected. A few considerations:

- The automated Wi-Fi recognition of your phone and the subsequent look-up of previous purchases is no different than if a store associate who has previously helped you recognizes you and recalls the items you previously purchased. Good personal shoppers already do this.

- The store only knows who you are if you have chosen to load the store app and activated a store account, which is inherently an "opt in."

- To give away personal data, consumers expect a quid pro quo. Shoppers should get something in return for being recognized, in this case, an improved personal styling service.

That said, privacy issues must remain a key consideration of any automation project. Companies should inform people how their personal data is being used and always ask them to opt in to a service like this, rather than just giving them the choice to opt out.

Your CIO and CHRO Just Became Best Friends

Leaders will soon preside over a blended workforce: a collaboration of digital and human intelligence, working together closely in teams.

Digital assistants, collaborative AIs, robots, and drones will become teammates. Any effort to develop such a workforce, improve productivity, strengthen business culture, reorganize, or otherwise deploy new labor strategies necessarily involves both HR and IT since each presides over key parts of the workforce—the human intelligence and the digital intelligence. The entire blended workforce must to be aligned behind the core purpose of the organization and motivated to execute against it. With the continued advance of AI and robotics, this fusion will seem natural and essential.

Empower Your Employees, Elevate Their Work, and Maintain the Humanity in Your Brand

Technology should augment the efforts of humans. Well-designed, thoughtful automation will elevate human work so that people find their jobs more meaningful, satisfying, and rewarding.

Any major automation effort should involve ethnographers and experienced designers on the front end of the project to understand the important steps where the innate humanity of the organizations adds value within the business process. Poor awareness of where humans add unique value may lead to overautomated business processes that destroy market differentiation and reduce the company's ability to deliver against their brand promise and purpose. Well-executed automation projects will support and *enhance* the humanity in a business process, rather than limiting or removing it. Our semi-automated fitting room retains all the usual human-to-human interactions that we expect in the shopping experience. The store associate's friendly, helpful, and speedy service is what differentiates the experience.

The Importance of a Thoughtful Approach to Automation

Companies may be tempted to deploy AI aggressively throughout their operations as a way to reduce labor costs, boost efficiency, and increase profits. Leaders should proceed with caution and be mindful of being overzealous. Overautomation strips away the differentiation that humans bring to the brand. Consider the consequences of every brand in an industry taking automation to the extreme. If we assume that all companies have similar access to capital and technology, the logical conclusion of this exercise is that every company looks alike. Differentiation is limited to scale, market reach, and historical brand equity. If they all deliver the same level of service and capability to customers, the undifferentiated offering becomes a commodity and everybody fights to the bottom on price. That is no fun for either the businesses or the customers they serve.

Thoughtful leaders will keep an eye on the long term and take a balanced approach to automation. Organizations must remain cost competitive *and* support their people, so they can deliver ever-improving experiences to customers. Spiral up, not down.

As I discussed in my 2013 TED Talk (www.baldfuturist.com/ted), machines must ultimately make us better humans. Machines should also make our companies better companies. Every company should reflect on their purpose and clearly define what being a better company means to them. Deploy automation that is fully aligned with your values and that accelerates the execution of your core purpose.

8 The Data Ultimatum

Data as Fuel for Business Innovation

Data is crucial to the future of every company. It will improve the quality and speed of decisions, feed your future AIs, fuel customization and personalization efforts, create new revenue streams, and elevate your offerings. Every company is now a tech company, and every company is now a data company, even if they haven't figured that out yet. Companies that don't embrace data to make operations more efficient, create new products and services, improve customer experiences, and open new channels will fall behind. They will join Kodak, MySpace, Xerox, Yahoo!, Sears, BlackBerry, and Blockbuster and be remembered as companies who withered after failing to innovate.

Invest and plan accordingly. Because whoever has the best data wins.

The Strategic Importance of Data: Data-Driven Decisions, Hungry AI, and Frictionless Experiences

Every company is now a data company. Data has become the lifeblood of every business, vital to its future success. Data is raw material for business model innovation and product differentiation. Data is fuel to power future AIs. Data offers insight needed to fine-tune every aspect of operations. Data should underpin every business decision. Data allows you to understand your customers better than they understand themselves. Without gathering, preparing, and analyzing data, modern companies cannot hope to remain competitive. Data is power.

Data-Driven Decision-Making Kills the Gut

By now, every company should be using data to make the majority of their business decisions. Decisions made without data are just educated guesses. In some industries, this is still accepted practice. Workers make important decisions with their guts. They draw on their intuition and experience to make the highest-quality decisions they can.

The head fashion designer of an apparel company might make decisions on colors and styles more than two years in advance. If they are right more than 50% of the time, they are pronounced a hero. For years, fashion designers have dispatched "cool hunters" to urban hot spots—nightclubs, trendy New York bars, high-end Parisian restaurants, Tokyo shopping malls—to figure out what the cool people are wearing, and thus where fashion might head next. The rise of social media sites like Pinterest provides a new source of information for fashion designers. Artificial intelligence processes millions of images from social media and other visual sources to spot patterns, clusters, and trends and to make predictions. This new capability is vital for apparel companies. Half of all clothing is sold on markdown and the lead time from design trend to store shelf is dropping below 6 weeks for fast-fashion brands like Zara and H&M. Speed and accuracy means viability.

Human brains are designed for efficient decision-making. For most decisions, our brains use shortcuts or heuristics (rules of thumb). While these often work well, human decision-making is plagued by cognitive biases and heuristic errors that lead to poor decisions. Humans aren't good at assimilating huge, complex data sets to find correlation and insight. Sophisticated analytics software, often turbocharged with AI, will usually lead to higher-quality, speedier decisions.

Here are two important questions every business leader should ask their organizations:

1. Which business decisions could be improved by informing them with data?

2. What new data sources must we develop to support data-driven decision-making?

These two questions often lead to discussions about an organization's sensor strategy, social media strategy, data hygiene strategy, data security strategy, and a "gather versus buy" strategy for data. They also lead to a review of the disconnected data silos currently spread across the organization and how they might be integrated or unified.

Process Automation Coordinates Human and Machine Resources

The labor force of the future will be a blend of humans and machines, working together in teams. Some tasks will be performed by people, some by robots, and some by AI.

As businesses reengineer their processes to embrace automation, they build bridges between the physical and the digital worlds. AI lives in the digital world, humans exist in the physical world, robots straddle the two worlds . . . part digital intelligence and part physical presence. For these three elements to work effectively together, data has to flow back and forth between the physical and digital worlds. Like a baton in a relay race, data is the handoff between tasks as they execute one after another and occasionally in parallel. Sensors gather data so a model of physical events can be built in the digital world. This model, together with operational data, is then used to coordinate the actions of physical and digital resources.

Feed the Voracious Hunger of Your AIs

AI, at least in the form of the deep-learning platforms that are popular today, requires lots of input data to train it. While the law of diminishing returns applies, generally, the more training data, and the higher the quality of that data, the more capable your AI.

In 2017, Google announced their decision to embrace AI throughout their entire product line and throughout business operations with their "AI first" strategy. As every company follows Google's lead and embraces AI top to bottom, access to data becomes a strategic imperative. Data feeds AI, and AI drives competitiveness. Determine what data you will need in the future. Gather and store whatever data you (legally and ethically) can. If you can't gather it yourself, make the alliances or develop the products you need to get it. Today's data will fuel tomorrow's AI. And tomorrow's AI will be a vital ally in your next competitive battle.

Use Data to Deliver What Your Customers Want: Customization versus Personalization

In a crowded world of 7.5 billion people, we all want to feel distinctive. Consumers expect brands to honor their uniqueness and to help them manage their busy lives. They will build relationships with brands that take the time to get to know them and that save them time.

People want control over what they buy and to express themselves through their purchases. In an era of abundant choice, shoppers crave the ability to customize products. Decal stickers and covers for phones and laptops are an expression of this desire, but barely scratch the itch.

Marketers sometimes confuse customization and personalization. With customization, some aspect of product, service, or experience design is controlled by the customer. When you order a tall mocha latte with two shots, extra foam, and vanilla sprinkles at Starbucks, that's customization. Personalization describes a scenario where choices are made by the seller, not the buyer. Choices are informed by observations the seller makes on the customer's prior behaviors and expressed preferences. Personalization has the power to delight and saves people time. Netflix and Spotify analyze your previous media habits and make personalized recommendations designed to simplify and aid your decision process. Personalization feeds on data and customization choices are expressed as data. Data is key to honoring uniqueness and delivering the friction-less experiences that customers demand.

Customize Your Products, Services, and Experiences

Consumers can customize a sandwich at the sandwich store, change the look and feel of their phones, and customize shoes from Converse. In the coming decade, customization will be expected in every aspect of life. To deliver customized products or services, you must first capture prefer-ences in the form of data. Some customers will have neither the time nor the desire to customize everything, so well-considered default settings and easy-to-use interfaces are vital to make life easy for consumers.

Use Personalization to Create Frictionless Experiences

Consumers are busy, and sometimes lazy. Anything brands can do to make their lives easier is appreciated (and expected). Customer data can be analyzed to make predictions about preferences. Why ask your customer a question (requiring time and cognitive effort on their part) if you're 95% confident you already know the answer? Personalization delights customers by accurately guessing needs and wants or making intelligent suggestions that save consumers time. For example, a person-alized Starbucks app would note that you only order a mocha latte in the winter months, and that you get a tall hot green tea in Spring, a venti iced coffee in summer, and some pumpkin-spiced monstrosity around Halloween. The app would elevate the most likely customized menu choice based on the time of year. Service can be personalized, too. Some mortgage companies use CRMs to track how customers choose to con-tact their brokers—by phone, email, or text—and guide the broker to reach out using the same preferred communication method when they have a great refinance rate to offer.

Consumers are fickle. They are loyal to brands until the moment they are offered a slightly better experience elsewhere—perhaps just one less click to achieve a task. Personalization removes friction from experi-ences so they feel delightful to customers and remove reasons to switch.

Create New Value with Data

Every company should seek ways to gather, refine, and use data as a way to create new value. Data can also be monetized and used to elevate your offerings.

Turn Data into Dollars by Monetizing Your Insights

Data is often compared to oil in that it's not much use until it's refined. Oil is refined into gasoline, jet fuel, bitumen, plastic, and all manner of other oil-based products. Data is refined into information, knowledge, and wisdom. Raw data describes observations, signals, or facts about the world. On its own, it lacks context and is fairly useless. Information is created by examining relationships inside data and applying context and interpretation. Information typically answers "who," "when," "what," and "where" questions. Further understanding is reached by examining patterns inside information to create knowledge. Knowledge typically answers "how" and "why" questions. Wisdom comes from applying experience and sound judgment to integrate and evaluate knowledge, to understand the organizing principles of a system, and to extract insights on what is the best, most moral, or most beneficial course of action. Future AIs may venture into this territory, but for now this is an exclusively human capability.

Data can be monetized to create value. A simple method is to gather internal operational, product, and customer usage data and infer insights that are used to improve operational efficiency and the design of future products. Data can also be turned into valuable information that is monetized externally. Car makers could gather data about road surface quality using accelerometers and GPS sensors, data they sell to local governments in the form of maps that show the location of potholes. Cameras fitted to autonomous vehicles can map open parking spaces in a city, information that can be sold to parking assistant applications.

Grocery stores use loyalty cards to gather data on how we shop. They sell that data to consumer goods companies eager to learn how our shopping habits evolve over time. Data-driven insights gathered for external sale can also guide internal decisions. British grocer Sainsbury's saw low sales of Grape-Nuts cereal and considered discontinuing sales. Analysis of loyalty card data revealed that Grape-Nuts are mostly bought by high-spending and loyal customers. Using this insight, Sainsbury's decided to keep selling Grape-Nuts, despite low volume.

Elevate Your Offering: Products to Services to Experiences to Transformations

Companies are paid to create value. The more value they create, the more they get paid. A metalworking shop is paid to turn sheet steel into widgets. A restaurant is paid to turn groceries into a meal served in a pleasant environment. A tour operator combines transportation and lodging services to deliver you a vacation. WW (formerly Weight Watchers) delivers ready-made meals, a dietary plan, and motivational resources to help customers fight the flab. Each of these examples demonstrates a step in an important hierarchy: raw materials to products, products to services, services to experiences, and experiences to transformations. Each level in the hierarchy creates additional value, value that consumers will pay extra for.

Sensors, data, and processing can elevate your offering and move you up the value hierarchy. Let's consider how sensors and data might elevate a doggie daycare service.

- **Additional service levels.** An RFID reader tracks the location of each dog using an RFID tag located in its collar. A microphone in the collar records how often the dog barks, and an accelerometer records the dog's activity: running, walking, sitting, and sleeping. Sensors in food and water bowls measure how much each pet eats and drinks. These data are used to build a new remote monitoring service, marketed as a silver level of service. An app shows Fido's owner his activity level, how social he is with other dogs, his food intake, and so on.

- **Create an experience.** Additional sensors, processing, and the provision of context yield an experience. Fido's data is contrasted with other pets at the facility so the owner can see how active,

sociable, noisy, and gluttonous he is compared with other dogs.
Names and photos of Fido's friends are shown, ranked by how
long Fido plays with each. Cameras hidden inside pet toys and
located around the facility automatically compile a one-minute
video summary of Fido's day that shows highlights of his play, as
determined by data from RFID readers, collar accelerometers, and
machine vision systems. A real-time camera feed of Fido is available
as a web stream to his owner. With these compelling experiences, pet
owners feel more connected to their pets and their day at the facility.
This experience is sold as a gold level of service.

- **Step up to transformations.** The platinum service includes
  a transformation, an intervention needed for an overweight,
  underweight, noisy, or antisocial pet. Instrumented food dispensers
  with integrated RFID readers restrict food availability to animals on
  a diet. Trainers review a dog's sociability score, perform necessary
  interventions, and track its progress over time using sensor data. This
  data is presented to the owner as proof of progress and evidence of
  transformation.

By using sensors to gather data and computational resources to
process and act on that data, we have elevated simple products—dog
collars, food bowls, and pet toys—to deliver services, experiences, and
transformations. At each level, pet owners are likely to pay more for the
incremental value they receive.

Data Spirals: Create Increasing Levels of Value Using Moore's Law of Data

Engineers have kept Moore's Law going for more than half a century by
designing the computer chips of tomorrow using the computer chips
of today. These new chips are then used to create the next generation
after that, and so on. This self-sustaining loop of increasing computing
performance benefited us all. Fast hardware let us run more complex
and demanding software. New software created a market for faster chips.
And so, the world turned.

A new counterpart to Moore's Law has emerged: This time it's all about data. Here's how it works: A service is created that collects data in the process of delivering that service. These data are used to build a new, more sophisticated service that wasn't previously possible. That service gathers yet another set of even more sophisticated data, forming an upward spiral of value creation. At each turn of the spiral, services become more capable and more intimate, and the data sets gathered become bigger, more complex, and more valuable.

Companies like Google, Amazon, Baidu, and Facebook build data spirals all the time. Let's examine a familiar example from Google. The foundational data sets that underpin Google Maps and Google Earth are satellite images, topological data (that capture the shape and interconnection of roads), and location data. Google packages these data to create their mapping services. These "free" services gather personal data as they are used. Google logs every search you make on Google Maps and tracks your location while you're using the app. This personal data is used to deliver new, more sophisticated and more valuable services.

By analyzing your location, Google figures out where you live and work, where you buy your groceries, where your kids go to school, and gains insight into your personal interests. From your location data, Google calculates your driving speed and direction. This data is aggregated to build accurate traffic models that add a traffic service to the navigation capabilities of Google Maps and Google's Waze service.

The spiral keeps turning. Traffic data is combined with data from Google Calendar to boost the capability of Google Assistant, which offers helpful advice on when users should set out for their next appointment, given current traffic conditions. Because Google Assistant is more valuable, people use it more regularly, and for a wide variety of other tasks including home control and voice searches. The voice data gathered is used to train Google AIs. Google Home products that feature the Google Assistant voice capability include a screen that displays a screen saver for personal photos. Google encourages you to upload personal images to Google Photos so you can enjoy family photos on rotation right on your kitchen counter. Google uses those photos to train their AIs.

You get the picture. Google has built multiple, interconnected spirals of value and data creation. More data, more value; more value, more data.

This data spiral began when Google realized the core value of gathering personal location data and calculated that the best way to get it was by delivering free mapping services. At the time, Google didn't have map data so in 2004 they made two strategic acquisitions: Keyhole Inc, the original creator of what became Google Earth, and Where 2, which became Google Maps. The total rumored price for both companies was less than $45 million. Quite a bargain.

Savvy companies like Google understand the strategic importance of investing to buy or build valuable data sets. Consider the effort Google puts into gathering images for its Google Streetmaps service. They know Streetmaps will let them gather even more valuable data in the future.

An important note: data spirals don't have to be built around personal data. Data spirals can be built around any data sets an organization might need. UPS and Fedex optimize their delivery driving routes using navigation data from their drivers. UPS estimates their ORION routing system saves them 10 million gallons of gas and reduces the distance their drivers travel by 100 million miles annually. Uber and Lyft use location, navigation, and traffic services to create their value (and gather passenger data in the process). Waymo self-driving cars use Google Maps to navigate as their lidar and radar sensors gather high-fidelity mapping data on street layouts. Tesla's cars build detailed maps of the road network as they are driven by their human owners; this data trains and improves its autonomous driving systems. Spirals are everywhere.

As the original Moore's Law stalls, the "new Moore's Law" of data spirals is ascendant. Companies that rode Moore's Law through the 1980s, '90s, and 2000s created enormous value. Companies that embrace data spirals in the 2020s will find similar levels of success. What service can your company build to get you the data needed to offer higher-value services and access to even richer sources of data? What is your data spiral strategy?

9 The Future of Work

What to Expect and How to Make Yourself "Robot-Proof"

Technology has always changed work. As businesses deploy the technologies outlined in this book, workplaces will evolve rapidly. To understand the future of work, it's helpful to review how technology changed work in the past.

The History of Work: From the Physical to the Knowledge Era

At the dawn of the industrial revolution, most people survived by working the land. In 1790, about 90% of the U.S. population worked in agriculture (Source: USDA). Workers were measured by the amount of physical work they could do in a day. What mattered was strength, stamina, and technique.

The industrial revolution moved people out of the fields and into factories and offices. Today, less than 3% of U.S. jobs are in farming (Source: USDA). It's a similar situation in much of Western Europe, Canada, South Korea, Japan, Israel, Argentina, Australia, and other industrialized nations. This happened because we created mechanical muscles: The steam engine, mechanization, electrification, production lines, and computer control boosted production and created enormous wealth. Mechanical muscles commoditized most physical labor and many workers transitioned to knowledge work.

In the knowledge era, workers are valued for their experience, their knowledge, their creativity, their cognitive abilities, and their capacity to tap into their personal network to get things done. Most of today's knowledge jobs were unimaginable in 1790. Millions of people now make a living as web designers, pharmacists, and party planners. The average standard of living has risen dramatically. People live longer, healthier lives. While some people still do jobs that involve physical work—construction workers, truckers, janitors, warehouse workers, manufacturing technicians, baggage handlers, and so on—many of them are assisted by tools and machines.

The Next Era of Work: Augmented Work

Mechanical muscles launched us into the knowledge era. With the advent of artificial intelligence, we are creating mechanical minds. These mechanical minds will fundamentally reshape work.

AI Commoditizes Some Knowledge Work, and More Physical Work, Too

Powerful AIs are already doing some knowledge work. They leverage using diagnostic, decision making, and other capabilities previously only possessed by humans. Autonomous machines fitted with powerful sensors and controlled by AI will commoditize more physical work, work that was impossible to perform using previous generations of automation. Robots that can hang drywall, repair potholes, and sort recycling are all in development.

Automation won't replace all work. Some physical work will remain—jobs that require dexterity, craftsmanship, and physical interaction with humans are all safe for now. And not all knowledge jobs are doomed either. Far from it. Many knowledge jobs will be elevated rather than replaced by automation. Automation will reduce repetitive, dangerous, and boring work and enable workers to focus on meaningful work that is more rewarding. That said, the rise of AI is a major inflection point on the scale of the industrial revolution. For decades, software has eaten jobs. The advent of artificial intelligence accelerates this process and pushes technology into places that seemed like science-fiction fantasy just a decade ago.

Our ability to make and wield tools is one of the skills that differentiates us from other animals. From hammers and fishing rods to combine harvesters and computers, we use tools to get stuff done. These tools are subordinate to us. We are in control. With AI, machines are gaining autonomy and our relationship with technology is changing. Rather than controlling tools to perform a task, we will collaborate with them. Technology will have agency and make some of its own decisions. We will partner with technology to co-create content and we will think of AI and robots more like teammates than tools.

Collaborative technology boosts our existing capabilities. Super sensors and wearable technology will help us to see more, hear more, and feel more. Digital intelligence will augment our own intelligence. Robots will help us to achieve more. The SAM-100 robot, made by Construction Robotics, works in partnership with a bricklayer. Together, they can lay six times as many bricks as the human could alone.

The future of work is a tight collaboration between human intelligence and machine intelligence. Mechanical minds will augment and extend our own capabilities, both cognitive and physical. This doesn't require a physical merging of our bodies. We can augment ourselves without taking such drastic measures. My sense of direction is improved without having to implant a GPS in my brain; I simply need the mapping capabilities of my phone.

Welcome to the augmented era of work . . . an era when humans work in partnership with cognitive machines to get work done. I've already presented many early examples of augmentation technologies throughout this book. To make my case for this new augmented era of work, let's quickly review four of them.

1. **Cobots** are a class of robot specifically designed to work in partnership with humans. Cobots will work alongside humans in retail stores, warehouses, research labs, food service, and many stages of the manufacturing process.

2. **Collaborative AI** co-creates content in partnership with human workers. This type of AI will swiftly invade many roles, going far beyond its origins in engineering and architecture as generative design. Ten years from now, a collaborative AI might help me to write my next book or put together my presentation materials. Collaborative AI will help programmers to code, teachers to teach, and lawyers to build prosecution and defense strategies.

3. **Digital personal assistants** will support most workers. A digital intelligence will guide us through our day, help us stay focused on key tasks, and take care of errands.

4. **AR workers** blend the physical dexterity and intelligence of a human with the digital intelligence and vast online resources of a machine. Augmented reality (AR) will offer step-by-step visual instructions to workers, showing them what to do next. The result is a hybrid of human and machine, intimately combined to create an augmented worker.

Cobots, collaborative AI, digital personal assistants, and AR workers are just four examples of the ways that technology will augment humans in the workplace. We are entering the augmented era of work. And nothing will ever be the same again.

Automation Armageddon: Plan a "Robot-Proof" Career

As we enter the augmented era, two things are clear: Some jobs will be elevated through a deeper partnership with intelligent technology, while other jobs will be replaced entirely, putting millions of people into a state of turmoil.

Which Jobs Are at Risk?

There is much debate on the topic of job automation. Many factors and dynamics will determine how the next phase of automation plays out. Just because a job function *can* be automated doesn't mean that it *will* be. To project the impact of automation on employment, we must consider economic factors (sometimes a human will work for less than a robot costs to build and maintain) and technical, political, regulatory, and other practical issues. It's often not the right business decision to replace a human with an AI, even if it's technically possible. For example, nobody wants to be told they have stage-three liver cancer by a robot.

Well-informed and intelligent analysts have researched AI's likely impact on the global workforce. Their conclusions vary wildly but they all agree that a substantial number of jobs are at high risk of automation in the next 10 to 25 years.

A 2013 study by the University of Oxford kicked off much of the interest in this topic. The study, by Carl Benedikt Frey and Michael A. Osborne, concluded that 47% of U.S. jobs are at risk of automation. A 2017 PricewaterhouseCoopers (PwC) study suggests that 38% of U.S. jobs are at risk of automation by 2030. In a 2014 study, Bruegel concluded that 54% of EU jobs—European jobs skew heavily toward the service sector—were at risk of automation. Global studies by the Organisation for Economic Co-operation and Development (OECD) came to a less startling, but still sobering conclusion. In 2016, the OECD concluded that only 9% of global jobs were at risk of automation, though by March 2018 they updated their estimate to 14% of all jobs.

Varied predictions make it difficult to decide quite how concerned we should all be about the impending automation tsunami. Comparisons are difficult because each prediction model uses different assumptions and different input variables and makes predictions for different markets in different time frames. Models vary because they must estimate complicating factors that include the rate of job destruction versus job creation, the likely speed of technology development and adoption, and the amount of short-term labor market contraction caused by the retirement of the baby boomers (i.e., how long will boomers linger in the workforce).

Historically, technology has always created more jobs than it has destroyed. Typically, new jobs require higher levels of skill, create more value, and thus command higher wages. Jobs created by new technology tend to be less physically demanding and provide more job satisfaction. Some analysts argue this process will continue, and that AI will create more high-quality jobs than it will destroy. A 2018 PwC report focused on the United Kingdom predicts that while artificial intelligence will destroy 7 million UK jobs, it will create 7.2 million new jobs in the process. Another PwC report predicts that AI will deliver a $15.7 trillion boost to global GDP by 2030. Almost half of this increase comes from AI enhancements to products that make them more affordable, more personalized, and available in a wider variety. This, predicts PwC, will stoke increased consumer demand and boost the economy.

If we assume that the average of these predictions is accurate, it leads to two major challenges for society. First, newly created jobs typically require higher skills than the jobs they displace. Accessible adult education programs will be vital for society to safely navigate this transition. Social safety nets may be needed to help people who aren't able to make the leap. A 50-year-old truck driver from Omaha, Nebraska, may not be able to learn how to design virtual objects for augmented reality interfaces.

The second challenge is the speed of the transition. In the industrial revolution, people moved from agriculture to industry over 10 generations, a 200-year period. The coming automation tsunami may require half of the workforce to transition in a *single generation.* Our current education system, designed 150 years ago to move people from fields to factories, does not scale to cope with this challenge. Government, employers, and the education system will all need to step up. An August 2019 declaration by the Business Roundtable acknowledges as much. The statement on the evolving purpose of business, signed by 181 CEOs of major corporations, specifically refers to the need for companies to support employees "through training and education that help develop new skills for a rapidly changing world."

AI automates tasks, not jobs. Jobs that consist of a few routine, repetitive tasks are more likely to be automated than jobs that comprise a high variety of nonroutine tasks. Truck drivers perform one main task: they drive. Once the task of driving is automated, the whole job of a truck driver can be automated. Some of the many, varied tasks performed by a marketing manager can be automated, but the majority of tasks cannot. Automation will allow the marketing manager to focus more of their time on tasks where they add unique value. To accurately predict job losses, models must comprehend all the major tasks involved in every job on the planet and whether each task can be automated. A tall order, and another reason that models disagree.

Whether you choose to believe the OECD model, the PwC predictions, or another analyst, the issue is clear. In the next two decades we must remobilize huge chunks of the global workforce. The debate now is only over the scale of the challenge to society: merely massive, or monumental? This challenge should capture everyone's attention. Efforts like the Emma Coalition (emmacoalition.com) seek to raise awareness of the issue, engage policy makers, and prepare the workforce for change.

The Sky Isn't Falling . . . Yet

The scale of the challenge is uncertain, and we still have some time to plan for the coming transition. But time is short, and this should be an issue we are all talking about. If we get this transition right, we will enter the augmented era in a way that elevates human work, creates a higher standard of living, and makes work more emotionally rewarding. If we get it wrong, the economy could collapse.

People and politicians remain in sweet denial on this topic. Amazingly, 94% of Americans think that it is unlikely they will lose their job to automation (Source: NPR/Marist). In 2017, U.S. Treasury Secretary Steve Mnuchin was asked by *Axios* whether he was concerned about automation. His disconcerting response was that it's "not even on our radar screen" and that he thought the issue was "50 to 100 years away." Automation-related job losses are already happening. The National Bureau of Economic Research reported in March 2017 that 670,000 jobs were lost to robots between 1990 and 2007, a time period when robots did not yet have the benefit of modern AI-based intelligence. Research conducted by Daron Acemoglu at MIT and Pascual Restrepo at Boston University shows that every robot installed in a manufacturing environment displaces an average of 5.6 workers and depresses average wages by 0.5%. It's harder to ask for a raise when you're competing for jobs against robots that never get tired, call in sick, or request a paycheck.

Over the next two decades, AI-powered automation will affect a wide variety of jobs. Some roles—including farm laborers, radiologists, underwriters, polishers, telemarketers, cashiers, bookkeepers, tax preparers, butchers, bank tellers, clerks, paralegals, taxi drivers, auditors, customer support specialists, and food preparers—may become fully automated. Roles that involve high levels of creativity, empathy, human interaction, collaboration, adaptation, cultural understanding, systems thinking, complex problem solving, or that involve a high variety of nonroutine tasks will remain safe from automation. These roles will incorporate AI in a way that allows workers to elevate their efforts and focus on tasks only humans can do.

Becoming "Robot-Proof"

The most common question from my keynote audiences is some version of "what can I do to survive the automation tsunami?" People ask for themselves, but more often out of concern for children and grandchildren. The high-level answer is simple. To survive, we must make ourselves robot-proof. We must nurture and improve the skills that machines will never master. We must double down on our own humanity.

AI will continually improve. Robots will become nimbler and more dexterous. Machine vision, speech recognition, and voice platforms will become more capable. Machines will improve their creative capabilities. As this occurs, human workers must shift their focus toward skills that are uniquely human. For some this may feel like a retreat. For others it will feel like liberation. Robots and AI will take on lower-level tasks and free us to focus on more meaningful, impactful, and rewarding work.

Robot-proof skills include complex critical thinking, creative problem solving, social intelligence, and what I'm calling a "twenty-first-century psyche."

Complex Critical Thinking

Our brains can understand the intricate linkages and interactions that occur between disparate parts of a complex system. We seek out the information needed to understand these relationships and step back to see the bigger picture. We analyze situations and contrast them with other situations, understanding parallels and differences that might exist. We apply judgment and test ideas against preexisting standards and expectations. These standards might be cultural, professional, societal, or other criteria that require complex knowledge and experience—insight machines have no concept of. Humans can weigh evidence and draw conclusions, even in highly complex scenarios. We can generate new ideas and judge these ideas on their merits. Machines cannot.

Creative Problem Solving

To solve complex problems, we use our ability to imagine new potential scenarios and plan ways to build solutions. To prepare children for the postautomation economy, we should fuel their imaginations and curiosity and teach them practical problem solving, for example, in Maker Labs. While machines have gained limited creative capabilities, they are mostly useful for co-creating content in partnership with people. Human creativity is still a powerful asset that makes us robot-proof. Entrepreneurial skills—the ability to see opportunity, create business and marketing plans, raise capital, attract talent, and build value—are unique to humans and will be even more important in the postautomation economy. We should invest in organizations that nurture these skills in children.

Social Intelligence

Understanding people—how to talk to them, motivate them, and work productively alongside them—will be a vital postautomation skill. Leadership skills, defined as the ability to inspire others to follow you, will remain important and highly relevant. Interpersonal communication skills enable us to share complex ideas, influence others, and gather important insights and wisdom. Teaming skills—the ability to work effectively with others—will become even more important as teams become more dynamic, cross-functional, and diverse. Empathy remains one of the main skills that differentiates us from machines. Many robot-proof roles require the ability to understand another person, to put yourself in their shoes, and to show compassion for their situation—for example, nursing, teaching, and counseling. "Culture" captures the wonderful weirdness of why humans behave the way they do. To understand culture is to understand all the rich subtleties of people's origin, background, identity, and outlook. Culture informs how we see the world, how we see ourselves, how we behave, what is important to us, what our unique needs are, and many other things that machines find baffling. Machines can't understand cultural constructs. This difficulty is often used to provide comic relief in science fiction; consider the *Star Trek* characters Spock and Data.

Twenty-First-Century Psyche

Careers for life are long gone. People entering the workforce today may have two, three, or more careers in their lifetime. They may enter careers that don't exist today and that will become obsolete before they retire. To navigate a world of constant change, people will need to be adaptable, mobile, constantly curious, optimistic, and always learning. They will need to take charge of their destiny in a way that perhaps their parents and grandparents never had to. They will need tenacity and grit. This twenty-first-century psyche will enable people to navigate a vibrant, rapidly shifting labor market, transition into exciting new roles, and participate fully in the postautomation economy.

You might also hear this set of robot-proof skills described as the 4Cs of the twenty-first century: creativity, communication, collaboration, and critical thinking. However you slice it, to thrive in a postautomation economy you should focus on building uniquely human skills.

Complex, Diverse Teams of T-Shaped Individuals

The next set of human challenges are big and complex. They cannot be solved by any one organization or any single approach. These challenges will only be addressed by high-functioning, diverse teams that span many disciplines.

Consider the evolution of the automobile. A car-design team in the 1950s needed mechanical, petrochemical, electrical, and industrial engineers who worked with aerodynamics experts and designers. Cars were made of steel, copper, wood, leather, glass, and rubber. A modern car design team adds new disciplines: electronic engineers, semiconductor design, programmers, experience designers, safety engineers, and so on. Designs incorporate aluminum, metal alloys, carbon fiber, plastics, and electronics. Autonomous vehicles require yet more expertise in AI, machine ethics, simulation, data science, and sensor technology.

To collaborate effectively, people from different disciplines and backgrounds must understand something about each other's expertise. Importantly, they must have respect for other disciplines. All too often, liberal arts students are dismissive of engineering, and engineers pour equal scorn on the liberal arts. Our education system must create well-rounded specialists with a working understanding of many other disciplines and a curiosity to learn beyond their chosen field. These "T-shaped" or "π-shaped" individuals will combine deep knowledge and problem-solving capabilities in at least one discipline with a working understanding of many other disciplines. These people also have skills that allow them to cross boundaries: strong communication skills, interpersonal networking skills, and teaming skills.

To produce world-changing results, companies must build diverse teams of T-shaped (or π- or m-shaped people!) people. For those teams to flourish, leaders must foster a culture of constant curiosity and mutual respect.

New Technology Creates New Types of Work

As new technology solves new problems and creates new capabilities, new types of work are generated. These jobs are rarely predicted at the time. When James Watt's steam engine burst onto the scene in the late eighteenth century, few would have predicted it would lead to a wide range of train-related jobs. Aside from all the people needed to build trains, tracks, and stations, many people were employed to manage station operations, run the signals, maintain the tracks, create timetables, check tickets, load luggage, and serve food in the dining car. When the first computers were built, nobody imagined the roles of web designer, game physics programmer, PowerPoint presentation coach, computer-aided designer, smartphone screen repair technician, or cybersecurity tsar.

Full deployment of the six technologies outlined in this book has only just begun. Some new roles have already emerged. Most exist beyond our current imagination. We will certainly need more data scientists, robotics engineers, and machine learning experts. We will need people who can apply these disciplines to solve problems. People with domain expertise that spans multiple disciplines—an engineer with expertise in both AI and medicine—will be in high demand. High-impact projects will require cross-disciplinary collaboration by teams of people from a wide variety of expertise. New roles will be created at the intersection of previously separate disciplines—machine ethics will combine knowledge of artificial intelligence with the philosophy of morality and ethics.

New roles will emerge as technology is used to create new value in new ways. When augmented reality matures, "virtual object designer" may become a bona fide job. A vibrant market may emerge for a wide range of interactive virtual objects: branded sports team avatars, virtual intelligent mirrors, and interactive digital sculptures for the coffee table. Object designers might combine expertise in visual design, experience design, and programming. Advances in biotech may create organism designers. As people live longer, longevity coaches may help us imagine and plan how to live out our golden (and platinum?) years. New roles will be associated with replanning our cities for autonomous vehicles. Autonomous platforms will create new roles—mobile hairdresser? The energy industry will create new roles associated with smart grids and the transition to a carbon-free society. Many jobs will be created that can't be imagined today. Just as they always have.

Keeping the World Spinning in the Postautomation Economy

Automation may displace hundreds of millions of people from their current careers in just the next two decades. Some will need support as they transition to new roles.

Identity, Purpose, and Life 2.0

Many people feel lost when they are asked to imagine what "Life 2.0" looks like for them. Think about your own career. If somebody snapped their fingers and your job, and all jobs like it, disappeared forever in an instant, what would you do instead? What if all your experience and skills training was suddenly irrelevant? How would you choose a new career for the next phase of your life? Often our jobs become a facet of our identities. They help to a form our sense of self. They are one way that we create meaning in our lives and feel a sense of purpose. A major disruption in the workplace can leave people feeling lost, abandoned, worthless, and hopeless. Career-counseling services help people to find a new sense of identity as they plan their path to a new career. Society should invest in these services and scale them to cope with inevitable future demand.

Upskilling and Reskilling Millions

We will need to prepare millions of people for the coming transition. This burden will fall on government, business, and the education system. Businesses must play a key role. They won't be able to rely solely on others to provide the educated talent they need for future jobs. It may be more cost-effective to retrain existing employees than to lay them off and fight in the open market to recruit scarce talent. In July 2019, Amazon announced a plan to spend $700 million to retrain about a third of its workforce by 2025. Workers will gain new skills that either allow them to take on new challenges at the company, or that prepare them for a new role outside Amazon.

The World Economic Forum predicts that by 2022 "no less than 54% of all employees will require significant re- and upskilling. Of these, about 35% are expected to require additional training of up to six months, 9% will require reskilling lasting six to 12 months, while 10% will require additional skills training of more than a year."

Lifelong learning is the new normal. On-the-job training has been part of most career progressions, but automation will accelerate the need for constant learning and personal development. The era of a single education for life is over.

Businesses will compete to maintain a well-educated, adaptable workforce that can perform in a rapidly evolving work environment with skills that complement the latest capabilities of technology. To avoid high turnover and high talent acquisition costs, companies will need to build robust training departments or make strong alliances with third party training providers.

A New Social Contract

While the long-term prospect for new job creation might be strong, the rapid speed of automation and the urgent need for reskilling may create a short- to medium-term (think next 10–15 years) challenge that some conclude will create a class of permanently unemployed and underemployed people. The single-generation transition is unprecedented and may place an enormous strain on society.

To keep the global economy going, we may need to consider changes to the social contract. The three-day week, often discussed in the 1970s, may need to become a reality, at least for some. We may need to find a way to provide people with a decent income in return for just 25 hours of work each week. Some advocate for a partial decoupling of work and income, for example, with schemes like Universal Basic Income that provide a fixed income to all citizens, regardless of their employment status.

Sir Richard Branson, Elon Musk, Mark Zuckerberg, Stephen Hawking, and Ray Kurzweil all seem to have concluded that some kind of Universal Basic Income (UBI) will be required in the future. U.S. presidential candidate Andrew Yang is passionate about the need for what he called "a freedom dividend" to navigate the coming waves of automation. Elon Musk, who endorsed Yang, said, "There is a pretty good chance we end up with a universal basic income or something like that, due to automation." Sir Richard Branson said of UBI, "The hope is that policies like these can help people struggling just to survive, and allow them to get on their feet, be entrepreneurial and be more creative." In a 2018 interview with Reddit, the late Stephen Hawking remarked, "If machines produce everything we need, the outcome will depend on how things are distributed. Everyone can enjoy a life of luxurious leisure if the machine-produced wealth is shared, or most people can end up miserably poor if the machine-owners successfully lobby against wealth redistribution. So far, the trend seems to be toward the second option, with technology driving ever-increasing inequality."

Hawking's insight indicates that automation-related job losses will quickly become a major political issue. Rapid automation will be disruptive to society and an absence of government intervention may lead to extreme inequality, increased poverty, and more homelessness.

As businesses automate, they trade out human labor for capital equipment in the form of robots. Microsoft co-founder Bill Gates has suggested that corporate taxes be updated to reflect this reality. "Right now, the human worker who does, say, $50,000 worth of work in a factory, that income is taxed. . . . If a robot comes in to do the same thing, you'd think that we'd tax the robot at a similar level."

Others advocate for a negative income tax that provides supplemental pay from the government for people earning below a certain threshold. The advantage of a negative income tax system is that it provides incentive for people to work, even in low wage jobs. This has been a major criticism of UBI, though early trials of UBI seem to indicate that only a very small percentage of people take advantage of the system and shirk productive work. Most people, it seems, work for many reasons that go beyond generating income—they work for the challenge, social interaction, self-worth, status, to stay occupied, and to contribute to an effort they feel is worthwhile.

There are early signs that populations may seek government intervention to slow the pace of automation: 58% of U.S. adults say that limits should be placed on how many jobs can be replaced with robots and computers, even if that technology makes a business more productive (Source: Pew Research Center). Widespread automation and unemployment may lead to labor strikes and social unrest. The Luddites destroyed the mechanized looms that took their textile-weaving jobs. If we are to avoid a "Luddite 2.0" moment, society will need to address the rising inequality that automation may bring. Societies in Europe and Asia, where people are more receptive to the need for social programs, may be in a better position than the United States to embrace this approach.

All Hands on Deck

When it comes to the topic of automation and job losses, there are more open questions than answers. The scale of the challenge for the 2030s will become clearer in the first half of the 2020s. Corporations, the education sector, and all of our institutions will have to step up with an appropriate and rapid response. We can all play an important role, too. Help others to understand the challenge ahead and encourage meaningful and nonpartisan conversations about potential solutions. We will neither unionize nor deregulate our way out of this one. By virtue of having read this book, please consider yourself deputized as a futurist.

Spread the word. Start the conversation. Today.

Part III

Lessons from Industry, Sector by Sector

10 Keeping Healthcare Healthy

What Every Business Can Learn from Healthcare Tech

Technology will transform the delivery of healthcare, a revolution that is already well under way. Super sensors, boosted by sophisticated AI, will enable clinicians to "see" their patients in a way that they have never seen them before. AI will augment the diagnostic capabilities of doctors, offering them a second pair of eyes and a valued second opinion. Ultimately, AI may take on lower-level diagnosis and care, allowing doctors to focus on the more challenging cases and spend more quality time with the patients that need it most. Remote sensing, using a combination of wearables and in-home sensing, will maintain a constant connection between patients and clinicians, transforming the nature of their relationship and turning the current healthcare model upside down.

The Challenge: Meeting the Needs of an Aging Population

This shake-up of our pre-internet healthcare system can't come soon enough. Without it, the existing system will struggle to handle the increased demand for health services that is predicted for the coming decades: patients will suffer, costs will spiral, and eventually the system will collapse. To meet future demand, improve the quality of care, and improve outcomes, we must reimagine healthcare.

The global population is aging. Americans over the age of 65 will outnumber children by 2035 (Source: U.S. Census Bureau). By 2060, almost one quarter of the American population will be seniors, up from about 15% today.

In China, population aging is acute. Despite the repeal of the government's one-child policy, birth rates in China are still dropping and the fertility trend looks bleak. China has more people over the age of 65 than the entire population of Russia. By 2050, almost 40% of the population will be over the age of 60 (Source: ChinaPower).

If you want to glimpse the future of the United States, China, and Western Europe, you need look no further than Japan, where the number of people over the age of 65 has *quadrupled* in the last 40 years. They account for more than a quarter of the population and sales of adult diapers now outnumber the sales of diapers for babies (Source: Wikipedia). By 2050 there will be 20 million fewer Japanese people than there are today.

As a population ages, it places an increased burden on the healthcare system. Older folk rely on more frequent and more expensive healthcare services. Almost 80% of a person's lifetime healthcare expenditure occurs after the age of 40, and almost half occurs after the age of 65 (Source: HSR). Paradoxically, new disease cures that result in a boost to life expectancy may lead to an overall increase in the lifetime cost of care.

The world's aging demographic is a ticking time bomb. The current care model will not scale to meet the expected demand. We cannot build enough hospitals, train enough doctors and nurses, or afford to run a healthcare system at the scale required to meet future demand.

Artificial Intelligence Improves Patient Interactions and Outcomes

AI is a fabulous technology for the healthcare industry. Medical diagnosis is largely about finding patterns of symptoms in test data. AI is ideally suited to find patterns in oceans of data, including patterns that humans might miss.

The Predictive Capabilities of AI Transform Public Health

Dengue, a mosquito-borne disease, is nasty enough to send a person to the hospital. If the disease progresses to dengue hemorrhagic fever, also known as severe dengue, and is left untreated, it has a 40–50% mortality rate. Dengue is a major issue in tropical, subtropical, and even some temperate areas. Roughly half of the global population is at risk of dengue fever, according to the World Health Organization. In Asia alone, authorities spend $300 million annually on mosquito control.

AIME (Artificial Intelligence in Medical Epidemiology) is an AI trained with vast data sets to predict future outbreaks of dengue. The AI takes many variables into account—including wind speed, local roof architecture (flat roofs pool water where mosquitoes can breed), the location of water accumulations, rain patterns, and population density—to predict the timing and location of outbreaks. To make its predictions, the AIME system considers 276 variables, a set of factors far too complex for human analysis. It predicts outbreaks up to three months in advance with 80% accuracy. Amazingly, the AI can predict the location of the outbreak to within a 400-meter radius. AIME predictions are used to focus limited resources and optimize the impact of vaccination and mosquito control. The predictive capabilities of AI might be used to predict other public health issues and inform the deployment of appropriate resources.

Artificial Intelligence Discovers Drugs and Designs Prosthetics

Pharmaceutical companies use AI to suggest chemical compounds that might be candidates for therapeutic drugs. Technology companies like

Atomwise train their AIs with data about the molecular structure and efficacy of known drugs. With exposure to enough data, the AI can establish complex relationships between the molecular structure of a compound and its associated impact on the body. Some correlations are entirely coincidental and not causative. Other correlations may illustrate the potential for a breakthrough drug that interrupts a disease path. AIs like Atomwise's can be given a set of desired characteristics as an input and will output the molecular structure of compounds that may have those characteristics. Pharmaceutical companies use Atomwise to build a short list of drug candidates. This narrowed list of candidates informs first-pass exploration and saves pharmaceutical companies many millions of dollars. Future AIs might also make intelligent suggestions on the most effective and efficient ways to synthesize new compounds, too.

Business Insight: Pharmaceutical AIs Might Aid the Discovery of Drugs That Save Millions of Lives

An AI might help to discover a drug that one day saves your life or the life of your child or grandchild. Artificial intelligence could unlock cures for Alzheimer's disease, Parkinson's disease, and many types of cancer. In many ways, we are only just beginning to realize the full power of AI to solve significant human problems. In a fearful world, we must be careful to balance concerns on the risks of runaway AI development with an understanding of the huge potential upside AI presents to humanity. Every business should consider how AI might be used to deliver breakthroughs that allow them to reach higher and do things that had previously seemed impossible.

Digital Diagnosis Complements Traditional Care

DeepMind, an Alphabet company based in the UK, has built an AI that aids the early screening and triage of a range of eye conditions. The AI reviews Optical Coherence Tomography scans, known as OCTs, to diagnose eye disease. These 3-D retinal scans take about 10 minutes to perform but reveal an incredible amount of information to clinicians and to the

DeepMind AI. The AI was trained on an anonymized database of 15,000 OCT scans and can recognize the symptoms of 50 different diseases, including macular degeneration and diabetic eye disease. The system uses a set of competing algorithms, each trained independently but designed to operate in parallel. Results are compared and the majority rules. This improves the overall accuracy of the system by eliminating occasional false positive or false negative results. In trials, the DeepMind eye AI (say that phrase out loud) made the same treatment recommendations as 94.5% of eye doctors. The AI mitigates for a shortage of specialist technicians and eye health clinicians. By triaging patients and allowing eye doctors to focus on more challenging cases, DeepMind's AI helps the healthcare system to scale. In the future, many other AI-based diagnostic tools will emerge to support doctors and scale the reach of healthcare systems.

Business Insight: AI Offloads Routine Tasks so Humans Can Focus on More Complex Tasks

DeepMind's eye scanner AI performs triage on ophthalmic patients. It doesn't seek to replace eye doctors but to support them and augment their capabilities. It offers an effective screening service to identify and offer a preliminary diagnosis on disease. This boosts the efficiency of eye doctors, enabling them to see more patients in a day and to spend more time on challenging cases. Look for ways that you can use AI in your organization to free your staff from routine tasks and to support them in the execution of their jobs.

Artificial Intelligence "Sees" Patients in New Ways with Super-Sensing

As we have previously discussed in the chapter on artificial intelligence, AI is a wonderful tool that helps us to see the world more completely. Clinicians will use this "super-sensing" capability to see their patients more fully and in ways that weren't possible before.

An Israeli start-up, Beyond Verbal, is building an AI to screen voices for a particular set of biomarkers. These vocal biomarkers may indicate specific healthcare conditions or changes in a patient's emotional state. Beyond Verbal claims early success with their effort, specifically to indicate COPD, sleep apnea, and congestive heart failure (CHF). They also claim to be able to predict the need for hospitalization and the likelihood of mortality for CHF patients. Through joint research with the Mayo Clinic, Beyond Verbal has also demonstrated that their AI can detect coronary artery disease (CAD) just by listening to a patient's voice. Further, they are working to find significant correlations between voice and a range of other health conditions, including hypertension, diabetes, and cancer. The hope is that future tools will constantly monitor a person's voice and raise flags when vocal biomarkers are detected.

Another Israeli start-up, Sonovos, has developed an AI-enhanced smart stethoscope, branded CompuSteth. AI analyzes audible body sounds and infrasounds—sounds that are beyond a human's audible range—to diagnose health conditions. Sonovos claims their product can avoid the use of expensive CT and x-ray scans.

As well as being able to "hear" health conditions, AI can also be trained to "see" them. A blood draw is typically required to predict a patient's risk of experiencing a cardiovascular event such as stroke or heart attack. Verily built an AI that predicts a patient's cardiovascular health risk with 70% accuracy (the same accuracy as achieved with traditional methods), with no blood draw. The AI reviews retinal scans of the fundus—the area at the rear of the eye—to deduce a patient's approximate age, blood pressure, and whether the patient is a smoker—factors that are all indicators for cardiovascular health. The AI can effectively "see" health risk in the patient's eye.

Boston start-up FDNA has developed a suite of smartphone-based apps that provide genomic insights from phenotypic information. For the nonmedical reader, let me translate that last sentence. FDNA's Face-2Gene app use facial scans of a patient, snapped using a smartphone's camera, to detect fine-grain facial traits it can correlate with genetic diseases. In effect, the AI "sees" small abnormalities in the shape of a face and extracts insights that would otherwise have gone unnoticed—insights that reveal the presence of disease-causing genetic variations. The software scans for more than 7,500 genetic disorders and gives doctors a probability that a patient has certain syndromes, for example, Kabuki syndrome, KBG syndrome, or Cri-Du-Chat syndrome. The app is used in children's clinics around the world including the Mayo Clinic, Mount Sinai Hospital, Istanbul Medeniyet University, Duke Medicine, and the Sydney Children's Hospital Network.

Your genotype is your genetic identity, described by your genome. Your phenotype is a description of your actual physical characteristics: your height, hair color, eye color, how easily you gain weight, how happy you are, and so on. Your phenotype also includes your disease history, your overall current health, your behavior, and even your general disposition. Not all phenotypes are a direct result of your genotype. But your genotype plays a huge role in determining your phenotype and your health. Another way to think about phenotype is that it is the clinical manifestation or expression of the genotype as a result of its interaction with the environment.

FDNA is building a huge database of genomic and phenotypic information, crowdsourced from clinicians, labs, and researchers. They are encouraging the medical community to share data and insights, share cases, and consult with each other using their platform. FDNA claims their platform is used by 70% of the world's geneticists at 2,000 clinical sites spread across 130 countries. Their secure, cloud-based database holds anonymized phenotypic and genotypic data associated with more than 10,000 diseases. FDNA plans to go beyond facial analysis and search for

Business Insight: Super-Sensing Transforms Our Ability to See the World

We are only just beginning to explore how AI can help us to lift the veil from the world and see it in exciting new ways. Recent advances in the medical world demonstrate great promise: sensors that can see through walls, detect genetic disease in the shape of our faces, and hear disease in our voices. Every business, no matter their focus, should consider how super sensors might be used to create new products and services, optimize operations, or improve customer service.

new diagnostic tools that can be used to test and prescribe treatment for the hundreds of millions of people living with genetic disease. Future AIs may help us to discover unknown linkages between genotype and phenotype that lead to breakthroughs in human health.

Healthcare Gets Personal with Precision Medicine

FDNA's efforts are part of a broader effort by the healthcare industry to personalize medicine.

For the entire history of modern medicine, healthcare services have been designed to serve the broad population as a whole. By and large, treatment plans are rarely individualized. A typical experience at the doctor's office goes something like this: The doctor examines you, figures out what's wrong with you, and then prescribes some kind of pharmaceutical medication. Often, the doctor will say something like, "Let's try you on ABC medication and if that doesn't work, or if you experience XYZ side effects, we will try something else." The reason the conversation goes like that is that doctors have no idea if a particular medication will actually work for you, or if you will experience any side effects. Treatments assume we are all like the general population. Only, we aren't all alike. Our genetic makeup is different, and thus the interaction of pharmaceuticals on our bodies, and on disease paths in our bodies, is different. When a doctor prescribes a medication, they might know the percentage chance it'll work on you, based on how trials went on the general population. But they don't know how it'll work on *you*. They play a statistical game, trying the medication with the best efficacy on the general population and the lowest known number of side effects.

Precision medicine could change all that. With access to your genomic data, a physician will use a powerful computer to choose the best medication for you. Artificial intelligence is really good at finding correlations hidden inside massive data sets. An AI will review the genomes of all previous patients who have been prescribed medications for your condition. Based on your specific genetic makeup, it will then recommend the medication likely to have the highest efficacy and the fewest side effects. For you.

Precision medicine will also improve cancer treatment. To treat cancer effectively, doctors must identify molecularly distinct cancer subtypes and potential drug combinations for targets. This requires a high-quality analysis of vast amounts of data. By ingesting electronic medical records and molecular diagnostics, an AI can filter through the data and recommend the best personalized cancer treatment for a specific patient.

Business Insight: Big Data Is Essential to the Personalization That People Have Come to Expect

Personalized medicine is just one example of a broader trend to personalize and customize the delivery of services. Every customer wants to be treated as a unique individual. We want our uniqueness to be acknowledged and honored. We want control over the way we receive services, and we want services to be tailored to our needs and wants. As we explored in Chapter 8, data is an essential ingredient needed to deliver customization and personalization capabilities. Healthcare is no different.

Drones Save Lives

Zipline, a robotics company based in California, builds drone networks that deliver urgently needed medical supplies to remote locations. Their first trial focused on the country of Rwanda, where challenging terrain, heavy rains, and poor infrastructure make it impossible to access some locations by road for several months of the year. Zipline's drones sail over mountain ridges and washed-out roads to reach remote rural communities with urgently needed blood supplies, vaccines, and medicine. A fixed-wing design lets drones travel greater distances than quadcopters (Zipline claims up to 10 times farther) and fly in challenging weather conditions. Drones cruise at about 70 miles per hour (110 kilometers an hour), carry up to 3.3 pounds (1.5 kilos) of cargo, and have a round-trip range of 100 miles (160 kilometers).

In Rwanda, the number one cause of death for women is postpartum hemorrhage after childbirth. Blood transfusions save women's lives. Transfusions can be the difference between life and death after a bout of malaria, too. Here's how the service works. A clinic worker places an order for blood supplies to the central blood depot via WhatsApp, SMS, or by going online. The depot picks the correct blood product, wraps it, and places it inside the Zipline drone. The drone is catapulted into the air and autonomously follows a predetermined flight path that leads it to a drop zone over the clinic. This can be a small clearing, or even the roof of the clinic. On approach, Zipline sends an SMS to the clinic to advise that delivery will occur in the next minute or so. The drone circles the clinic and drops the package to the ground with the aid of a small parachute. The drone returns to the depot, ready for the next job. The average time from order to delivery is 30 minutes or less. Zipline drones also saves the lives of snake-bite victims. Rarely needed medicines like snake antivenom are not widely stocked. After a bite, antivenom must be administered within hours if the victim is to be saved.

Rwanda is only the beginning of this story. More than 2 billion people around the world have inadequate access to essential medical supplies due to geographical and infrastructure challenges. Zipline is working with the Tanzanian government to launch the world's largest national drone-delivery network. Tanzania is more than twice the size of California; only 8% of its roads are paved. Distribution of goods is challenging there. More than 100 drones will link four distribution centers to more than 1,000 local health centers and run up to 2,000 flights per day, serving a population of 10 million people.

Drones also treat heart-attack victims. Almost 1,000 people experience out-of-hospital heart attacks every single day in the United States alone. For some victims, quick access to a defibrillator machine can mean the difference between life and death. Every minute that passes between sudden cardiac arrest and cardiopulmonary resuscitation, a victim's chance of survival drops by 10%. After 10 or 12 minutes, only 1 in 10 victims survive. Ambulances can't reach most victims quickly enough, but defibrillator drones arrive much faster. Start-up Flirtey (how do they pick their names?) partnered with ambulance provider REMSA to run drone trials in the state of Nevada. A remote-piloted drone and an ambulance are dispatched to victims simultaneously. The drone gets there first and lowers a defib machine to the ground so anyone on the scene can use it to save the victim's life. A similar trial by the Swedish Transport Agency found that defib drones arrive an average of 16 minutes sooner than ambulances. When every minute counts, that's a huge difference.

Business Insight: Drones Aren't Just for Taking Pictures

Drones now do a lot of useful work and may become the workhorses of the twenty-first century. They are widely used in agriculture, construction, surveying, maintenance, and now healthcare applications. Consider ways you might be able to use drones to do useful work.

The Remote-Monitored Patient: Sensors and Wearables Flip the Model

Think about today's healthcare model. You don't feel well so you call the doctor's office to make an appointment. Unless your symptoms indicate an emergency, you'll be offered a 10- to 20-minute time slot in the schedule of a doctor, likely sometime in the next week or so. When you arrive at the doctor's office, you may or may not still be exhibiting the symptoms that you were experiencing when you first called. Perhaps you had a crazy headache, felt light-headed, or had pain somewhere. But now, you feel fine. The doctor examines you and asks you to describe how you felt the previous week. You do your best to remember and describe how you felt. This is not a very effective use of anyone's time. A more worrying scenario is that you continue to get sicker while you wait for your appointment, perhaps infecting others with your ailment, and ultimately need emergency treatment and a more expensive intervention.

How do we flip this picture around and make the process more efficient? How could we design a system where your doctor is automatically

alerted when you fall ill, and she calls you? For years, corporate IT has remotely managed the health of computers on a network. Soon, doctors, supported by algorithms and sensors, will remotely monitor and manage our
health. An algorithm might detect a heart attack and automatically dispatch
a defib drone and an ambulance. A spike in body temperature and a low
heart rate might alert a nurse to check in with a patient by phone and assess
the need for care. This conversation might result in a suggestion to retreat
to bed, an appointment with the doctor, or directions to the nearest ER.
A patient might not even be aware that they are experiencing an episode.
They might receive a notification to let them know that there is a minor
issue and no need to come in just yet, but that the doctor is watching the
issue from afar and will intervene if it doesn't resolve or gets worse. With
the advent of inexpensive sensors, 5G networks, the popularity of wearable
technology, and the use of AI, this vision of proactive, real-time response
and remote care management could quickly become a common reality.

Wearable devices, such as those from Fitbit, Samsung, Withings, and
Apple, have become popular, particularly with people wanting to monitor physical activity and sleep patterns. Wearable devices will continue
to gain in sophistication and evolve the ability to track more about our
health. Apple's latest watches include heart rate monitoring and simple
ECG (electrocardiogram) capabilities. The watch alerts the wearer if
it detects heart arrhythmias, such as atrial fibrillation, unusually low
or unusually high heart rates. The data gathered by the watch is stored
securely on the patient's phone where it can be displayed and shared with
a doctor as part of a conversation about health. Personal health data will
be gathered by evermore sophisticated wearables, sensors located in the
home, and eventually sensors inside our bodies. Sensors that can be swal-
lowed to monitor for gastrointestinal or stomach issues are already
in trial.

Blockchain-Based Medical Records Reward Healthy Behavior and Take Us beyond Accidental Wellness

Data from wearable devices, digital scales, and other home health devices
can be gathered and stored in private healthcare records stored on a

> ## *Business Insight: Remotely Manage Resources to Cut Costs and Reduce Downtime*
>
> IT managers remotely manage PCs and soon doctors will remotely manage patient health. Cheap, abundant sensors and computing enable all objects and infrastructure to be connected, monitored, and remotely managed. Review your product line and infrastructure. Look for opportunities to add remote monitoring and management capabilities to boost reliability and allow you to improve function over time.

Blockchain. When secure data from doctor and hospital visits are added, a complete, private picture of a person's health can be built.

Longitudinal health records, built over decades, will give doctors better insight into what keeps us healthy. Today, we are "accidentally well." That's a term coined by my friend, Dr. Brigitte Piniewski, who is both a medical doctor and a leading mind on the healthcare application of Blockchain technology. The healthcare community has some understanding of the behaviors and choices that keep us healthy, but as demonstrated by ever shifting dietary advice regarding the amount of coffee, red wine, or butter we should or shouldn't consume, there isn't deep knowledge on what actually keeps people well. To truly understand wellness, we need to review longitudinal behavioral data on the population that's gathered over the course of their lives. Blockchains provide the foundation of trust that enables data to be gathered, stored, and shared while honoring individual privacy. Compare this to the current model where data brokers sell five-year chunks of health system data to pharma companies. Piniewski's view is that we must stop treating old people as cost centers and instead look at them as national treasures. She contends that our biology is unable to keep up with the rapid environmental changes wrought by the modern world. Today's elderly people are our last opportunity to benchmark the health of people who lived in pretechnological times. Piniewski is a passionate advocate of digital therapeutics, the use of data to inform and encourage behavioral and lifestyle changes. As more sensors are deployed in homes, in wearables, and ultimately inside our bodies, digital technology will be used to help us all understand more about our own health, and to prescribe the steps we should take to remain well.

Token economics can reward desired behaviors. The more data that a patient submits on their health Blockchain, the more tokens they receive. Additional tokens are awarded for data that signals healthy behaviors and lifestyle choices are being followed. In this way, a digital health identity and records scheme could evolve into a system that encourages and rewards an individual's efforts to promote their own wellness, reducing the burden on the healthcare system.

Augmented Reality and 5G Transform Telesurgery and Telemedicine

High-speed internet connections, robotics, and virtual or augmented reality will enable clinical and surgical talent to reach across huge distances. Autonomous robot surgeons are still decades away. To maximize the reach of human surgeons, particularly into far-flung rural communities, we will need to use telesurgery. Robot-assisted surgeries have been conducted since the mid-1980s, and telerobotics, where the surgeon operates at a distance from the robot and patient, was introduced in the late 1990s. Telerobots from companies like da Vinci are used to perform routine laparoscopic abdominal, spine, heart, and urological surgeries. Typically, the robot, physician assistant, and other support staff are scrubbed in and positioned at the operating table while the surgeon controls the robot from the other side of the room. The robot enables the surgeon to make fine-grain movements and doesn't even require them to scrub in. For patients, these keyhole surgeries are minimally invasive, heal faster, and result in less trauma, less blood loss, and less pain.

The first true remote surgery was performed in September 2001. A surgeon in New York City performed an operation on a patient located in Strasbourg, France. The connection was made over dedicated fiber

optic cables laid beneath the Atlantic Ocean. While such remote surgeries are possible, they are not optimal. Even with dedicated and reliable
data connections, the time lag involved makes it hard for surgeons to
perform delicate manipulations and defeats haptic feedback systems
that help the remote surgeon to "feel" what they are doing. Low-latency,
high-reliability 5G networks and satellite constellations will make it
possible for more remote surgeries to be performed, making specialist
surgical talent available to far wider areas.

Augmented reality (AR) is changing surgery, too. Patient vital signs
can be displayed in the surgeon's field of view, making them easily accessible at all times. Presurgical scan data can be overlaid on the surgeon's
view of the patient, allowing them to see x-rays, CT scans, and other
imaging projected onto the patient in three dimensions. This essentially
gives the surgeon "x-ray vision" so they can better plan surgeries and
avoid major blood vessels and nerves. Augmedics' xvision system is an
early example of research in this area. Without AR, many surgeons have
to continually look away from their patients to review images and charts.
By bringing this imagery to the patient, the surgeon's eyes are kept in
one place. This improves the speed, accuracy, and safety of procedures,
which leads to better outcomes.

Business Insight: Augmented Reality and 5G Networks Will Transform Collaboration and Work

The combination of AR and 5G technologies is potent. Speedy 5G
connections reduce lag for long-distance communications and AR
provides a rich new modality for people to communicate complex
ideas across space. Together these technologies will enable improved
collaboration between distant parties and change the way that we work.
Find ways to use AR and 5G to improve the way you collaborate with
suppliers, customers, and from employee to employee.

11 Transforming Human Mobility

What Every Business Can Learn from Transport Tech

We are about to experience the next major shift in human mobility, the likes of which we have not seen since the arrival of the steam engine. This transformation of the global transportation system provides useful insights for every business.

The Challenge: Climate, Traffic, and Moving Deathtraps

Today's global transportation network is amazing. A journey to the other side of the planet takes less than a day and costs the same as a laptop. But our cities are crowded and becoming more densely populated every year. Existing transport systems are overwhelmed, which limits economic activity and reduces livability. We need new ways to move people and goods safely from one place to another.

Automotive Accidents Claim More Than a Million Lives Each Year

Each year more than 5 million fender benders injure 4.5 million people and kill more than 40,000 more, just in the United States alone (Source: National Safety Council). Globally, 1.35 million people are killed in car crashes each year, one human life every 23 seconds, with almost half of those killed being pedestrians, cyclists, or motorcyclists (Source: World Health Organization). Road accidents are the eighth-leading cause of death globally and account for 2.2% of all deaths. Car accidents are the leading cause of death in people aged 15 to 29. Beyond the human suffering, this motorized mayhem has a significant economic impact. Property is destroyed, accident victims miss work, and people require expensive medical treatment for injuries. Road accidents cost well over a trillion dollars annually: that's 1–2% of global GDP (Source: WHO).

Human error accounts for 94% of all road accidents in the United States (Source: U.S. Department of Transportation). If machines can be built to drive more safely than humans, we could reduce accident frequency, and ultimately, we might make them a thing of the past, saving millions of lives. Autonomous driving won't eliminate all accidents, but might significantly reduce them. Car body repair shops should take note.

One Sixth of All Greenhouse Gases Spew from Our Transport Systems

Internal combustion engines pump out billions of tons of carbon dioxide and other greenhouse gases each year. Globally about 15% of all emissions come from transportation. In the United States, transportation accounts for about 30% of greenhouse gas emissions (Source: EPA).

Traffic Chokes Cities, Slows Economic Activity, and Wastes Time

The average American driver loses 97 hours each year to traffic congestion, which translates to a national economic impact of $87 billion (Source: INRIX). In the world's most congested city, Moscow, drivers lose 210 hours per year to congestion and travel at an average speed of just 11 mph. Global traffic causes lost productivity, increases the cost of transported goods, wastes fuel, creates extra pollution, and causes stress to drivers.

The Next Revolution in Human Mobility: Horseless, Driverless Carriages

In the nineteenth century, the best way to get around was by horse and cart. The horseless carriage changed human mobility forever. With internal combustion engines, people could travel great distances in relative comfort. Goods could be transported to distant markets, a significant boost to commerce. New industry giants were created—Mercedes-Benz, Ford, and General Motors—while horse breeders, blacksmiths, cartwrights, and buggy whip makers went out of business.

The next major transition in human mobility—to the horseless–driverless carriage—promises to free us from the stress of driving, make mobility more accessible, improve carrying capacity for our transportation networks, and cut the cost of transportation. The first fully autonomous vehicles should be launched in around 2021 and will be sold at a premium. As sensor and computing prices tumble, the cost of autonomous capabilities will drop substantially. Around 2030, autonomous car sales will really take off. By the mid-2030s, autonomous cars will represent half of all sales and by 2040 the vast majority of all cars sold (94%) will have fully autonomous capabilities (Source: Loup Ventures).

Business Insight: Advances in AI Solve Problems Thought Impossible Just a Decade Ago

In the late 2000s, well-informed and highly credible scientists were saying that a computer would never be able to handle the complex task of driving a vehicle. Self-driving cars seemed improbable. Yet autonomous vehicles, powered by sophisticated AI, will soon take over the transportation landscape. Capable engineers with bold visions for the future will continue to surprise us with new breakthroughs in AI. Business leaders should pay close attention to the latest developments, brainstorm contingencies in the case of such breakthroughs, and should seek to inspire their IT teams to continually push to solve the improbable.

Vehicles Morph from Products to Services

Transportation will become an on-demand service you use rather than a product you own. Some people will continue to own cars for a variety of reasons, but many in urban areas will find the economics of on-demand transportation services too compelling.

Loup Ventures estimates that by 2040, 68% of road vehicles will be part of a fleet service. That compares to around 5% today. Simple economics will drive the shift. The average car is parked for 96% of each day, doing nothing. More than half of the cost of a taxi or ride-share transportation is the driver. It's estimated that as cars become both autonomous and electric, the cost of a ride may drop to one tenth of the cost of a typical Uber ride today.

The race is on to see who will become successful fleet operators. Traditional rideshare companies—Uber, Lyft, Ola, Grab, and Didi Chuxing—are a natural fit and are well-positioned to be big players. Tech companies may also make a bid to become operators. Google has autonomous car ambitions through its Waymo subsidiary. Apple has a billion-dollar stake in Didi Chuxing, which in turn has invested in Uber. Elon Musk revealed plans to put a million "robo-taxis" on the road, presumably operated by Tesla. Amazon may be the dark horse to watch here, too. Traditional car OEMs may become operators. Major car rental companies—Hertz, Avis, Enterprise, National, and others—will pivot their businesses if they are to remain relevant in the future. Local governments might become operators as part of a public transportation strategy. Small fleets of on-demand autonomous vehicles might make better economic sense to connect local rural areas than traditional, underutilized bus services operating on standard routes.

The autonomous car market feels like the gold rush of the 1850s. At this stage, it's anyone's game. Established players will go head-to-head with well-funded new entrants. As cars morph into services new business models will emerge, for example, some journeys may be supported by in-car advertising.

On-demand vehicle services will improve access to mobility services for people who are unable to drive: people with disabilities, people who are too young/too old to drive, and people who could not previously afford to travel by car.

People will summon the type of vehicle that matches their particular need. Cars will become spaces where we spend time; spaces where we do things other than driving. Cars will evolve to provide a range of in-journey services and we will expect a range of in-car capabilities. For longer journeys with kids, we might book a movie theater van. We might grab breakfast on the morning commute in a personal dining car. Busy mobile workers might summon a business car, complete with desk workspace, video-conference facilities, and high-speed connectivity. Other vehicles might provide sleeping or exercise facilities.

Business Insight: In-Vehicle Services Offer Significant Opportunities

As we cease to drive and all become passengers, we will want to achieve more while on the go. With a captive audience, vehicle operators have the opportunity to create new revenue streams by offering travelers a range of in-journey services. Riders may be willing to pay for conferencing services, entertainment services, food and beverage services, connectivity, and information services. The market will segment with vehicle interiors purpose-designed to meet specific in-transit needs. Business will have opportunities to partner with operators to provide these services. What partnerships could you build?

On-demand autonomous transportation will show up in a broad range of shapes and sizes. Most Uber and Lyft journeys have an average of 1.1 passengers, plus the driver. Once the driver is removed from the equation, most rides are just one person. Smaller autonomous "pods" that carry one or two passengers will likely emerge to minimize costs, emissions, and congestion.

On-demand autonomous vehicles will operate as part of a wider, overall transportation network featuring autonomous trams, trains, buses, and other rapid transit. Journey planning software will coordinate and orchestrate journeys as we move from A to B. You might be driven from your home to a transit center by an autonomous car, transfer to an autonomous train whose departure is coordinated with your arrival, and then move to a shared autonomous transit pod that drops you at your destination before dropping other passengers who are headed to locations nearby. To deliver a seamless end-to-end journey experience for riders, multiple transportation networks, perhaps operated by entirely different entities, must be coordinated. Systems will be needed to handle ticketing and billing that spans these various transport networks.

Less Parking, More Drop-Off Zones

Autonomous vehicles will reshape our cities. Shared vehicles, operating as a transportation service, don't spend much time parked. Once they drop off their passengers, autonomous vehicles move on to collect their next fare. Fewer parking structures will be needed. Some will be repurposed, others demolished. With less need for street parking, city planners will have the choice to either increase traffic flow on major arteries or widen sidewalks to increase space for pedestrians and improve the aesthetics of our streets.

As vehicles become autonomous most will also become electric. Corner gas stations will become a thing of the past. Individually owned cars will be charged at home or at work; fleet cars will use centralized charging facilities located on the outside of town.

Autonomous vehicles will communicate with each other constantly to coordinate their movements. With faster reaction times than humans, autonomous vehicles will be able to drive closer together than human-driven cars. This should improve the carrying capacity of our roads and lead to improved traffic flow and reduced journey times. Traffic signals may eventually become a thing of the past as vehicles at intersections negotiate with each other to maximize traffic flow. Smart algorithms might use split-second timing to coordinate vehicles as they move through intersections. Most of the time vehicles might not even need to slow down. The passenger experience might be scary at first, but eventually we will likely get used to it.

Autonomous Platforms Bring Services to Your Door

For millennia, service delivery has been connected to physical premises. I need to shoe my horse; I visit the blacksmith. I'm hungry; I visit a restaurant. My hair gets long; I visit the barber. In each case, the consumer visits the service provider. With the rise of autonomous vehicles, brands have a new platform on which to deliver mobile services. As a complement to fixed infrastructure, brands can now add autonomous mobile platforms that take services to busy customers.

Wheelys, a company based in China and Sweden, has a bold vision for the future of retail. They make a range of small, portable stores designed to operate without staff. Their flagship store, the Moby Alpha, is a fully automated corner store, *on wheels*. The store is registered as a slow-moving vehicle, so it bypasses all typical building and zoning laws. Moby Alpha is designed to shift the economics of retail. I spoke to Wheelys Chairman of the Board, Per Cromwell, who told me "physical retail has seen very few major changes the last 50 years. Lack of innovation is the main reason why physical retail is dying. By reinventing retail using automation and AI, we will not only stop the bleeding; we will enable new retail in new areas."

The store is summoned with the MobyMart app. Moby Alpha comes to the customer's location and access to the store is granted using the app. Shoppers browse the store, select items, and pay with their phone before exiting the store, which moves on to the next customer. The Moby Alpha is currently on trial in the streets of Shanghai, China.

San Francisco–based Robomart envisions an autonomous, on-demand farmer's market. The vehicle uses RFID and machine vision technology to enable a "grab and go" experience. The vehicle automatically senses what produce a customer selects and bills them automatically via a companion app. Retailer Stop & Shop is operating first pilots in the Boston area.

*Business Insight: Project Your Brand Promise
with Autonomous Platforms*

Autonomous vehicles create the opportunity for companies to project
their brands and deliver new services in new ways. Consider autonomous
vehicles as a new platform on which value can be built and through
which you can project your brand promise. Brands can use autonomous
platforms either to deliver in-transit services or to bring service capabilities
to a consumer's location. The meaning of "mobile strategy" just expanded
beyond apps to comprehend physical mobile platforms, too.

Autonomous Trucks Transform Haulage

Every major truck company is heavily invested in autonomous technology. Haulage companies face a shortage of truck drivers and legal restric-
tions on the number of hours their employees can drive without a break.
Depending on the country, drivers typically need to stop and rest every 8
to 10 hours or so. An autonomous truck can power on through the night
and is limited only by the occasional need to refuel or recharge.

Autonomous trucks will reduce shipping costs. TuSimple, a Chinese
autonomous driving company, claims its technology reduces the cost of
shipping goods via tractor trailer by 30%. In 2019, both UPS and the
United States Postal Service ran tests with TuSimple's Navistar autonomous trucks, and UPS has taken a minority stake in the company. The
average truck is replaced after five years. Once autonomous trucks pass
regulatory tests, expect a rapid turnover in the fleet.

The future of trucking likely involves out-of-town hubs located near
major highways. Human drivers will perform the more challenging task of
driving trucks through city traffic to the hub. The load is then transferred to
an autonomous truck that drives it across the country on major highways,
eventually arriving at another hub. Here, the load is transferred to a human
driver who drives it to the final destination. With this approach, truck drivers will be able to spend more time at home with family and friends, and
less time on the open road, sleeping in their trucks at night.

Going 3-D: Tunnels, Gondolas, and Passenger Drones

Beyond the occasional underpass and overpass, our road networks are largely two-dimensional, which limits traffic flow. For tech entrepreneurs, the solution to traffic congestion seems obvious: Use the third dimension. Take traffic underground or into the skies.

Tunnels

Elon Musk's Boring Company seeks to build a network of narrow-gauge tunnels for traffic to bypass the ground-level road system. Narrow-gauge tunnels are faster and cheaper to build. The Boring Company claims a 10-fold reduction in costs versus traditional tunneling. Musk's vision is to use these tunnels for his Hyperloop system and to host high-speed autonomous carriers for standard cars to ride on, like a kid riding on a skateboard. The system, known as Loop, aims to carry 4,000 vehicles per hour, moving at a speed of 155 miles per hour (250 kilometers per hour) along its main arteries. Cars enter the system on side tunnels known as spurs and drive onto autonomous carriers that automatically merge into the traffic flow and rapidly accelerate to speed using electric motors. Hyperloop takes things to the next level, removing the air from tunnels to reduce wind resistance. It will zoom passengers along in pressurized autonomous electric pods at up to 600 miles per hour (970 kilometers per hour). Each pod will carry up to 16 passengers. Early trials look promising, though many municipalities are wary of letting a private company dig a network of tunnels beneath their cities. Musk's bet is that as traffic jams become apocalyptic, cities will come around to his point of view.

Gondolas

To complement underground transportation, cities are also looking to the skies. Urban gondolas have become efficient systems to transport people from one neighborhood to another. Gondola systems already operate in Medellín, Colombia; La Paz, Bolivia; Caracas, Venezuela; Ankara, Turkey; Hong Kong; Singapore; London, England; Nizhny Novgorod, Russia; and Mexico City. Gondolas are cheaper to install than bridges or underground train networks. La Paz's gondola system has 11 lines, 39 stations, and covers

21 miles (33.8 km). It cost just $750 million to build and carried 50 million passengers in its first two years of operation, saving commuters 652 minutes. A typical subway system costs up to $700 million per mile to build. Cities including Edmonton and Toronto in Canada, New York, Chicago, Austin, Seattle, San Diego, Oakland, and Boston in the United States, and Oxford in England, are looking to gondolas to relieve transit pressures.

Passenger Drones: *The Jetsons* Becomes Reality

Mark my words: A combination of airplane and motor car is coming.
—Henry Ford, 1940

For decades, flying cars have struggled to move from fantasy to reality. The advent of efficient electric motors, powerful batteries, cheap sensors, artificial intelligence, and drone flight control systems have led to significant breakthroughs. Passenger drones will become part of the public transportation system in the 2020s. More than 100 companies are racing to build what essentially amounts to a flying car. I estimate that about 20 of these companies have a viable shot at building commercially successful products. These companies include big names of the aeronautical industry—Airbus, Embraer, and Boeing—together with start-up companies like eHang, Volocopter, Joby Aviation, and Lilium. Traditional car manufacturers—most notably Volvo, Daimler, and Toyota—have placed bets and made investments in the leading start-ups. Daimler backed Volocopter, Volvo parent company Geely acquired Terrafugia, and Toyota has invested in Joby Aviation. Porsche, a Volkswagen company, is rumored to be exploring passenger drones of their own.

Some passenger drones, like Terrafugia's TF-X and NFC's Aska, look more like traditional fixed-wing aircraft and require a short runway. They have foldable wings and double as a traditional (but ugly) car. Most passenger drones are eVTOL designs, fully electric vehicles designed for vertical take-off and landing (VTOL). Some passenger drones are single-seaters, others will carry up to 16 passengers. Flying speeds vary between 40 and 300 mph with the average being about 150 mph. Electric drones appeal to city managers because of their zero-emissions operation.

Drones are designed for safety with many redundant rotors. Many can lose up to three rotors and still land safely, and some are equipped with parachutes in case of a catastrophic failure of the flight systems.

In a signal of market viability, Uber has discussed bold plans for their Uber Elevate service, which seeks to build an aerial ridesharing network. Uber predicts that 15-minute flights could cost as little as $60. When you consider how far you can fly in 15 minutes compared to the distance you'd travel for $60 in choked city traffic, that pricing starts to look very attractive. Long term, Uber's goal is to bring the cost of drone flight down below the cost of a gas-powered car today, on a per mile basis. That would be an incredible turning point.

Bell Helicopter recently shortened their name to Bell in recognition of the fact that their future lies beyond traditional helicopters. The Bell Nexus passenger drone, due to launch in 2023, was first displayed at the Consumer Electronics Show in January 2019. This electric-hybrid VTOL beast carries four passengers and a pilot. Once fully autonomous flight control systems are approved by the FAA, the pilot seat will be used for a fifth passenger.

Passenger drones will finally make urban aviation a reality. Semi- and fully autonomous flight controls will remove the need for qualified pilots and make the technology accessible to the masses. Before cities open their airspace to these machines, rigorous testing must be completed and air-traffic management protocols must be agreed. First trials are expected in Singapore, Dubai, Dallas, and Los Angeles, with an initial focus on short hops between the rooftops of tall buildings. Over time, ground stations will be built to bridge ground and air traffic. Uber has ambitious plans to connect Uber Air and ground-based rideshare services into a comprehensive end-to-end mobility service.

Passenger drones offer an alternative to building more roads. A vision from the Swiss Energy and Climate Summit imagines a drone network that eases congestion on the nation's freeway system. The Swiss spend 33 million hours in traffic each year, resulting in an estimated economic impact of 1.62 billion Swiss francs ($1.65 billion). Adding a third lane to Switzerland's two-lane highway network would cost 60 million Swiss francs per kilometer ($98 million per mile). Flight corridors along the freeway may prove significantly cheaper. Twelve-passenger Volocopters would shuttle passengers from hub to hub along the length of the route. Up to 120 drones would operate in each direction between Bern and

Zurich, carrying up to 1,500 passengers per hour. The network would run off renewable energy and remove the need for a third lane on highways, saving huge costs and retaining many square miles of farmland.

Whether to alleviate traffic in cities or on major rural arteries, passenger drones look like a promising new layer to our complex transportation networks. The build-out will begin in the first half of the 2020s and continue through the 2030s and 2040s.

Business Insight: Innovations Created to Solve One Problem Often Scale to Solve Another

Innovation occurs in interconnected webs. A breakthrough piece of innovation developed in one sector can be combined with innovation from another and then scaled to solve new problems. Passenger drones provide a great example. The autonomous flying taxi services of the future will use battery and electric motor technology developed for use in hybrid and electric cars, flight control software developed to stabilize camera drones, and ridesharing platforms developed on mobile devices from the 2010s that makes use of GPS technology developed in the 1970s. Future innovation stands on the shoulders of today's breakthroughs. Leaders should pay close attention to technology innovation in adjacent industries and find ways to leverage those advances to make breakthroughs of their own.

Decarbonizing: Electric Cars, Trucks, Trains, Ships, and Planes

The shift toward electric vehicles (EVs) is underway. EVs are quieter, do not emit pollution, don't contribute to carbon emissions if electricity is generated from renewable sources, and have far fewer moving parts, making them more reliable than traditional cars.

New regulations will accelerate the transition from carbon-fuel-based vehicles. Athens, Paris, and Madrid will ban all diesel vehicles by 2025. India has mandated that 30% of all vehicles sold by 2030 must be electric. Scotland is committed to 100% zero-emissions vehicle sales by

2032, with England, Wales, and France following in 2040. The city of London has bold plans to move toward zero-emission vehicles. They will create a zero-emissions zone in the center of the city by 2025 and require all taxis and minicabs to be zero-emission by 2033 and all buses by 2037. The city wants a 100% zero-emissions transport system by 2050.

Car companies are responding. Volkswagen AG makes cars under the Volkswagen, Audi, Porsche, SEAT, Škoda, Bugatti, Bentley, and Lamborghini brands. Volkswagen will launch 50 new EV models and 30 new gas–electric hybrid models by 2025 and will offer EV options for every one of their 300 vehicles by 2030. General Motors has committed to 20 new EV models by 2023, and BMW to 12 new EV models by 2025. *Bloomberg New Energy Finance* predicts that sales of electric vehicles will pass 50% of all global vehicle sales by 2033 and reach 86% of all sales by 2040.

Tesla's electric semi-truck has the potential to transform the haulage industry. Tesla trucks will have a 500-mile range when fully loaded and traveling at highway speeds, and a peppy 0-to-60 mph of just 20 seconds when pulling an 80,000 lb load. They charge to a 400-mile range in just 30 minutes, the time taken to load and unload a trailer. Autonomous driving and jackknife prevention, using independently controlled motors on each wheel, are both featured as standard. Batteries are stored in the base of the vehicle to lower the truck's center of gravity and reduce the risk of tipping. Tesla guarantees trucks will not break down for 1,000,000 miles and claims brake pads never need to be replaced since most braking is done electrically, recharging batteries in the process. Most compelling of all, Tesla claims operating costs are 20 cents per mile cheaper than diesel-powered trucks, which gives the electric truck a two-year payback period.

Electric transportation will also spread to the oceans. The world's first all-electric ship is in service in China. It transports 2,200 tons of cargo up to 50 miles on a single charge with a top speed of 8 mph. The 2,400 kWh lithium-ion battery recharges in just two hours, the time needed to unload cargo. Paradoxically, the ship is being used to transport coal. Norwegian company Yara will soon launch a zero-emission container ship named the *Yara Birkeland*. The ship will

replace 40,000 truck journeys per year and link two densely populated urban areas in Norway. It carries up to 150 containers and will
initially operate with a human crew. Within a few years of operation,
the ship will become fully autonomous. Ultimately, Yara imagines a
ship that is loaded and unloaded at ports by fully autonomous cranes.
Longshoremen beware.

   The International Civil Aviation Organization predicts that aero-
space emissions will triple by 2050. Decarbonizing aircraft is a significant challenge. The energy density of fuel is substantially higher than
even today's best battery technology. A Boeing 787 carries more than
100 tons of fuel for a flight. With today's battery technology the batteries needed for the same flight would weigh more than 10 times the
maximum landing weight of the 787. The approach used to remove
carbon-based fuels from roads makes sense for the skies, too. Hybrids
provide a bridge to fully electric operation. Boeing's SUGAR volt is a
hybrid plane designed to operate quietly and reduce fuel consumption
by 70% over today's planes. The SUGAR volt uses jet fuel for take-off
but switches to electric for some portion of the flight. Its longer wings
fold so it can operate out of existing airport gates. Currently a research
project, launch isn't expected until the 2030-to-2050 time frame. Electric flight projects are under way by other major aeronautical players.
Airbus is collaborating with Siemens and Rolls-Royce on their E-FAN
X test concept. Boeing and JetBlue are funding an effort by start-up
Zunum named *Aero*. *Aero*, a 12-passenger hybrid plane with a range of
700 miles and a cruising speed of 340 mph, can take off on a runway
just 2,200 feet long and may come to market as early as 2022. Low-cost
European carrier Easyjet has lofty ambitions for a transition to electric
planes. Easyjet is working with Wright Electric to develop all-electric
planes designed for short-haul routes (335 miles or less). Economics are
driving Easyjet. For low-cost carriers, fuel is a significant component of
their cost structure. Easyjet's goal is to fly their first electric plane service
within a decade.

Business Insight: Watch for Change in Other Industries That Might Affect Your Own

The demand for electricity will increase dramatically in the coming decades. An expanding population, more electric gadgets, data centers, digital ledgers, vertical hydroponic farms, and air-conditioning for a warming world each add to the demand forecast. But all that new demand is dwarfed by the future needs of transportation networks as they transition away from carbon-based fuels. Electricity generation and distribution capabilities will require significant investment. Today's energy grids are flimsy and in urgent need of upgrade. Transportation's transition to zero emissions will need to be carefully managed in lockstep with the evolving capabilities of the energy sector. This is a great example of how changes in one industrial sector can have huge implications for another. Every business should be on the lookout for ways that changes in other industries may provide challenges or opportunities.

12 Surviving the Retail Apocalypse

What Every Business Can Learn from Retail Tech

It wasn't until the beginning of the twentieth century that retail began to look like it does today. In 1909, Harry Selfridge opened the first department store on Oxford Street in London and introduced stunning window displays, the promise of excellent service, and an enjoyable shopping experience that turned stores into destinations. Then, in 1916, Piggly Wiggly popularized the self-service model. Prior to this innovation, goods were served over a counter by a shopkeeper, and products—coffee, flour, and sugar—were measured and placed in a paper bag.

Since then, we have seen the emergence of big box stores, malls, membership stores, and the mighty Amazon. Grocery stores operate like the early Piggly Wigglys, and department stores still look very much like the original Selfridges. We pay with plastic (or our phones and watches) and we order some of our stuff online, but in-store retail looks very much the same as it has for as long as anyone reading this book has been alive.

Change is coming. Retailers should expect more change in the next decade than the industry has experienced in the last century. Shoppers will browse differently, choose differently, buy differently, and expect to communicate with retailers through new channels, some of which don't yet exist.

The Challenge: E-Commerce and the Retail Apocalypse

The fastest growing stock of the 1990s was Circuit City. In 2008, Circuit City filed for bankruptcy and by 2009 they had closed their doors for the last time. Many of the iconic retailers of the twentieth century are either mortally wounded or gone. But all is not lost. Retailers that invest in technology to reimagine the shopper journey will continue to thrive in this $17 trillion sector.

With annual sales of a quarter-trillion dollars, Amazon has become the juggernaut of the e-commerce era, dwarfing even their nearest competitor. In 2019, the average American spent more than $2,000 per year online (Source: Statista). Global e-commerce sales of $2.2 trillion in 2020 will rise to $2.8 trillion by 2023 (Source: Statista). While people value the convenience of online shopping, they still prefer in-person, physical shopping for many of their purchases. In 2020, U.S. e-commerce sales will reach only about 12% of all retail sales. People shop in stores for many different reasons, seeking social, fun shopping experiences with friends and family that allow them to explore new possibilities in an appealing environment.

The End of the Middle: The Great Bifurcation of Retail

Retail is splitting into two distinct halves. The low-end is focused on price and speed, and the high-end is focused on quality, brand, and the shopper experience. Retailers left in the middle are neither one thing nor the other and have struggled to make their business models work. As this bifurcation continues, successful retailers will deploy technology to optimize either for low-price, high-speed fulfillment, or for high-touch, service-oriented, experiential shopping.

Consumers Want Customized Products, Personalized Shopping Experiences

Consumers are becoming less interested in off-the-shelf products that look just like everyone else's. Three color options no longer count as offering personalization. Shoppers will expect to customize many of the things that they buy. This has obvious implications for the retail experience and the entire supply chain that supports it. Within the decade, it may not be unreasonable to walk into a clothing store and say, "I want this shirt, in that color, in my size, in five minutes."

Massive Choice and the Tyranny of Choosing

Shoppers love choice. But too many options can be time-consuming and stressful. A quick stroll down the toothpaste aisle of any supermarket highlights the problem. The simplicity of "good, better, best" has been replaced by myriad options, flavors, and packages. Shoppers need help to narrow choices with curation, personalized recommendations, and guided customization.

Friction-Free, Fast-Fulfillment for a Busy World

Sometimes we want to take our time and enjoy the experience of shopping. Other times, we need to grab and go. Trained by e-commerce experiences and trying to navigate busy lives, shoppers want options for fast fulfillment of their needs in a frictionless shopping environment. Frictionless means no queues, no waiting, no hassle, no checkout.

Digital, Frictionless, and Unstaffed Stores

Physical store operations are changing as digital technology begins to blur e-commerce features with brick-and-mortar retail.

The Digital-Physical Store

Physical stores are being fitted with digital technology. And pure-play digital retailers, including Amazon and JD, have started to build physical stores. Stores now make use of digital signage, sensors, beacons, and mobile payment terminals to boost the shopper experience. Digital-physical stores gather data on shopper behavior, which is used to optimize the selling environment and boost sales.

Some Stores Become Showrooms

New shopping and fulfillment models are emerging. Shrinking delivery costs and sub-one-hour-delivery times might split browsing and fulfillment for some product categories. In this model, shoppers visit showrooms to browse and try product samples. Customers don't buy from in-store inventory; goods are shipped to their homes from centralized fulfillment centers. Men's clothing brand Bonobos has already embraced this direction with their "Guideshop" locations. These stores only hold enough inventory for customers to try sizes and styles. All purchases are shipped directly to customer's homes from centralized warehouses.

As retail footprints shrink, it may make sense to centralize inventory and split fulfillment away from the rest of the retail experience. As the desire for customization rises, we might see manufacturing or final finishing of goods colocate with fulfillment.

Frictionless Checkouts and Unstaffed Stores

Amazon led the way on frictionless checkouts with their Amazon Go stores. Their "grab and go" experience feels magical. As you enter the store you scan a special barcode generated by the Amazon Go app on your smartphone. Once scanned, you put your phone away and forget about it. You wander the store and pick up whatever you want. If you change your mind, you simply put things back. When you're ready to leave, you just walk out. No checkout, no lines, no wait. Within seconds, your Amazon account is billed automatically and accurately. Honestly, the experience feels like you're stealing. Amazon Go stores feature a plethora of cameras and other sensors mounted in the ceiling and on shelves. AI keeps track of customers as they walk around the store and notes which items they take. Amazon plans to build 3,000 similar stores in the coming years.

Other brands have built automated stores that streamline the shopping experience and do away with almost all staff. Alibaba's Tao Café is a staff-less cafeteria and boutique located in Hangzhou, China. To use it, you must be a member of Alibaba's Taobao service. Facial recognition technology identifies shoppers and as they leave the store, goods are automatically scanned by RFID readers, which even capture goods placed inside bags. The checkout process takes about 10 to 15 seconds. JD's X unstaffed convenience store works the same way. Human labor is needed only to clean stores and to restock shelves at the end of each day.

Suning runs a number of unstaffed stores in China, selling sporting goods, personal electronics, food, and fast-moving consumer goods. Like the Tao Café, Suning uses face recognition and RFID technology. Cameras, AI, and analytics track in-store traffic flow and optimize product placement and store operations. In the future, Suning plans to use augmented reality to display additional products virtually, optimizing the use of physical space.

French supermarket giant Auchan plans to build hundreds of Auchan Minute convenience stores across France and China. These fully automated minimarkets are open 24/7, contain 500 different products, and are accessed with the scan of a smartphone app. Shoppers scan products at the cash register and pay with WeChat or Alipay before they exit the store. Auchan representatives are available by live video chat if any problems occur.

Generally, consumers like these unstaffed stores. In surveys, people say they are quick, easy to use, and avoid social friction—meaning any interaction with other people. Sad, but true. On the downside, some people report stores can be dirty and not well-maintained. They also worry about products being tampered with, an issue that can probably be resolved in the future with the use of sensors and AI.

> ### *Business Insight: Consumers Expect Frictionless Experiences*
>
> Busy consumers quickly lose attention. A realization of a need or want may not survive the next distraction. Amazon's Echo platforms and one-click "Buy Now" website buttons show the power of removing friction from the purchase process. Fickle shoppers will switch to other suppliers in a heartbeat if they offer a more efficient way to find, choose, and buy what they need.
>
> No matter your business, pursue a relentless effort to remove unwanted friction from every customer interaction, remembering that sometimes friction is a desired part of an experience for customers. Use AI to predict needs so customers don't have to invest the cognitive effort to express them. Automate away all transactional pain and use technology to support sales associates and customer service agents so they can deliver unparalleled service. Make it so easy to do business with you that customers never want to go anywhere else.

Shopping with Smart Shelves, Chatbots, and Robots

Grocery store Kroger has begun deployments of its EDGE (Enhanced Display for Grocery Environment) smart shelf technology. These high-definition, color digital displays line the edge of store shelves and replace traditional printed signage, which speeds store operations. Price changes, special offers, and coupons can be deployed with the touch of a button. Displays offer additional information to customers, including nutritional information and suitability for special dietary needs. Kroger generates additional revenue by selling advertising on the displays. The brightness of the displays allows them to lower overall store lighting, saving money.

Smart shelf technology like Kroger EDGE may one day offer fully personalized shopping experiences. These could include personalized offers that are triggered by the proximity of your phone and personalized shopping guidance: As you walk down each aisle in the store, specific items on your digital shopping list are highlighted in a chosen color, speeding the shopping process.

Chatbots may be integrated into next-generation store shelving and fixtures to answer simple questions and provide additional information about the products on display: specifications, online customer reviews, and warranty information. Chatbots could help consumers to make purchase decisions and answer questions: "What's the difference between the V200, V300, and V500 models?" As they gain sophistication, sales chatbots might engage in full sales conversations, answer more complex queries, understand the customers' needs, preferences, and price sensitivity, and recommend the right product solution for them.

Beyond store infrastructure, sales chatbots may be embedded in a store's mobile app and inside store robots. Robots at hardware store Lowe's can answer simple customer queries and guide shoppers to products inside the cavernous stores. The LoweBot speaks multiple languages and has a touch screen. When not helping customers, LoweBot roams the aisles, running visual checks of store inventory.

Bossa Nova Robotics makes robots for retail stores. Martin Hitch, Bossa Nova's Chief Business Officer, told me he estimates that up to 40% of grocery store workers' time is spent auditing the shelves. Bossa Nova's robot uses both 3-D and high-resolution 2-D cameras to count products on shelves. It then builds a picklist for the human shelf-stackers to work from—more cornflakes on aisle 7 and more aspirin on aisle 4. The robot spots misplaced products, too. Shoppers are notorious for putting products in their basket, having second thoughts, and then dumping them wherever the mood strikes them. As it audits, the robot builds a map of the store (known as a planogram) and learns exactly where every product is located. To perfect their technology, Bossa Nova ran multiyear trials with several big box stores. Their partnership with Walmart is perhaps the most visible. Giant have deployed a similar robot named Marty. Marty searches their stores for safety issues, using eight cameras to find spills, debris, and other trip hazards. Marty warns nearby shoppers and alerts store employees by paging them over the store PA system. Ultimately, Marty will also be used for inventory monitoring and to do price checks. Expect robots to become a common sight in the aisles of a retail store near you.

Auto retailers Carvana in the United States, Autobahn motors in Singapore, and Tmall in China have created gigantic, robotic car vending machines. The Autobahn robot holds up to 60 high-end and classic cars. Tmall is a collaboration between Ford and Alibaba in Guangzhou. Customers must have at least two social credits to access the program via Alibaba's Taobao mobile app. Customers are given a three-day test drive and qualify for discounts at the dealership if they go on to make a purchase.

AI Transforms the Shopper Journey

The shopper journey describes the entire shopping process, from the moment someone becomes aware of a need, through exploration, discovery, selection, purchase, delivery, and then subsequent use of a product. Retailers are turning to AI to help them improve the shopping experience and deliver better service throughout the shopper journey.

AI Revolutionizes Discovery and Curation

The Campbell Soup Company built AI-enhanced online ads that, when clicked, hold a conversation with the customer and recommend recipes they might like, based on ingredients they have at home.

Target added visual search capabilities to their smartphone app. Customers snap a picture of items they're looking for using a phone app, which responds with links to similar products that Target has in stock. Next-generation visual search tools may use AI to disassemble entire scenes, for example, a shopping app shown an image from a home decor magazine would identify every item in the room and provide purchase links for each one.

Some retailers use AI to help their customers discover new products and services. Travel company Thompson's "inspiration engine" guides holiday-makers to find the perfect vacation using a conversational chatbot feature. In a Thompson survey, 77% of people said they wanted a virtual travel agent feature. The 1-800-Flowers group of companies, including Harry & David, Cheryl's, Wolferman's, and The Popcorn Factory, have deployed an AI-based curation chatbot named Gwyn. This personal gift concierge assesses the needs of customers and curates a short list of products to help them find the ideal gift. Outdoor wear company North Face offers a similar curation tool.

Brands like to know how their customers are feeling, so they can offer assistance when they are confused, respond appropriately when they are upset, or understand moments of delight. Bentley's Inspirator app uses a device's camera to assess the sentiment and mood of customers as they flick through a catalog of cars. The app automatically creates a customized "dream" car for customers in the background, based on a customer's reactions. Future in-store applications of sentiment analysis might use smart cameras to anticipate when a customer needs service, automatically alerting the nearest store associate.

Box-fashion company StitchFix curates and mails a box of clothing based on a client's personal taste. Customers keep what they like and return what they don't. StitchFix uses AI to curate these clothing collections and to predict overall demand for styles. While AI makes recommendations for clothing kits, human stylists review the kits and act as final decision-makers. Such personalized outfitting and styling may extend to other categories in the near future, for example, home furnishings. A customer would submit a photo of their living room and offer guidance on their tastes and goals for a new look. Artificial intelligence, using GAN technology, would respond with a photo-realistic image of that same room, now filled with furnishings that are curated based on the customer's expressed tastes.

AI Turbocharges Store Operations, Merchandizing, and Design

AI plays a vital role in the operation of retail stores. Smart cameras spot safety issues and optimize the planogram (the layout of the store) based on sales data and observations of customer traffic. Robots perform stocktaking and AI-powered algorithms predict future demand at a granular level—by line item, by distribution center, and by store. AI sifts through social media feeds to assess customer sentiment, observe emerging trends, and gather customer needs and wants. The task of "cool spotting," where hip observers populate hip locations—nightclubs, major city streets, trendy bars—to observe what the cool and groovy people are wearing, is being taken over by AI.

AI designs new products, too. Myntra, an Indian clothing company owned by Flipkart, uses Generative Adversarial Networks (GANs) to design clothing. They claim the sales of AI-designed garments is growing 100% per year. Another AI-based tool helps Myntra's purchasing department to assess how well a new item will sell based on past sales of items with similar colors, sleeve lengths, fabrics, etc. Buyers are empowered to ignore these projections but often find the guidance to be invaluable.

Le Tote, an online retail store for women's clothing, has a tiny six-person team that does *all* of the buying for their site. They use AI to augment their intuition and help them find dresses, tops, pants, and jackets to sell on their site. The AI analyzes digital wish lists, online ratings, and recent purchases to predict future demand and set stock levels.

> ## *Business Insight: Decision Support Is Important in Every Industry*
>
> Retailers must sell the right products, in the right way, at the right time, at the right price, to the right people. Success requires many decisions to be made accurately and quickly.
>
> Data-driven decision-making is transforming retail. AI crunches data to spot trends and design new products with high chances of market success. Store operations are measured and optimized to boost sales, limit markdowns, and maximize profits. Gut decisions are being replaced by data-driven decisions. Gut decisions have no place in retail. They have no place in your business, either.

AI Predicts What Customers Will Want, and When They Will Want It

Predictive analytics find patterns in customer purchases and predict what they might buy next. Unexpected but statistically significant patterns emerge. A white goods retailer worked in partnership with Intel to review sales data. Initial findings were unsurprising: customers who bought a TV were likely to buy a replacement television 10 years later. What shocked the retailer was that customers who bought a TV were highly likely to be in the market for a new washing machine seven years later. Weird, but true. This insight led to a successful shift in the retailer's marketing strategy.

Home Shopping with Voice, Gesture, and Augmented Reality

Retailers are eyeing your home as their next, and perhaps most important, piece of real estate. People lead busy lives, and there is little pleasure in sourcing toilet paper, milk, and shampoo. We are fundamentally lazy, and retailers know it. They want to make it as easy as possible to supply you with the goods you need on a regular basis. Google and Amazon have invested heavily to place retail outposts into millions of homes. Amazon Echo and Google Home platforms are designed to reduce purchase friction by moving the point of purchase close to the place where customers realize they have a need. Authors Chip and Dan Heath call this "shaping the path" in their excellent book *Switch*.

One of the major challenges for v-commerce platforms (voice-based shopping) is to establish specifics. If you order "milk" do you want soy, whole, 1%, 2%, almond, coconut, chocolate, lactose-free, lactose-free 2%, or lactose-free 2% milk with added calcium? Amazingly, this list of choices is just a small subset of the milk options available at some grocery stores. One solution is to build v-commerce systems that learn your preferences over time and reduce the number of times clarification must be sought. Another is to use another communication modality—gesture—to express selections naturally and efficiently.

Augmented reality (AR) will turbocharge home shopping, creating delightful, natural shopping experiences in the living room. Issue a simple voice command, "Show me gray sweaters under $60" and a range of gray sweaters appear all around you. You browse, point, and say, "Show me more like this one." Perhaps you'd prefer to experience a private, personalized fashion show in AR, complete with catwalk models parading through your living room, each wearing garments that have been selected to match your personal style and taste. You might use AR to try a new piece of artwork on your wall or to explore a kitchen remodel.

Virtual browsing affords the possibility of being able to shop for items that don't yet exist. Manufacturers might create a product digitally, test it with a variety of potential customers, and only manufacture it once they find sufficient interest. AR and VR (augmented and virtual reality) offer an excellent interface for shoppers to design customized products, choosing colors, configurations, finishes, and adding unique personal details before placing an order. With 78% of millennials expressing interest in customized products (Source: The Cassandra Report), retailers should be ready to offer customization in every category.

Business Insight: Boost Your IT Budgets Now to Avoid Catch-Up Later

The retail sector underinvested in technology for decades. New lighting and a zigzag checkout queue passed for innovation. The graveyard of dead retailers is testament to a stagnant sector that failed to invest forward. In retail, a long-range strategic plan has a horizon of perhaps two years. Most managers are focused on the next few weeks of operations. Complacent retailers were outmaneuvered and left bewildered by the rise of Amazon, which invested billions in technology and infrastructure as part of a multidecade strategy for domination.

Caught flat-footed, retailers are playing catch up. They know they must double down on WACD (What Amazon Can't Do) and leverage their physical assets to delight shoppers in ways that Amazon cannot. Historically, retailers invested only 1–2% of revenues in IT. They probably need to increase that spend to 5–8% of revenues if they are to remain relevant. Already operating in survival mode, this is money that struggling retailers just don't have. For many, it's too late.

Don't wait for an Amazon-like tech company to start eating your lunch before you reluctantly increase your IT budgets. As a strategic exercise, imagine that Jeff Bezos lays eyes on your industry next (because he might). Consider WWJBD (what would Jeff Bezos do?), look at your current assets and business processes, and determine where you can invest in technology infrastructure to remake your business and remain competitive. Don't wait. Invest *now* to build capabilities that will streamline operations, delight customers, and stave off competitive attack.

Never assume that your future is ensured just because you were fine in the past. A failure to increase IT budgets now is essentially a surrender of your future. This is the crux of *The Innovation Ultimatum*. Bite the bullet and innovate now or face painful catch-up and possible destruction later.

13 Cheap, On-Time, Safe, and Genuine

What Every Business Needs to Know about Future Supply Chains

Supply chains matter. A healthy supply chain is essential to the success of almost every organization. History is filled with stories of mighty armies that were defeated not by superior enemies, but by a poor supply chain. The British in the Revolutionary War and the German advance on Russia in World War II are just two examples.

The Challenge: Shifting Expectations and Widespread Fraud

Modern businesses are highly interconnected. Complex products may contain thousands of components, sourced from hundreds of suppliers. Supplies often cross continents, oceans, and customs borders. Businesses need dependable supply chains. In 2011, devastating floods in Thailand sent shockwaves through the entire IT industry. At the time, Thailand was the world's number two supplier of hard disk drives (HDDs) and the flood resulted in a 30% shortage in HDD supply for several quarters.

211

Nobody in the PC industry escaped. Beyond the obvious impact to HDD companies, every PC manufacturer's results were crushed because they couldn't meet demand. Vastly reduced PC sales hit every other supplier to the PC industry, devastating their results, too. Many corporate IT projects were delayed by a year due to a lack of PC supply. The Thai flood had global consequences. In a complex, interconnected world, supply chains matter more than ever.

Consumers Want Lightning-Fast Delivery, Low Prices, and Transparency

We live in a 24/7 world of rapid consumption. Consumers demand low prices, bountiful choice, high quality, and near-immediate delivery. Delivery speed expectations have collapsed from weeks, to days, to hours. The next bar is delivery in minutes. Last-mile delivery is costly and complex. It is still a highly manual process involving delivery vehicles, drivers, and handheld carriage to the doorstep. This labor-intensive process is too costly and too slow to meet future market expectations.

Consumers expect to track the location of purchases as they make their journey to their front door. They also want to know where products are sourced and how they are made. Led by millennials, consumers vote for and against brands with their wallets. My friend Jamie Gutfreund, a former CxO of several global companies, once explained to me that fundamentally, shoppers care about only one brand: "Brand Me." The brands that we purchase accrue to our own personal brand, whether in our own minds or in the minds of the people we care to impress. Educated by a series of investigative journalism reports, many consumers have an elevated awareness of the impact of consumer culture and want to buy responsibly. In the future, consumers will demand to understand the true cost of their purchases so they can make informed choices. Since a product is the sum of all its component parts, consumers will expect rigorous transparency that spans the entire supply chain, right back to raw materials. In the early 2010s, the semiconductor industry underwent a massive effort to eliminate conflict minerals from their supply chains after unflattering media reports resulted in sustained pressure from buyers. As consumers become more sophisticated, their buying criteria will evolve. Consumers will demand to know a product's carbon footprint and the amount of water, energy, and other resources used to make it. They may require details on the labor, sustainability, fair-trade, and safety practices of manufacturers before voting for them with their wallets. And they will want audited proof of all claims. Brands caught making false claims pay dearly in the market. PepsiCo was caught making false claims that their Naked Juice products were "all natural" and "non-GMO." Customers were awarded a substantial settlement.

Beyond understanding origin, consumers want to be told the story of the products they buy. People will pay more for products that come with an origin story, and research shows that people actually perceive this story in their brains. Tests with fMRI machines show that if you tell a group of people that the wine they are drinking was made at a small family winery in a remote French village using methods that were handed down for generations, the pleasure sensors in their brains will light up far more than a control group given the exact same wine and told that it's local supermarket plonk served from a box. People can literally taste the story. Eyewear maker Warby Parker uses TV advertising and their website to tell the story of how their eyeglasses are manufactured. McDonald's in Australia, known affectionately there as "Maccas," created the Track My Maccas smartphone app to help customers understand that ingredients are all farmed locally. The app used augmented reality and 3-D animation to tell the story of where the wheat in a customer's bun was grown, where the beef came from, and even to show a photo of the farmer who raised the cattle. The app grabs a barcode scan from the burger packaging and uses the GPS location of the store to access a detailed supply chain database and render the experience.

Transparency on the provenance of all goods will become a market requirement. The ability to tell the origin stories of products will have commercial value. Build your supply chains with that in mind.

Food Fraud Is at Least a $50 Billion Problem: Diversion and Counterfeiting Are Rife

Is your food safe to eat? Is it really what you think it is? Answers to these questions are not always straightforward. In 2010, the Grocery Manufacturers Association estimated that the global market for mislabeled seafood is $15 billion a year. A study by the University of California Los Angeles (UCLA) and Loyola Marymount University checked the DNA of fish ordered at 26 Los Angeles sushi restaurants between 2012 and 2015. They found that 47% of the sushi was mislabeled. The same study found that 100% of the "halibut" and "red snapper" served was not the species advertised. Nine out of 10 times, the fish sold as halibut was actually flounder. Across the United States, the international conservation group Oceana found that red snapper is mislabeled on menus between 77% and 90% of the time.

We don't always get what we pay for in restaurants. This might happen because the restaurateur is a crook, because the restaurateur was unwittingly sold food that was deliberately mislabeled somewhere along the supply chain, or due to an honest mix-up at the packing plant. Whatever happened, the result is the same: Consumers don't get what they paid for. The supply chains that serve us are opaque at best.

Seven percent of food contains fraudulent ingredients (Source: World Customs Organization). There is a very good chance you have consumed fake olive oil. Journalist Tom Mueller wrote a major exposé on the fake olive oil industry. He estimates that up to 70% of the olive oil sold globally is either totally fake or has been adulterated with cheap substitutes. Canola oil is colored, chemically deodorized, and passed off as extra-virgin olive oil. Buying higher-priced oil doesn't inoculate you from the problem. In a 2012 test of olive oils by the Australian government, not a single olive oil purporting to be "100% extra-virgin olive oil" passed their tests. The Italian mob is said to be heavily involved.

The World Customs Organization estimates that fake food is a $49 billion industry, annually. That estimate is probably on the low side. Beer is watered down, food is cut with cheap fillers, and items are repackaged. As the excellent documentary *Sour Grapes* explores, fraud and fakery are a problem in the luxury wine market, too.

Counterfeit and adulterated food isn't just dishonest, it can also be dangerous. In 1981, more than 20,000 people suffered food poisoning after consuming olive oil that had been mixed with aniline, a toxic chemical. About 800 people died. In 2008, 300,000 Chinese children were made ill when milk was deliberately contaminated with melamine. Melamine bulks out the product, saving manufacturers money. An estimated 54,000 children were hospitalized, and six children died. In 2013, the British Food Standards Agency found that the meat in a Findus "beef" lasagna was not beef. Their analysis revealed that "up to 100%" of the meat came from horses. It was a huge scandal in the UK. In 2014, *NPR News* reported that most shredded cheese sold in American supermarkets has had cellulose (extracted from wood pulp) added to it.

Clothing, footwear, cosmetics, handbags, pharmaceuticals, watches, and electronics are all routinely counterfeited. The Global Brand Counterfeiting Report of 2018 estimates the global market for counterfeit goods will reach $1.82 trillion in 2020. Another big issue for brands is diversion. Here's how it works: A brand orders 1,000 items from their supplier. The supplier makes 1,100 items, ships 1,000 to their client, and then sells 100 on the gray market, reaping value that was created by the brand.

Adulterated, counterfeit, and diverted products cost brands trillions of dollars and put consumers at risk. Technology solutions are needed to address these glaring holes in our supply chains.

Today's Supply Chain Is Complex, Still Runs on Paper, and Does Not Favor Brands

Modern supply chains are complex. The tracking of materials, piece parts, and goods through the supply chain is only partly digitized. Many transactions are still tracked with paper, particularly toward the front end of supply chains, before piece parts are assembled into finished goods. Paper-based tracking systems reduce traceability and increase the risk of fraud. For some more unscrupulous brands, a flaky paper trail and a sea of dodgy middlemen offers plausible deniability when their suppliers are revealed to have unsavory labor practices.

Brands are generally at a major disadvantage. As well as diversion and counterfeiting, they must also deal with "shrink," the polite industry term for stealing. Shrink occurs throughout the supply chain: from shoplifting in retail stores, through products "falling off the back of a truck" during transportation, to deliberate shorting of goods. This is where a supplier marks a box as containing 100 items, but only ships 98.

Goods are constantly counted and recounted as they move through a supply chain. Even with electronic product codes and barcode scanners, items are miscounted. Some retailers take advantage of this, deliberately miscounting incoming goods from brands. They order 500 pieces, receive 500 pieces, but report they only received 489, and bill the brand for the 11 "missing" items. Brands have long known they are being taken advantage of by a leaky supply chain, but there was little they could do about it. They wrote the issue off as the cost of doing business, built the losses into their business model, and passed the price on to consumers. In some sectors, the combined forces of counterfeiting, diversion, shrink, and dubious bill backs from retailers have become untenable. Brands urgently need to regain control over their supply chains. That all begins with transparency.

Streamlined Logistics with IoT, Autonomous Vehicles, Robots, and Drones

A number of start-up companies, and some logistics titans, are embracing autonomous machines as a way to cut the cost of last-mile delivery.

Starship Technologies, a London-based company launched by two of the co-founders of Skype, builds autonomous delivery robots. Each robot can handle cargo the size of two bags of groceries. Starship Technologies has conducted extensive trials in London and the San Francisco Bay area. Partner Mercedes-Benz built specially configured vans with the capacity to house up to eight robots. The van acts as a mobile minifulfillment center. The van, which is not yet autonomous, is driven to a safe, central location from where the robots scatter to make their deliveries. As each robot exits through a side door, the driver loads it with a package. An RFID tag on the package conveys the package's destination. The bots are fully autonomous, travel on sidewalks, cross roads, and safely navigate around obstacles, hazards, and pedestrians. They have a range of up to 3 miles, a distance they can travel in less than 30 minutes. Customers track delivery progress on a smartphone app and receive an alert when the robot is about to arrive. Customers enter a code to open the secure pod and retrieve their package. The robot then returns to the "mothership" van, enters the back of the vehicle, and lines up for the driver to load it with another package. Starship Technologies built a special version of their delivery robot for Domino's Pizza. Known as the DRU (Domino's Robotic Unit), the robot has special compartments to keep pizzas hot and drinks ice cold. Domino's conducted autonomous delivery trials in Australia, New Zealand, Germany, the Netherlands, and the UK. They see autonomous delivery as a way to expand their business without being constrained by the availability of (human) delivery drivers.

Kiwi claims their delivery robots are 65% faster than couriers and have an average delivery time of 27 minutes. Their goal is to make $1 delivery a reality. Amazon has also announced plans for last-mile autonomous delivery with their Amazon Scout robot.

Continental AG, based in Germany, partnered with robotics company ANYbotics to demonstrate their autonomous delivery vision at the Consumer Electronics show (CES) in January 2019. ANYmal autonomous delivery robot "dogs" are carried by Continental's autonomous CUbE vehicle to a centralized location. The ANYmal robots carry packages on their backs and make their way to customers. The robot dogs can climb steps, and even reach up to ring doorbells before dropping their package on a porch. The CES demonstration was extremely slow, but advances in hardware and software will speed operations and make such solutions viable in the future.

Delivery drones will use a similar "mothership" approach. An autonomous vehicle, loaded with 10 to 20 package-bearing drones, will drive to a central location where the drones are dispatched. This combo model of drone and delivery van has already been explored by UPS. UPS modified one of their delivery vans to house a drone launch pad in its roof. The drone handles small deliveries that deviate from the main delivery route. The driver places the package in the drone and launches it. While the driver continues on their route to make deliveries, the drone flies to the "off route" location, drops the package, and returns to the van where it lands and descends through the roof to recharge, ready for its next delivery.

FedEx's delivery robot, designed by Segway inventor Dean Kamen, uses a technology similar to that included in high-tech wheelchairs. This gives it a limited ability to climb curbs and stairs. FedEx is conducting trials with partners that include Walmart, Target, Lowe's, Pizza Hut, AutoZone, and Walgreen's. FedEx claims that 60% of these retailers' customers live within three miles of a store, making robotic delivery an attractive option.

Nuro's delivery robot is larger than the delivery robots mentioned so far and drives on roads. Their electric delivery vehicle drives at speeds of up to 25 miles per hour. It has multiple storage bays and is primarily designed for grocery delivery. Nuro has done a number of trials with grocer Kroger.

Business Insights: Autonomous Delivery Changes the Economics of Last-Mile Delivery, Which Reshapes the Shopper Journey and the Overall Shopping Experience

Once the technology and the economics of the approach are proven in trials, it's sure to spark a vibrant cultural conversation on whether the low cost and convenience of robotic delivery is worth the hassle of sharing our sidewalks with a near-constant stream of robots. If trials in London are anything to go by, the answer to this question may be "no." Sensors embedded in delivery robots track how often they are kicked or punched by people as they pass by. They get kicked a lot. As well as ensuring their robots are safe and reliable, innovators will need to find ways to minimize social friction. Robots will need to be sufficiently courteous and respectful of humans if they are to gain our trust and be welcome in our world.

The era of one-hour, one-dollar delivery will change the landscape for every consumer-facing business and may shift consumer behavior. Consumers have figured out that it can be smarter to lease rather than own high-price, low-utilization products. This is also true for fashion items or products that undergo regular cycles of innovation. Low-cost, rapid delivery may accelerate the shift away from ownership by making products available on demand as a service, for example, a tool kit or professional camera equipment service. New services businesses will emerge, built around the sharing of goods via one-dollar local delivery services. What new services could your business launch using a one-dollar delivery service as its foundation? How could superfast, low-cost deliveries create a more sustainable business model where occasionally used goods are shared by many people?

Blockchain Speeds Audits, Builds Provenance, Aligns Incentives, and Fights Fraud

As consumers demand more transparency around the products they buy, and brands grapple to control costs and quality, more will be demanded of the supply chain. Blockchain technology improves transparency and ensures compliance throughout the process.

Everledger, a start-up operating in the diamond business, uses Blockchain to capture the vital characteristics of a diamond (cut, color, clarity, carats, provenance) and reduce fraud, trafficking, and theft. Blockverify, Gem, and Factom use Blockchains to confirm the authenticity of high-value assets. These platforms identify counterfeit products, stolen merchandise, and diverted products, and catch fraudulent transactions. Their initial focus is on luxury goods, pharmaceuticals, electronics, and gemstones. Ultimately, these platforms ensure that customers get what they are paying for. The immutability of Blockchains helps to fight fraud by making it harder to hide the true origin of product, change item counts, or misrepresent commercial shipments by falsifying documentation. Start-ups working in this area include SkuChain, VeChain, Provenance, Waltonchain, TEMCO, and Ambrosus.

When things go wrong, it's important to investigate the root cause of an issue and fix it quickly, as a part of a process of continuous improvement. Rapid resolution also limits fallout. The investigation of food-borne illness sometimes takes weeks or months. In November 2018, the Centers for Disease Control and Prevention issued a warning about romaine lettuce infected by *E. coli* bacteria. The Food and Drug Administration investigated another romaine *E. coli* outbreak just the year before. Each time, hundreds of U.S. consumers were made sick, many were hospitalized, and several people died. In an attempt to limit infection, romaine lettuce was pulled from the shelves of every grocery store in America. Without good information on the source of infection, all romaine was considered suspect and was destroyed. It was a huge waste of mostly good lettuce, a major effort for retailers and distributors, a big financial loss for producers, not to mention the emotional pain and suffering caused to Caesar-salad lovers.

IBM worked with major retailers Walmart and Kroger and food suppliers including Dole, Driscoll's, Tyson, Nestlé, Unilever, and Mc-Cormick to add additional traceability and audit capabilities to the food supply chain using Blockchain technology. Based on IBM's Hyperledger fabric, the new supply chain system stores secure records and offers easy audit trails. The system can be used to investigate food-borne illness outbreaks in seconds rather than weeks, which reduces exposure and risk when issues arise.

To establish the provenance of a product, we need to chronicle every step of its journey—from raw materials to finished goods—and record that origin story in a tamperproof database. The immutability of a Blockchain makes it the perfect technology to underpin a supply chain platform that records and guarantees provenance. As a shorthand, let's call this a provenance chain. A provenance chain stores all the information needed to establish the origin story of a product. This information will vary depending on the category of product being tracked. For example, temperature and humidity information is relevant for the storage and transportation of fresh food or temperature-sensitive medicines, but not for plumbing supplies.

As they move through the supply chain, products are handed off from one entity to another—subcontractors, manufacturers, integrators, ground transportation, warehousing, shipping, customs, and so on. At each stage, goods are counted, and quantities are recorded on the provenance chain. Counts are made by a range of different sensors. Smart cameras might use machine vision technology to count items as they move down each production line. Warehouse workers might scan barcodes with a handheld scanner as they are loaded onto trucks. RFID scanners mounted in trucks might read the RFID tags mounted on packaging. For food items, temperature and humidity information is read from sensors in trucks, loading docks, and storage facilities. All this information is stored immutably on the provenance chain.

The full origin story of a product goes far beyond details of the physical journey it took from manufacturer to end user. Sophisticated supply chains will track the amount of labor, waste, emissions, and water involved in the production and delivery of a product. Provenance chains will evolve to capture this additional information on the manufacture of a product. Connected sensors will meter the use of factory resources such as water, energy, and processing chemicals. The source of a factory's energy will be recorded, noting the percentage that came from fossil fuels versus renewables. Audited information on the factory's labor practices, employee benefits, pay, and working conditions will be added by independent and accredited inspectors. As goods are assembled from piece parts, all of the data on all their constituent parts is added into the provenance chain.

Transparency builds trust. By providing an immutable audit trail on the origins of a product, manufacturer claims for sustainability, freshness, and responsible manufacture can be backed up with data. Ultimately, farm equipment and other sensors might add data to provenance chains that capture how much water, fertilizer, insecticide, and herbicide was used to grow produce.

That's *a lot* of data to gather and store on each product. This may sound like unreasonable overkill. Why would farmers, factories, warehouses, logistics companies, retailers, and all the other entities involved in a supply chain invest in the sensor technology needed to gather all this data? Why would they agree to submit to additional scrutiny and audit? A few simple answers: (1) Some are already gathering this data to help them optimize their business processes. (2) Consumers and brands will demand it. (3) Added supply chain visibility quickly resolves disputes and saves money by making audits a breeze. (4) Brands will make it worth their while using token economics.

Let's explore what a brand-centric supply chain might look like.

How to Build a Brand-Centric Supply Chain

A provenance chain is only as strong as its weakest link. Any opaque stage of the journey could be a moment of spoil, adulteration, counterfeit, diversion, or shrink. To build trust, full provenance, end-to-end visibility of a product's origin story, must be established. To build a complete record of its history, we must get eyes on the product right from when it is grown or made and follow it through every step in its life. Miss a moment, and provenance can no longer be ensured.

Gathering data at every step of the journey is challenging. Enter the power of token economics. Since a provenance chain is built on top of a Blockchain or similar distributed ledger technology, it generates tokens. Tokens are used to reward participation in the chain. Those that invest in equipment to supply data to the provenance chain receive tokens. So, a cold chain trucking company that provides temperature and RFID scan data to the chain for items in transit is rewarded. So is a manufacturer that installs smart cameras on their production lines and contributes data. Warehouses that connect barcode scanning tools to the provenance chain are paid for the data they submit, too. Entities are persuaded to participate with financial incentives.

Tokens incentivize desired behaviors throughout the chain. This provides brands with leverage and a tool to align supply chain interests with the brands' interests. Suppliers who guarantee (and prove with data) that their production lines aren't being used for diversion get extra tokens. Logistics companies that don't experience shrink get extra tokens. Retailers that have accurate counts and reduce bill backs get extra tokens. Such a process could go further, rewarding retailers for shelf compliance. Compliance is the retail term for when products are displayed properly, per prior agreements between the brand and the store. For example, food companies pay supermarkets to display items at eye-level or on a promotional endcap. Compliant retailers that display items correctly (as audited by robots, perhaps) and remove items from display when they are out of date would be rewarded. Machine vision technology would play an important role here.

The powerful provenance chains described here don't exist yet. Parts of them do, but the full vision described here is still a number of years away. As brands wrestle with huge hits to their bottom line wrought by continued rises in shrink, diversion, counterfeiting, and fake retail bill backs, they will no longer be able to write these issues off as the cost of doing business. Brands will look to provenance chains to enforce good behavior and align the interests of supply chain players with their own. An effort akin to the ISO 9000 quality push of the 1990s may be needed to drive change through industries and certify compliant organizations.

Business Insight: Token Economics Can Shift Incentives

Networks of interdependent companies often have to collaborate within a broader ecosystem to create value. These collaborations don't always equally favor all participants. The brand-centric supply chain example shared here outlines how token economics can be used to encourage participation in a common data network built on a distributed ledger. Further, token economics can be used to reward certain behaviors and align business priorities. Such an approach can be used by any industries to align and reward the efforts of people or organizations that operate together in a loose cooperative network.

14 Smart Factories and Augmented Factory Workers

What Every Business Can Learn from Manufacturing Tech

The global manufacturing industry is the backbone of the modern world. It builds the "stuff" of our lives: paper towels and blue jeans, frozen pizzas and SUVs. With an output of $40 trillion (Source: Interact Analysis), the sector accounts for 16% of global GDP (Source: World Bank) and 14% of global employment (Source: McKinsey). By 2025, the majority of global consumption will be in developing economies where billions of new middle-class consumers will seek high-quality, low-cost products. Manufacturing demand will soar.

Successive innovations—mechanization, mass production, electrification, outsourcing, Six Sigma, just-in-time, automation, LEAN, and others—have boosted manufacturing efficiency, quality, and output. The next set of transformations will focus on distributed manufacturing, mass customization, next-generation automation, supply chain innovation, additive manufacturing, and new materials.

The factories of the future will be highly automated, cloud-connected facilities where robots, AIs, and people work side-by-side. Engineers will design enhanced, easier-to-manufacture products in partnership with collaborative AIs. Workers will receive real-time training and work instructions through augmented reality. These hybrid workers will gain knowledge as if in a scene from *The Matrix*. Sophisticated AI will quietly coordinate suppliers and schedule maintenance. Manufacturing is about to get a makeover.

The Challenge: Mass Customization and Globalization

Markets are highly segmented and hyper-specialized. Consumers expect vast choice and products that closely or exactly fit their needs. People don't just want to buy a spatula, they want one in a color that matches their kitchen decor. Demand has shifted from high-volume, low-customization products in the 1980s to lower volume, high-customization products today. In the future, consumers will seek fully customized goods and services, built to their specifications and exactly tailored to their needs and desires. Consumers, used to fully customizing their coffees at Starbucks, will expect similar levels of control over every aspect of their lives.

Globalization, low-cost shipping in standard shipping containers, and outsourcing have hollowed out big chunks of the manufacturing sector in mature markets. The U.S. Bureau of Labor Statistics estimates that 7.5 million U.S. manufacturing jobs have been lost since 1980, despite rapidly expanding domestic consumption, with the vast majority of those jobs (5.5 million) lost since 2000. These losses are partly attributable to automation, but mostly to overseas outsourcing to cheap labor markets. As shipping costs and developing market wages rise, tariff wars rage, and consumers seek customized products and rapid delivery, AI-powered automation will stimulate manufacturing companies to move production closer to consumption markets.

Paradoxically, automation may lead to manufacturing's slow return to mature economies as production is repatriated.

Generative Design Melds Human Creativity and Machine Intelligence

There are many ways to design an industrial valve, a chair, or a shopping cart. Generative design tools use AI to "riff" on an engineer's design and generate many variants. Engineers specify design goals—size, shape, weight, cost—and the AI creates design options that meet these criteria. Variants adhere to design goals but may be subtly or radically different from the original design.

Generative design pioneer Autodesk makes a suite of generative design tools. These tools create design variants and run simulations on each to assess its reliability, manufacturability, tensile strength, and so on. The tool auto-generates a bill of materials for each design to estimate manufacturing cost. The AI even offers suggestions on how to improve quality, reduce weight, reduce cost, improve structural integrity, or make the design easier to manufacture. The designer chooses the option they like most. The final design is a collaboration of human and machine intelligence.

When Autodesk first applied generative AI to product design, they expected the main benefit would be improvements to the quality of designs—lighter, stronger products that are easier to make. The tools certainly delivered that, but the new design process also unlocked creativity and took productivity to new levels. Greg Fallon is VP of business strategy and marketing at Autodesk. Fallon told me, "A designer can explore many—think tens, hundreds, or thousands—of valid design options simultaneously, which allows her to consider options she didn't have time to consider before. Often, some options are designs she would never have thought of. She can see all these options in a matter of minutes or hours. This compares to a manual process that would have produced a single result on a timescale measured in weeks or months."

Fallon continued, "Generative design is in its infancy. In the near future, it will go way beyond design and engineering to manufacturing, where it will simplify how products are made—everything from programming the machines to laying out and managing the factory. It could eventually extend to the supply chain, helping to optimize where, when, and how a product is built."

Generative design will enable semi-or fully automated customization of products, helping brands to meet consumer demand for customized goods. And it will propel design to new heights, encouraging designers to explore radical new options and leverage the full potential of the latest manufacturing techniques, particularly additive manufacturing.

Business Insight: Collaborative AI Will Aid Workers in Every Industry

In the futurist trade, we constantly watch for market signals: early examples of new trends that indicate the shape of the future. Generative design is a clear signal. It shows us how artificial and human intelligence can collaborate to co-create. The result of that collaboration is something that neither the human nor the AI could have created on their own—a result that is *better* than either could have created alone. Generative design is an example of "collaborative AI." These AIs are designed to work in partnership with a human, not as a subordinate but as a collaborative entity. AI will collaborate with people in many different industries and in a variety of roles. Every company should take inspiration from generative design and find ways to build and deploy collaborative AI capabilities across their workforce.

Robots and Cobots Boost Productivity and Reduce Worker's Comp Claims

Despite decades of mechanization and computerization, many manufacturing processes still involve a significant amount of human labor. Jobs that require sophisticated vision, practiced dexterity, and the complex application of years of experience have been immune to automation and remain the exclusive province of people. Advances in machine learning, machine vision, and robotics will chip away at some of these jobs. Roles that combine sophisticated muscle memory with creativity and judgment, such as glassblowing, remain at very low risk of automation. Others, like industrial polishing, will become partly automated within the decade.

Polishing, which determines the finish of surfaces, is traditionally an extremely manual process. It's tough to teach robots to manipulate objects with the required dexterity, and to recognize when an object is "shiny enough." SYMPLEXITY, a European partnership between industry and academia, is attempting to build a robotic polisher. Using surface metrology and a set of sophisticated sensors, the SYMPLEXITY machine scans surfaces to find imperfections and rough spots, and to assess shininess. Using machine learning, the robot teaches itself the best approach to use given a particular metrology result. It makes decisions about the angle of approach for the polishing tool and how much force to exert. With time, these robots will be able to handle simple- to medium-complexity polishing jobs. Today, these robots are slow, but they will eventually outpace human finishers on all but the finest grade polishing jobs.

Beyond polishing, AI will automate several other skilled jobs in the coming years. Robots are attractive to bosses because they boost productivity, work through the night, don't take sick days, and never claim worker's comp when they're injured.

Robotics companies—including Universal Robots, Rethink Robotics, Fanuc, KUKA, and Stäubli—build robots designed to work safely alongside and in partnership with humans. Robots aren't just about replacing jobs. Cobots, collaborative robots, are estimated to represent about 25% of all robots sold in the future. Cobots use force-torque sensors to sense human presence and power off instantly if a worker gets too close so they can exist safely in the same space. Some manufacturers use cobots for tasks that require more than one person to perform but don't justify the time of two people. Cobots have been found to improve workplace satisfaction by handling tiring, repetitive operations and freeing workers to focus on more complex and rewarding work, including programming, training, and maintaining the cobot.

Business Insight: Elevate Human Work and Leave the Rest to the Machines

AI and robots will be capable of taking on many routine, dangerous, and physically demanding jobs that humans don't want to do. We should let them do it, and focus our time on more meaningful, impactful, and challenging work. Before the invention of the automatic washing machine, clothes were washed by hand, mostly by the hands of women. Even with the new-fangled technology of the washboard, invented in the 1700s, clothes washing was backbreaking, exhausting, and time-consuming work. The work was dangerous, too. Women were exposed to water-borne disease, respiratory disease, and the perils of the mangle. Clothes washing could consume six hours per day up to three times per week. Automatic washing machines freed many women to enter the labor market and lift themselves and their families out of poverty. While more than half of the world's population still doesn't have access to automated clothes washing, those that do have reaped huge benefits. By freeing up time to focus on other things, washing machines have made a huge difference in people's lives, particular the lives of women. So yes, automation will destroy some work. But much of that work is repetitive, strenuous, boring, or dangerous. Workforces will need to upskill. People will need help to develop the skills needed to participate in highly automated environments. But when trained and transitioned, they will do higher value, higher paid, and more satisfying work.

Digital Dexterity: Next-Generation Robots Learn to Manipulate Objects as Humans Do

To liberate humans from laborious, repetitive, and boring physical jobs that involve dexterity, robots must learn to pick up and manipulate a wide variety of objects, and do it as well as humans. To do this, robots must see an object, identify the best strategy to pick it up, execute that strategy without damaging the object, and then successfully manipulate the object into a desired position and orientation. As we reviewed in Chapter 3, progress is being made by researchers, but further breakthroughs are required before robots have anything approaching the dexterity of a human. Expect continued improvements in this area. Within a decade we may see robots with the speed, agility, and dexterity to participate in manufacturing roles that were formerly the exclusive province of people.

Exoskeletons Turn Factory Workers into Ellen Ripley

Exoskeletons are an attractive proposition in manufacturing. These wearable machines increase the strength and endurance of workers, distributing force away from limbs and out through the exoskeleton. Passive exoskeletons are purely mechanical devices, while active exoskeletons support limb motion with a system of sensors, motors, and hydraulics.

The Eksovest from Ekso Bionics is an entirely passive device, designed to reduce fatigue and injury in workers performing overhead tasks. Ford deployed Eksovests for factory workers who install parts on the underside of vehicles. They provide between 5 and 15 pounds of lift assistance using only springs and clever mechanics. Their use is supported by the United Auto Workers union as a way to improve health and safety. Daewoo's powered exoskeleton makes lifts of up to 30 kg (66 lbs) feel as light as a feather. The lightweight suit made of aluminum alloy, carbon fiber, and steel has a three-hour battery life. The exoskeleton is on trial with ship builders in South Korea, and Daewoo has ambitions to increase lift capacity to 100 kg (220 lbs) in the future. With that kind of support, workers are turned into superheroes.

ActiveLink, a Panasonic subsidiary, is developing a monster that dwarfs the Ekso Bionics and Daewoo devices. Their power loader, the Atoun NIO, is designed for construction, emergency response, and heavy manufacturing. NIO looks heavily inspired by the Weyland P-5000 Powered Work Loader used by Ellen Ripley to engage the alien queen at the end of the movie *Aliens*. Still an experimental device, the Atoun NIO features 20 powered motors and, according to the Atoun website, can lift 100 kg (220 lbs) "without breaking a sweat."

With continued improvements in battery efficiency, materials, sensors, and AI, intelligent exoskeletons will become a valuable physical enhancement for the manufacturing workforce. Properly used, they will boost productivity, reduce injuries, and improve job satisfaction.

Augmented Workers Improve Training, Aid Compliance, and Reduce Liability

In the U.S. and European manufacturing sectors, turnover rates of 20% to 30% are common (Source: European Parliamentary Research, U.S. Bureau of Labor Statistics). Most manufacturers face labor shortages and struggle to find skilled workers. Onboarding and training are lengthy and costly. Just when someone is trained to do the job, they move on.

Augmented reality (AR) platforms make workers productive on day one. An AR headset guides the worker using visual cues. A color highlight overlaid in the worker's field of view indicates which part to pick up. A digital arrow shows which way a lever or valve needs to be turned. A virtual screwdriver shows the worker where to insert and tighten screws. No keyboard, no mouse, no manual. A machine vision system tracks the worker's progress and ensures each step is followed correctly. Detailed work instructions, coded into the AR system, provide a step-by-step guide. The worker quickly learns task details and may eventually not need the visual instructions. To aid product customization, AR provides value to skilled workers by documenting any special instructions or customizations required for a particular order.

AR systems for factory maintenance workers will provide easy access to equipment information: real-time operational data, detailed maintenance history, and holographic notes left by co-workers. Voice interfaces will enhance the collaboration between AI and worker. To troubleshoot, the system asks the worker questions—is the wire properly attached to the gold connector?—and guides the worker based on verbal responses. The hybrid of worker and AI, connected through the AR interface, can diagnose and repair equipment the worker has never encountered before.

In the event of subsequent equipment failure, supervisors review the video to understand what happened. AR recordings insulate companies from liability by demonstrating work was completed to the required standard. If mistakes were made, any ambiguities in the AR system are identified and additional training is provided to the worker.

Business Insight: Augmented Workers Will Spread to Every Sector

We are moving toward a world of augmented workers that combines the best of human and machine. Machines and humans will work side by side as one. Powerful AI, trained to capture the expert knowledge of many humans, will have access to a vast knowledge database in the cloud. Humans bring instinct, experience, dexterity, and common sense. The powerful combination of AI and human, bridged with an AR interface, voice, and gesture, is unbeatable.

Augmented workers will initially be found in manufacturing, construction, and healthcare, but will quickly spread to other business sectors. Businesses should greenlight a few AR workplace experiments today. The results from early pilots will inform the most impactful areas for first deployments once the technology matures.

Your Next QA May Be an AI

Visual inspection of finished goods has long been done by humans, presumably chosen for their keen vision, discerning eyes, and powerful concentration. Landing.ai, a company founded by AI luminary Andrew Ng, creates AI technology for the manufacturing sector. One product uses machine vision and machine learning to perform visual inspection of parts. Landing.ai claims they can inspect a part in half a second and achieve accuracy that is similar to, or better than, a human inspector. Their system is equally comfortable finding defects on tiny printed circuit boards as it is looking for scratches on camera lenses. Their inspection AI can be trained very quickly, sometimes with just five images of piece parts. That's breakthrough technology.

Distributed Manufacturing and the Mega Corporation with One Employee

Manufacturing is becoming democratized and distributed. We are approaching an era when a mighty corporation might have just one employee. Such a company would outsource almost everything. The best way to describe this concept is to share a short science-fiction prototype story that I wrote on this topic a few years ago. It explores the key concepts behind distributed manufacturing and revisits a smart product idea from Chapter 2. As you read this story, consider how distributed manufacturing will fuel a new era of entrepreneurship and allow anyone with a good idea and a little business sense to participate in the global economy. Consider how such a capability might impact your business or change the way you go to market.

Mega-Corporation of One

A short story from the future by Steve Brown

Today, Alice would push a button and ship several million units of her new product to customers all over the world. It all started just three weeks ago with an idea she had in the shower. Alice was shampooing her hair and thinking about her young nephew, Peter, when the idea for MoJo came to her. She was struggling with what to get Peter for his fifth birthday. Nothing in the stores seemed quite right, so she'd decided to make something herself. And now she had the perfect idea—a teddy bear to read Peter a book.

Alice bounded out of the shower and almost slipped on the tile floor in her excitement. At this stage, she wasn't sure how to make her idea a reality, but she knew she could collaborate online with a few helpful strangers to get assistance. Wrapped in her towel, she sat at her computer and used simple gesture and speech prompts to create her design. She chose materials, modified an existing open source bear design to give it a more generous tummy (just like her brother's!), and selected a Raspberry Pi 7 as the component she'd use for the reading capability.

Alice's idea clearly had merit; an hour after she posted it on the IdeaZ entrepreneurial community, she had offers of help from a fabric expert, a pediatrician, and a programmer.

Her proposed product name, "BookBear," didn't test well with the marketing crowd she liked to use, so she ended up going with the crowd's favorite suggestion, "MoJo." She'd learned to listen to the masses when defining and marketing products.

On a whim, Alice decided to see if anyone else would be interested. Maybe 5 or 10 people would have an interest in her idea and would help share some of the development cost. She published her design to FundStarter, a popular venture site, and waited.

The next morning as she ate her breakfast, Alice almost spit out her cornflakes when she checked her FundStarter account. More than 40,000 people wanted a MoJo bear if she built it. Most had pledged more than her minimum asking price of $90.

"Wow," thought Alice, "I really am in business!"

Alice clicked a few keys and within five minutes had set up, registered, and been approved as CEO of her new company, FutureBear, LLC.

In return for 0.1% of the proceeds of her sales, Alice retained the services of a fabric expert, Mica. Mica recommended six different furry fabric options based on Alice's requirements for durability, softness, and moderate cost. Mica lived in Brazil but arranged for cloth samples to be delivered to Alice's home from a local distributor right there in Amherst. Alerted by the buzz of the delivery drone, Alice wandered outside to collect the samples and chose her favorites. She would offer three color options to her customers. Perhaps she could charge a little more for the nicest fabric and make it a special edition.

For a similar cut of profits, Jason Chen, a pediatrician living in Malaysia, helped Alice with recommendations on a voice tone that would be appealing to young children. Jason had worked in children's care facilities in Europe and offered insight into a range of voices most appropriate for European and Asian markets.

Finally, Alice held a quick Holo-con with Genevieve an Australian programmer based in Adelaide. For Genevieve it was a breeze to stitch together the open source OCR code, the natural language engine, and her preferred voice simulator platform. It

(continued)

Mega-Corporation of One (cont'd)

*was Genevieve's idea to include a language translation function.
Now MoJo would be able to read a book written in one language
and speak it in an other. Genevieve's other idea was pure genius.
The reading service would be included in the initial price of the
product, but for multilanguage reading (which would cost them
nothing to implement) she suggested that Alice could charge a
monthly service fee of $4 a month.*

*For her programming efforts, and for the translator idea, Alice
rewarded Genevieve with a full 1% of profits, a figure that seemed
to make her happy. Little did she know just how wealthy that
arrangement would make her in the coming months.*

*Alice would never meet Genevieve, Mica, or Jason. She didn't
need to. In fact, they would never talk again. The e-commerce
platform ensured everyone was automatically paid for their
contributions. Alice had no employees. How odd that word seemed
these days.*

*Things were starting to come together. Peter's birthday
was just two weeks away, but Alice still had plenty of time to
get everything done. With luck she should be able to get into
production later that week.*

*The design details for MoJo bear were stored in Alice's favorite
design tool, UcanMake, which connected her to a huge network
of suppliers and manufacturers around the world. Alice tested her
design with UcanMake's simulation tools. She laughed out loud
as she watched MoJo being subjected to physical stress tests on her
screen. MoJo had to be able to stand up to the rigors of life in the
world of a five-year-old.*

*Everything was going smoothly when Alice saw a flashing
red alert on her screen. MoJo had failed an important quality
certification in Germany. Without it, she would not be able to
sell MoJo in the German market. UcanMake showed that the
issue was with the material used to make MoJo's button nose. It
recommended a different type of plastic and estimated that the
change would add seven cents per unit. Helpfully, it also reminded*

Alice that 2,438 of her bidders were located in Germany. That made the decision easy.

"I think I can handle seven cents," thought Alice. "Okay, do it," she said to the design tool.

Later, Alice would realize this decision eventually cost her a quarter million dollars.

UcanMake automatically issued the necessary UL, CSA, CE, TUV, and other safety certifications and Alice moved on to selecting her manufacturing partners. UcanMake made it a breeze to use the manufacturing cloud. Alice swiped the "Bid" button on her Holo-screen and within half a second the tool had negotiated with 3,700 different manufacturers around the world and secured bids based on Alice's design specifications and projected volumes.

"Gold star only," Alice said to her computer.

UcanMake filtered the list and removed vendors that hadn't achieved a gold star rating for work practices, environmental standards, and sustainability. The cheapest bids from the remaining 282 manufacturers were from a Cambodian company quoting $32.25 per unit and a Polish company that quoted just 40 cents more. Both companies were highly rated and noted for providing healthcare services to their workers. Alice decided she would use them both. The design tool recommended she add a third manufacturer in Mexico to service the North and South American markets and reduce shipping costs. It proposed a suitable manufacturer in Guadalajara that was willing to discount their price to fill excess capacity and optimize factory utilization.

"Okay, sounds good," Alice said.

UcanMake distributed the order among the manufacturers to optimize manufacturing and shipping costs and presented a final average cost per unit on the screen.

"That price seems rather cheap," thought Alice. She had expected the unit cost to be double that. She wondered if her new suppliers were cutting corners. When Alice checked the size of her online order book, she couldn't believe it. More than 3 million people had signed up to buy a MoJo bear. Her mouth hung open. No wonder the bid price was so low with that kind of volume!

An influential toy blogger had spotted MoJo on FundStarter and mentioned it in a post. Over the last two days, MoJo had gone

(continued)

Mega-Corporation of One (cont'd)

viral. Millions of people were eager to have a toy that could help their children learn new languages.

Alice steadied herself with a hot cup of tea. The magnitude of the moment wasn't lost on her. With the press of a single button she was about to submit her design for manufacture to factories in Cambodia, Poland, and Mexico, three countries she had never visited. From there, the global distributor she had selected from the distribution cloud would ship her product to more than 3 million homes, in 143 different countries. The toy will delight millions of children and make her $100 million richer. MoJo will provide employment to hundreds of people in the customer support cloud she has engaged to handle queries, returns, and repairs on defective units. The ongoing revenue stream from the translation service might bring her another $500,000 a week, and it was looking like 3 million MoJos might just be the beginning. Not bad for a few days of effort. Alice sipped her Earl Grey tea and hit "Print."

This story explores the notions of crowdsourcing, gig labor, advanced simulation, and the concept of a range of cloud-connected, distributed services including design, marketing, funding, manufacturing, distribution, and customer support. Safety testing agencies morph into sophisticated software simulation algorithms. The story deliberately omits mention of security features, prototypes, and user testing to keep the story short, but these would be valid additions to the scenario described.

Business Insight

Design tools will become the front end to a virtualized manufacturing network, which is supported by distributed factories, distributed distribution networks, and distributed customer support. Design becomes collaborative and social. Distributed manufacturing and semi-automated design tools make the means of production accessible to any individual with a good idea. A stream of innovative products will come to market, igniting a vast economic boom. As technology displaces people from the traditional employment landscape, it will also birth a new generation of entrepreneurs for the postautomation age. That has to be a good thing.

Industry 4.0/5.0 and the Sentient Factory

The current focus of innovation in manufacturing, first coined by the German government, is "Industry 4.0." Industry 1.0 describes the first stage of industrialization, when mechanized factories were powered by water or steam. Industry 2.0 saw the arrival of mass-production techniques, the assembly line, and machines powered by electricity. Industry 3.0 applied computer control and automation. Industry 4.0 implements sensors, autonomous robotics, analytics, artificial intelligence, and the cloud to create cyber-physical systems that propel manufacturing to the next level. Industry 5.0 builds on the Industry 4.0 platform and cognitive AI to deliver mass customization at scale. It leverages many of the concepts explored elsewhere in this book—augmented workers, generative design, cobots, and wearables—to enable a tight and powerful collaboration between humans and machines in manufacturing.

Before the Industry 5.0 vision can be fully realized, we first need to move today's factories to Industry 4.0 and implement cyber-physical systems. In a cyber-physical system, machines fitted with an array of sensors share operational data with each other in real time. In this context, "machine" describes any automated manufacturing tool: looms, drills, ovens, mixers, hydraulic presses, sorters, sprayers, milling machines, and so on. A real-time, digital representation of the manufacturing environment is created using sensor data from machines. This digital model mirrors every aspect of operations. Advanced analytics software, powered by AI, "imagines" alternative ways that the production facility might be organized and operated. The software runs simulations on each alternative and assesses it for efficiency, quality, and throughput. The best option is then implemented on the production floor.

Control software intelligently manages production flow and maintenance schedules and communicates with suppliers and customers. Imagine a radiator factory that supplies automakers. When a machine at the radiator factory signals it would benefit from preventative maintenance, factory operations software automatically redirects production to other machines, schedules the maintenance, and, if necessary, reduces supplier orders for radiator piece parts and materials. It then communicates any production delay to automakers. The automaker's factory, receiving the delayed delivery date, determines an appropriate response and either places orders with a second source, or reconfigures the production flow to install radiators later in the assembly process. All this activity occurs automatically. Decisions are made based on predetermined operating parameters and business logic set by factory managers. Once these parameters are set, managers can focus on overseeing production and resolving issues the automated systems can't handle. Every machine makes as many autonomous decisions as it can.

In the Industry 4.0 model, machines and humans work together in a partnership. Machines automate dangerous, repetitive, trivial, and unpleasant tasks, freeing humans to focus where they excel. When machines can't figure out what to do, they request human guidance. Cloud analytics and visualization software present complex operational data to humans so they can make informed decisions rapidly.

The majority of consumers want customized products. Intelligent, adaptable Industry 4.0 factories can customize products as they flow through. Each product or job is usually identified with an RFID tag. A machine reads the tag to retrieve the desired specifications for the final product and deduce which steps, if any, it needs to perform before handing the product on to the next machine.

Let's consider a cake factory built on Industry 4.0 technology, fulfilling an order for a vanilla sponge cake with raspberry filling, chocolate icing, and a custom birthday greeting. Configuration details are stored in a database and linked to a job number. The job number is encoded on an RFID tag, which is taped to the underside of a metal tray. A reader at the head of the production line scans the tag and diverts the tray to the vanilla line, rather than the chocolate or lemon cake lines. A robot places a layer of vanilla cake onto the tray, which then moves to the filling station. The filling machine, able to dispense one of six different flavors, reads the RFID tag and determines that raspberry filling is required. It dispenses the filling and passes the tray back to the vanilla cake line for a second pass. Optical sensors perfectly align the second layer and the cake moves to the icing machine, which covers the cake with chocolate icing, per the job instructions in the database. Finally, the finished cake moves to a worker wearing AR glasses. The worker pipes the words "HAPPY BIRTHDAY JACK" onto the cake as shown by their display. When completed, the cake rolls down the line for automated packaging, labeling, and shipment.

Industry 4.0 changes the relationship between humans and machines, and also between suppliers, producers, and consumers. Agile supply chains, managed by algorithms, feed a global network of manufacturers. Products are built intelligently using local factory capacity, close to consumption markets. As developing markets mature in the coming decades, Industry 4.0 will be crucial to meet the incredible demand for manufactured goods. Building on top of the highly automated cyber-physical systems created by Industry 4.0, Industry 5.0 factories will leverage generative design and other cognitive AI capabilities to build mass customized products. Designers will use sophisticated cognitive AI design tools to co-create products and manufacturing workers will collaborate with cobots to create them. Personal data will be used as input to the design process, enabling products to be deeply personalized on behalf of clients. Fundamentally, the Industry 5.0 approach embraces and supports human creativity and brings the human touch back into the manufacturing process. This will be one of the topics of my next book.

Business Insight: Cyber-Physical Systems Demonstrate the Power of Data-Driven Decision-Making

Industry 4.0 offers a clear signal for the emergence of human-machine partnerships. Machine intelligence frees humans from routine decision-making and makes high-quality decisions based on data that improve factory efficiency, throughput, and quality. Every business should seek to make data-driven decisions. Where practical, routine decisions should be offloaded to machines, freeing human talent to focus on more complex decisions. Complex decisions, made by people, should be supported by machines wherever possible, for example, by preparing data visualizations. Organizations should steadily increase the percentage of decisions that are made with data as part of a continuous improvement process. Set goals, reward successes, and watch your business's decision speed and quality soar.

15 Removing Chaos from Construction and Intermediaries from Transactions

What Every Business Can Learn from Real Estate Tech

Construction is amazing. High-tech structures reach through the clouds and defy earthquakes. Beautiful architecture improves the livability of our cities. Millions of homes provide shelter to billions of people, giving them a place to raise families and live out their lives. Global real estate is valued at around $300 trillion (Source: Savills).

The Challenge: Mistakes, Margins, and Glacial Transactions

Construction is dangerous, difficult work that is plagued by human error and still runs off 2-D plans. Skilled labor is in short supply, project schedules are tight, and complexity is high. Real estate transactions are glacially slow and result in ridiculous piles of paperwork. The sector is ripe for change.

Costly Mistakes, Skills Shortages, and Safety Issues Constrain Construction

If you've overseen a construction project, or a home remodel, you know that mistakes and rework are all too common. Plans are imprecise, poorly specified, or impractical to build and creative workarounds are required on the job site. Construction is dirty, demanding, and sometimes inexact work that's prone to error. As testament, note how baseboards, light-switch covers, and door jambs all hide imperfections. Common estimates are that rework accounts for about 10% of the cost of most construction projects. With industry profit margins at 4–5%, that's significant. The number one challenge reported by 80% of construction companies is a limited supply of craftworkers (Source: AGC/FMI risk management survey, 2019). One in five deaths in private industry occur in the construction business (Source: U.S. Department of Labor). In 2017, there were 14 deaths in U.S. construction *per day*.

Transaction Friction Impedes the Real Estate Market

Markets operate more efficiently when transaction friction is reduced or removed. When stock exchanges left paper behind and moved transactions onto computers, global markets flourished. With the emergence of internet trading, broker fees dropped from hundreds of dollars to 10 bucks or less. Trades execute in fractions of a second. Contrast this with the real estate industry: In 2018, the average mortgage-financed U.S. home purchase took 45 days. Real estate transactions in the United States are horrible. To buy property you must sign a stack of paperwork two inches thick and grease the palms of many intermediaries along the way. The process isn't much different in other countries.

Purchases incur significant fees, errors in public records are common, bureaucracy is high, and transactions move at a snail's pace. High fees and a paper-based workflows deter sales and depress real estate markets.

Generative Design Transforms Architecture

Autodesk, the pioneer in generative design, makes a suite of architectural design tools that allow architects to enhance their design sensibilities with the smarts of an AI. Architects determine the high-level goals and constraints of a project and use computer-based tools to automatically generate hundreds or thousands of design options. The tools sort the options, assess each against project goals, and guide the designer toward optimal solutions. Architects co-create buildings with the AIs. The AI gives the architect greater freedom to explore radical ideas. The design tools find the best ways to bring those ideas to life. This approach enables designers to explore a far wider range of design options than they could alone.

> ### *Business Insight: Collaborative AI Increases Creativity and Boosts Productivity*
>
> Collaborative AI, in the form of generative architecture design, has proven a powerful tool. It enables architects to achieve more, and to produce more thoughtful, bold, and creative designs. The result is more beautiful architecture, more efficient buildings, better sustainability, lower cost, less waste, and reduced project times. Collaborative AI will show up in every industry. It has the potential to boost the creativity, impact, and productivity of most knowledge workers. Watch carefully for developments in your industry and get ready to embrace collaborative AI as a way to turbocharge your workforce.

From 2-D Plans to 3-D Augmented Reality Models

Most architecture is designed with 3-D software, yet buildings designed with a modern Building Information Model (BIM) are still described to construction workers using flat, two-dimensional blueprints. Augmented reality (AR) headsets keep plans in three dimensions and project them onto physical space to show workers where things need to go. This aids comprehension and reduces errors. AR headsets are suited to all phases of construction but are particularly useful for mechanical, electrical, and plumbing (MEP) systems. Seeing exactly where an air duct needs to go is way easier than trying to interpret 2-D paper projections.

Site inspection is a manual task. Building measurements are taken and compared against printed plans. SRI International's AR-based inspection system tracks the location of an inspector as they move through a site. The inspector visually compares what is being built against plans from the BIM, which are overlaid in her field of view. The solution speeds measurement, using sensors on the headset to measure distances and automatically highlight disparities with the BIM. Blue tape traditionally used to mark the punch list is replaced by holographic markers. The inspector attaches digital photos and notes to guide rework and create a detailed record of the issue so it can be tracked to closure. As AR capabilities improve, AR headsets will become a common sight on most construction projects.

Business Insight: Augmented Reality Limits Mistakes and Helps Hands-Free Workers

The use of augmented reality, particularly to translate 3-D plans onto physical spaces, aids comprehension and makes construction workers more efficient. As the capabilities of AR headsets improve, they will provide valuable support to a wide range of hands-free workers, guiding them to perform tasks and auditing their work. Plans, visualizations, and 3-D work instructions inhabit a worker's visual perception and align directly with the work in front of them. Relevant contextual working data is presented as a heads-up display. The result: increased productivity, quicker decisions, and fewer errors.

Robot Construction Workers, Drones, and 3-D-Printed Structures

Construction is labor-intensive, from architectural design, to building and final inspection. The industry employs many skilled workers—carpenters, electricians, plumbers, ironworkers, roofers, and joiners—and very little work is performed autonomously. In a 2019 survey, 63% of construction companies report using drones in their operations, while only 14% use on-site robotics (Source: AGC/FMI risk management survey).

Robots are starting to enter the construction workforce. A good human bricklayer can lay about 500 bricks each day. SAM-100, a robot made by Construction Robotics, lays up to 3,000 bricks in a single day. SAM-100 is a cobot designed to work in partnership with construction workers. A worker loads bricks onto the conveyor belt that feeds SAM-100's bricklaying arm, while another worker strikes the wall to remove excess mortar. SAM-100 is fast, but messy.

Hadrian X, a robot made by Australian innovator Fastbrick Robotics, lays bricks like a giant 3-D printer, using a 30 m (90 ft) boom. Hadrian X self-stabilizes and lays bricks with precision, even in windy conditions. It lays a combination of standard and large bricks, 12 times larger than standard house bricks, and fuses them together with adhesive that dries in just 45 minutes. The result is a home with improved thermal and acoustic properties over traditional mortar. Walls for an entire house can be built in one to two days. The process is cheap, creates no on-site construction waste, and is much safer for workers.

The Advanced Industrial Science and Technology (AIST) institute of Japan is developing a robot to hang drywall. The catchily named HRP-5P robot is not as fast as humans but is effective and methodical. Designers gave the humanoid robot additional limb joints to aid it in its work.

Construction drones conduct site surveys, oversee work, track worker productivity, assess progress to goals, document project milestones, perform safety audits, and ensure compliance against plans. These human-piloted drones will soon become autonomous, roaming sites and gathering data with a range of sensors. Machine vision technology will watch for safety violations—improperly secured ladders, trip hazards, and failure to wear personal protective gear. Laser scanners and other sensors will compare the built environment against plans and schedules, highlighting anomalies and project slips. Some construction companies use drones fitted with FARO laser scanners to compare construction progress with the building information model (BIM). Regular inspections matter. The sooner issues are discovered and addressed, the more money can be saved. Better to find a wall is misaligned before you install ducting, plumbing, electric, drywall, and paint on it.

Early detection and resolution of safety issues will save lives. Boston-based construction firm Suffolk is testing technology to predict where accidents will happen. The predictive AI, named Vinnie, was trained with 10 years of accident data and images of site safety hazards donated by a group of competing construction firms. Early results are promising. Vinnie predicted one in five safety incidents, a week ahead of time, with 81% accuracy. Technology partner SmartVid claims the system reduces incident rates by 30%. The drone also performs inspections, cutting 60% off the time Suffolk spends tracking progress and documenting milestones.

Additive manufacturing, better known as 3-D-printing, is coming to construction. Giant machines "print" with cement instead of ink. Icon's latest Vulcan II cement printer can build a 650 sq ft (60 m²) home in less than a day for just $10,000, with prices predicted to drop to $4,000 in the future. It has a build capacity 8.5 feet high by 28 feet wide (2.5 m × 8.5 m), enabling it to print homes of up to 2,000 sq ft (190 m²). Vulcan II builds resilient structures using a proprietary material named Lavacrete and lays 7 inches (17 cm) of material every second. The printer is delivered on a trailer, requires no on-site assembly, and can be operated by as few as four people. Icon claims their printer cuts construction costs in half. Their first commercial project is a 3-D-printed community, built to house more than 400 people and serve low-income families. 3-D-printed buildings increase design freedom, reduce build errors, and use less concrete than traditional construction. Dutch researchers are experimenting with 3-D-printed structures made from biobased plastics. These biomaterials can be either nonbiodegradable or biodegradable, enabling the sustainable construction of either permanent or fully recyclable, temporary structures suitable for disaster relief.

AI Aids Real Estate

Mortgage brokers and real estate agents always need to hustle for business, especially when the market is slow. AI embedded inside customer relationship management (CRM) tools guides brokers on their outreach strategy, prioritizing leads, and even forecasting the likelihood a deal will close. Many agents rely on their networks for leads. North Carolina–based real estate AI company First sifts through a real estate agent's personal network and predicts when people will be ready to sell, sometimes months in advance. First analyzes more than 700 insights sourced from data brokers—spending patterns, employment status, income history, credit status—to spot changes that signal a potential home sale. This allows agents to prioritize outreach and beat competitors to listings.

The natural language capabilities of AI speed data entry, automatically extracting customer data from documents, even if those documents aren't arranged in a standard format. AI ingests a document and identifies names, addresses, social security numbers, income, investment details, and more. Natural language processing analyzes the sentiment of incoming emails to highlight urgent issues or an unhappy client. Chatbots, like OJO and Roof.ai, answer real estate questions and help with home searches. For outbound marketing, AI recommends marketing mixes and outreach strategies. It ingests social media feeds to read thousands of online reviews and summarize them in natural language. AI even ingests the social media of competitors to make recommendations on changes to marketing strategies.

UK-based Proportunity uses AI to accurately predict the future value of London homes. They partner with first-time buyers of homes that their AI gives high future valuations. Proportunity supports buyers by taking an equity stake of up to 15%. This allows the buyer to afford a more expensive property than they could on their own. It also reduces the loan-to-value ratio for a mortgage, which allows buyers to secure a lower interest rate from lenders. When the buyer sells or refinances their home, they repay the equity to Proportunity, who make a profit based on the increased value of the home.

Skyline is an AI investment manager that analyzes 50 years of commercial real estate data to identify emerging trends and pinpoint locations that are about to see market gains. They analyze owner and asset behavior to identify investment opportunities, including arbitrage deals, off-market deals, predicted foreclosures, and mismanaged properties that could be performing better.

Disruptors Zest Finance and Underwriting.ai sell AIs that assess the risk of potential borrowers. Analyzing hundreds of data points, instead of the 10 or so that human underwriters consider, these AIs find low-risk borrowers that would not qualify under standard methodology, expanding the marketplace without increasing financial risk.

Fintech innovator REX uses AI to price homes and match sellers with qualified buyers, simplifying the sales process and replacing real estate agents. REX robots show houses and interact with potential buyers to answer questions. REX charges 2% to cover both sides of the real estate transaction versus the 6% fee common to most U.S. residential real estate sales. Not everyone will want to buy a home from a robot, but the economics provide a compelling alternative.

Blockchains Speed Transactions, Limit Fraud, and Create New Funding Models

Real estate transactions in the United States are notoriously overcomplicated and painful. Home buying is a stressful exercise that involves obscene amounts of paperwork, much of which you will never read, and payments to intermediaries that help broker a deal with a seller you will never meet. You work with a real estate agent, mortgage broker, escrow company, credit-scoring agency, property appraiser, home inspector, notary, title company, and maybe a lawyer. No wonder people hate this process. The escrow company holds money in good faith as a down payment on the deal. The credit-scoring agency checks that the buyer is likely to make their mortgage payments. The home inspector checks that the home has no significant, undeclared issues. The appraiser ensures that the home is worth the price being asked. The whole, painful process is designed to reduce risk and establish trust.

There is good news. Technology will bring the day when we are approved for a mortgage and buy a home with the single click of button. Innovators will use Blockchain and AI to cut out intermediaries and automate, or semi-automate, every step in the buying process. Mortgage applications will be streamlined and automated as buyers grant one-time access to relevant financial information stored on a Blockchain. Data accuracy is ensured, and sensitive financial data is shared easily between entities, speeding approvals. Blockchains will verify ownership and transfer titles, all while maintaining transparency and limiting fraud. Escrow and title exchange will be handled via smart contracts. Documents will be certified electronically without need of a notary.

Blend uses Blockchains for secure document transfer during the loan origination process. They claim their platform shaves 7–10 days off the average loan closing. Ubitquity, a Blockchain-based platform for real estate record keeping, is used by title companies, municipalities, and others to establish clean records of ownership. Imbrex is a Blockchain-based, community-owned real estate listing portal. Users maintain control over their data and earn rewards for contributing information to the platform.

Business Insight: Blockchain Limits Fraud, Speeds Collaboration, and Removes Intermediaries

Industries that involve contracts, suffer layers of intermediaries, or have complex process flows between multiple entities will benefit from the use of Blockchains. Smart contracts enable agreements to be captured in code and executed automatically when conditions are met. Blockchain creates trusted data sources, aids secure and speedy sharing of data between entities, and enforces rigorous process flows. This limits fraud, automates information flow, and eliminates risk. Intermediaries, which are there to mitigate for a lack of trust, are no longer needed.

Is everybody in the real estate market out of business? Absolutely not. Buying a home is, for most people, the biggest purchase they will make in their lives. Many people will seek a trusted human being to guide them through the stressful process. As Blockchains reduce paperwork and complexity in the house-buying process, the value offered by agents and brokers will naturally evolve. Filling out paperwork and writing up contracts will become a smaller piece of their value-add. Mortgage brokers and real estate agents will pivot to a primary focus on educating buyers and boosting their confidence in the decisions that they make. These are tasks that mortgage brokers and real estate agents already know how to do well.

> *Business Insight: Technology Is No Substitute for Human Connection and Reputational Trust*
>
> As the mechanics of loan origination and home buying are automated, mortgage brokers and realtors will need to focus on service, trust, and building the confidence of clients. Providers that deliver perfunctory service, or act only as gatekeepers to funding, will lose their business to pure-play digital services. Successful agents and brokers will focus on customers who demand the human touch: exquisite customer service, trusted advice, emotional support, and encouragement. Buyers need to feel confident in their choices. Ultimately, that is what brokers and agents are selling. Technology can't automate empathy. In an automated world, human connections and brand trust will matter more than ever, in every industry.

Tokenized Assets Democratize Property Investment

Very few people can afford to invest in commercial real estate. Tokenization, using Blockchains, democratizes access to real estate investment. Atlant, RealCrowd, and CrowdStreet crowdfund commercial real estate projects and make them accessible to individual investors. Atlant converts properties into tokens based on floor space: 1 mm^2 = 1 token. They check that a property's title is clean and create a new holding company designed solely to take ownership of the property. Atlant tokenizes the holding company, dividing the value of the company into tokens, based on the size of property. This forms a direct relationship between the number of tokens and the value of the property. Tokens traded on Atlant's trading platform, via a PTO (Property Token Offering), generate capital. Once all the tokens are sold, money is transferred to the seller. Investors profit from rental income and increases to the property's value, which are reflected in the price of the token. CrowdStreet enables an individual investor to buy a stake in a single property or a blended portfolio of properties, a bit like a mutual fund for commercial real estate. Minimum investments are as low as $25,000. Not for the faint of heart, but still substantially lower than having to stump up millions to buy an entire shopping mall yourself.

Business Insight: Democratize Investments Using Tokenization

By tokenizing assets, start-ups are democratizing the investment world. Inspired by early success in the real estate sector, crowdfunding entrepreneurs are entering new investment categories and creating new financial instruments aimed at individuals as well as institutions. Aurus, Digix, and GoldMint tokenize gold. Natixis and Trafigura tokenize crude oil. Breaker tokenizes entertainment rights. Other companies are working to tokenize stocks, works of art, rental properties, music, and patents so they can be bought and sold on markets just like anything else. Investment is being democratized. How will your company play a role, or take advantage of new investment opportunities?

Crowdfunded Mortgages Compete with Banks

Dharma Labs, ETHLend, and Homelend use Ethereum smart contracts to enable crowds of individuals to make loans and underwrite risk. Homelend's mortgage crowdfunding platform brings people together to collectively lend money to homebuyers. Homelend claims they will cut loan origination times from a typical 40–50 days to just 20 days. These new peer-to-peer lending platforms may someday democratize lending and reduce the need for large lending institutions.

Ultimately, AI and Blockchains will automate and speed every step of the lending and buying process. Empowered consumers will choose between full-service mortgage and real estate services and low-cost, streamlined digital services that lack the human touch. The day of the one-minute, paperless mortgage cannot be too far away.

16 Preparing Our Population for the Post-Automation Economy

Lessons for the Future of Education

The Challenge: A System Designed for a Bygone Era

Automation will profoundly impact the future of work, and to remain relevant in the post-automation economy, millions of people will need to reskill and upskill. A vibrant education sector will be vital to a functioning society and economy. To meet the challenges of the twenty-first century, we will need to reimagine education.

A Stagnant, Fragmented System Designed for a Bygone Era

Classrooms today look much as they did in the nineteenth century: students sitting at desks, facing the teacher and a blackboard. This model—which includes the notions of knowledge compartmentalization, recommended courses, standardized testing, multiple choice, and degree certification—was designed in the 1850s to prepare agricultural workers to transition into factory and office work. The same system persists to this day.

Educational institutions celebrate tradition and are designed to resist change. As former chief-of-staff to the U.S. Department of Education Joanne Weiss observed, "Education has been a place that is wildly resistant to innovation. It was designed [that way] so that crazy fads wouldn't use kids as guinea pigs. Now, when we are desperately in need of innovation, we have built a system that is really, really good at repelling it."

Some quirks of the current system:

- Teaching talent is trapped inside the walls of institutions. To access the best teacher in a particular subject, you must enroll at the school where they are tenured to teach, and once you enroll, you only have access to the teaching talent that works there.

- The current system doesn't scale well. To teach more people requires more physical spaces—schools, colleges, and universities.

- Students are sometimes treated more like products on a manufacturing line than as unique individuals. Students who learn quickly are left bored, and students who need more time and coaching to grasp key concepts are left bewildered.

- Students emerge from academia schooled in a discipline but with few of the skills needed to navigate the world of work.

The current school curriculum bores the pants off some kids and leads many to believe that education is not for them. In extreme cases, we may extinguish a child's curiosity for life. In the United States, 7,200 students drop out of high school *every day*. More than half say they drop out because they are bored. That's 1.3 million kids per year that are failed by today's system, just in the United States. Part of the problem is the curriculum, which feels irrelevant to some students, part of it is the pedagogy. Kids aren't engaged by today's teaching methods. We must use twenty-first-century technology to make learning significantly more engaging and tailored to the needs of the individual.

Half of the Workforce Is Not Prepared for the Post-Automation Economy

As they shift into new work in the 2020s and '30s, up to half of the workforce will need support to build the skills needed to thrive in the post-automation economy. Educators must prepare students for the world that will be, rather than the world that was. Spreadsheets revolutionized the skills needed to work in the accounting department. Word processors and laser printers made typing pools obsolete. Engineers had to embrace computer-aided design tools. In the era of robots and artificial intelligence, workers must develop the uniquely human skills needed to remain relevant in a heavily automated world.

Curricula don't fully serve the needs of students. More time is needed to develop skills people will need to thrive in the post-automation economy—workplace skills, communication skills, financial literacy, information research skills, entrepreneurial skills, grit, planning skills, critical thinking skills, self-awareness, ethics, optimism, creative skills, maker skills, technology skills, social skills, empathy, emotional intelligence, improvisation, home maintenance skills, additional language skills, the ability to judge information on its merits, and so on.

Competing with machines is folly. We must focus our time and passion on tasks that are beyond the reach of robots and AI. In the next decades, businesses will seek employees with the ability to generate new ideas, think critically about those ideas, understand and judge ideas in a social context, persuasively communicate ideas to others, inspire people to action, and develop the complex plans needed to execute on those ideas. These are not new skills. But they become the *primary* skills required in the 2030s and beyond. The humanities and the liberal arts will be as relevant as engineering and design skills.

Scale and Cost: Education Is Too Expensive and Is Inaccessible to Many

To keep people employed, we must boost the average educational level of the population. Dropping out of school at 16 will become a less viable option. More people will need to spend more time in school. Affordability is a major barrier to that happening.

Increased demand for education will come from two sources: (1) kids and young adults coming up through the education system for the first time will need to stay longer, and (2) millions of displaced workers will need to go back to school and develop new skills. In its current form, the global education system cannot deliver education at the scale and price point the market will need.

The cost of a quality higher education in the United States continues to skyrocket. The average four-year college degree now costs in excess of $100,000. More prestigious schools, like Harvard, cost three times that. Student loans are now the largest source of non-mortgage debt in the United States, where people incur crushing debt to get an education. Smaller colleges are being driven out of business as people either skip college (and the debt that comes with it) or move to online suppliers like Coursera, Knewton, Udacity, and Capella University, or the online programs of universities such as Purdue University Global and Southern New Hampshire University.

Harvard Business School professor and author of *The Innovator's Dilemma* Clayton Christensen commented in 2018 that he expects half of the 4,000 universities and colleges in the United States to go bankrupt in the next 10–15 years as a result.

Pedagogy must evolve and embrace technology to deliver a high-quality education to more people, at significantly lower cost.

How Technology Is Transforming the Sector

Our current educational model was developed more than a century before the invention of the internet. Anyone designing an education system from scratch today would build it very differently than the way it is.

Flip the Model and Free Teaching Talent from Geographic Limitations

Most students learn in the classroom and then do project work and exercises at home. Organizations like the Khan Academy promote a new model that turns the old one upside down. For many students, it makes more sense to learn at home using a range of media—from books, to video, to virtual reality—and do project work (formerly "homework") in the classroom where a teacher and fellow students can provide help when difficulties are encountered. Flipping the model allows students to learn at their own pace and on their schedule, rewinding video when they miss an important concept, taking breaks when needed, and accessing additional online resources when they need extra help.

In a flipped teaching model, a dashboard shows teachers the progress of each student. The dashboard highlights students having difficulty with certain topics so the teacher can plan individual interventions in the classroom and help students stay on track. Content that many students find difficult is flagged so teaching materials can be updated and clarified accordingly.

Internet video, VR, AR, and other modern media enable teachers to reach a broader audience, beyond their chosen institution. The internet makes the best teachers in the world accessible to everyone, wherever they are.

Some students do not have a home environment that's conducive to study. For them, a system built around technology-delivered study at home doesn't work. Some students may need access to learning technology in purpose-built connected study facilities that provide a safe, quiet space to access online learning.

Some subjects require a more interactive teaching style, but many lend themselves to the flipped approach. Teachers may not relish the idea of having their classes captured on video or other media, fearing it diminishes their value. A couple of thoughts here. First, this approach frees teachers to have more meaningful interactions with students, speeds the pace and quality of education, and allows them to reach more students in a given time frame. Second, as the internet pushes the cost of information down to zero (witness all the amazing information available with a simple Google search), this is a case of "get with the program or get out of the way." I hate to be so stark about this, but this is the harsh reality. If teachers act as gatekeepers to learning, they will fail. Good teachers have always fulfilled dual roles as instructor and coach. The instructor conveys information, explains key concepts, and enlightens while the coach provides guidance, encouragement, and inspiration. As learning systems evolve to capture more of the instructor side of teaching, teachers are freed up to spend more time as coaches, an empathetic and deeply human role that cannot be automated, and that has the most profound impact on students. Think of your favorite teacher in school and you'll know exactly what I mean.

The flipped model isn't a panacea, but it can be a valuable tool to increase access to learning and provide additional scale.

Building a Low-Cost, Scalable Education System

We must design an education system that is scalable enough to meet everyone's needs. Building new classrooms is not the answer. We must use technology to build virtual classrooms and high-quality educational experiences that connect teaching talent with students in new ways. We learn far more at school than just skills and facts. We gain social skills, teaming skills, communication skills, and more. Technology must connect remote students together in meaningful ways. Video conferencing and virtual and augmented reality can play significant roles, bringing people together in shared virtual spaces. Students don't only learn from their teachers; they also learn from each other. New technology must support student-to-student learning as much as it connects students to teachers.

From Flat Textbooks to 3-D Experiential Education

For some people, there is nothing like getting lost inside a good book. For others, books are neither an enjoyable or efficient way to learn. New media offers new ways to learn new things. Podcasts let us learn on our commute. YouTube videos explain assembly instructions and maintenance procedures better than words and static pictures ever can. Virtual and augmented reality take learning to a whole new level. Immersive VR transports us to new places and even takes us back in time. With VR, students can visit the Coliseum in ancient Rome, take in the view from the top of Everest, and explore the surface of Mars. Augmented reality keeps students anchored in their physical environment and introduces virtual objects and scenes for them to interact with. This enables more collaborative learning experiences. Medical students gather around a life-size hologram of the human body as their teacher uses gesture control to reveal the circulatory, lymphatic, and nervous systems. Engineering students interact with cut-away 3-D models of a wind turbine, an architectural design, or a representation of a complex molecule. Often, it's easier to understand the operation of a machine, a human organ, or a complex business process when it's presented in the primary format our brains evolved to process: three-dimensional images we can interact with and explore.

Virtual and augmented reality naturally lend themselves to experiential learning, which allows students to learn through doing rather than through instruction. Realistic simulations allow students to practice skills in a safe environment and guide them as they learn. With fine-grain controllers, haptic feedback, and high-definition displays, future VR and AR platforms will provide the perfect training ground for surgeons, mechanics, retail workers, engineers, construction workers, architects, scientists, and many other roles. AI-powered avatars within sophisticated VR and AR simulations will help people to develop and practice soft skills including conversational skills, language skills, negotiation skills, and more.

By working together to solve problems, students develop their ability to improvise, plan, create, and collaborate. Maker labs can familiarize students with the technologies that many of them will encounter in the workplace: AI, sensors, and 3-D printers. Whether they become engineers or not, this process teaches kids invaluable skills, builds their confidence, and prepares them to function in a highly automated world.

Sensors, Data, and AI for Personalized Education

A one-size-fits-all education system often progresses at the pace of the slowest student or leaves students behind to keep the majority moving forward. Consumers expect customized products and personalized experiences; expectations for education will be no different. Every student benefits when education is personalized. Sensors will gather data in the classroom and during personal learning sessions to analyze each student's level of attention and comprehension. Desk-mounted sensors, whether pressure sensors or more sophisticated sensors like Google's Project Soli sensor, sense note taking. Machine vision senses when students are paying attention, looking confused, or messing around. Learning tools can then adapt to an individual student's needs, pace, and interests.

Interactive training (multimedia, VR, and AR) will allow students to learn at their own pace, or to explore beyond the main curriculum and follow their unique interests. Adaptive learning platforms track how students learn and adjust their pace and approach based on what works best for each individual. Dreambox, an adaptive learning platform teaches mathematics to kids aged 5 to 14. It automatically personalizes learning plans based on each student's ability. Dreambox chooses the right lesson at the right time and uses the teaching approach that works best for each student.

AI-based voice agents will participate in team projects and assess each student's participation and capabilities as they go. Data analytics will provide the teacher with a dashboard that highlights the students who need additional attention. Real-time translation will allow all students to learn in their native tongue.

There is no reason why any student should receive a cookie-cutter education. Technology will assist educators to deliver a personalized learning experience even in large or virtual classes where personal attention from the teacher is more challenging.

Stagnant Sectors Will Experience the Same Pressures as Education

The academic world has been largely impervious to change for more than 150 years. Yet everyone I speak to who works in education recognizes the urgent need to drag the system into the twenty-first century. Retail, largely unchanged for 100 years before the e-commerce revolution turned it upside down, has been forced into a period of painful, grudging innovation that may prove to be too little, too late. Other stagnant industries—including healthcare, construction, transportation, financial services, and agriculture—will soon experience a period of rapid, long-overdue change.

New technology will burst through the institutional dams that have held back innovation for so many years. Bold innovators will break away, leaving the rest in the dust. The difference in capability between companies that fully embrace technology and companies that do not will become so profound that laggards will quickly become uncompetitive and irrelevant. Constant innovation is key to future survival. This is the harsh reality of *The Innovation Ultimatum.*

17 Embracing Technology in the Service of People

Strategies Lie at the Intersection of Possibility and Purpose

We live in an era of incredible possibility. Technology is improving exponentially and things that seemed impossible just a decade ago are now within our grasp.

Six powerful and complementary technologies—AI, IoT, 5G, AR, Blockchain, and autonomous machines—are ramping into the marketplace simultaneously. Individually, each technology would be a significant disruptor. Combined, they represent an unprecedented leap forward in technological capability and present extraordinary opportunity for every business. Organizations will combine these technologies to create new products and services, build new channels, automate operations, make higher-quality decisions, improve customer service, improve working conditions, cut costs, and solve major human challenges.

In a world of possibility, options are plentiful, and choices can be overwhelming. Strategic clarity is necessary to keep organizations focused and avoid distraction. When technology enables organizations to do so much, choosing what not to do becomes the overriding challenge.

Powerful new technologies bring rapid change to markets, industries, companies, and people. Change is disorienting and exhausting. To stand with you through inevitable tumult, employees need a north star to guide them, clear marching orders to align them, and an inspiring purpose that gives them the strength to endure. Strategic clarity and organizational alignment are vital if you are to navigate rapid change.

Clarity comes from an organization's well-articulated, inspiring human purpose. To successfully navigate the next decade, businesses must map the landscape of possibility and then use the lens of purpose to plot their course. With a clearly stated purpose, it's easier to focus efforts and avoid projects that detract from the core mission of the company. Employees will embrace change if you motivate them with a compelling vision for the future that gives them a reason to contribute discretionary effort. The late nights and weekends, the extra attention to detail, the extra push for results—these are all a function of discretionary effort, which is unlocked by giving people a reason to come to work that goes beyond a paycheck. Unless their compensation is directly and meaningfully linked to corporate profits, employees don't really care about quarterly results and delighting shareholders. They want to enjoy challenging work in a respectful workplace and successfully execute against a mission they consider worthwhile. Never underestimate the power of a corporate purpose that resonates strongly with employees.

As my friend Brian David Johnson taught me many years ago, when it comes to thinking about the future, there are two important questions that we need to ask and answer:

1. What is the future we want to build?
2. What is the future that we want to avoid?

To answer these two questions, organizations need to be crystal clear on their purpose, have a bold vision for the future, and have a mission that people believe in. Strategies will be found at the intersection of possibility and purpose.

It is leadership's job to ensure that everyone in the organization is crystal clear on the purpose, vision, mission, values, and strategies of the company. Invest more time in this than you think is warranted and you'll probably still not communicate these enough. Wordy, uninspiring vision and mission statements that are written by committee are worthless. Short, memorable statements, consistently and regularly shared with employees, make all the difference.

Be bold, be clear, and stay focused. Align, inspire, and motivate your teams to use these six technologies to change the world, in ways big and small.

Honor Individuality, Elevate Human Work, and Create Frictionless Experiences

Strong innovation plans focus on improving people's lives, specifically the lives of customers and employees. Evidence clearly shows that when their lives are improved, so are corporate results. Companies that focus on customers and employees automatically serve the interests of shareholders.

Here are six ways that the technologies described in this book can be used to improve people's lives.

1. Honor Every Customer as a Unique Individual

Every person on earth has a unique story, a unique life experience, and a unique way of looking at the world. On a crowded planet, where people can feel like a tiny cog in a giant machine, people cling to that sense of individual identity more than ever. They want brands to honor and celebrate their uniqueness, and treat them as valued individuals. Use technology to learn about customers, to let customers express themselves, to build customized products and services, to deliver personalized experiences, to communicate with customers in the way they wish to be communicated with, and to reward customer loyalty in the way they want it rewarded.

2. Value Everybody's Time by Creating Frictionless Experiences

Life is a blur. People are busy. Getting through the day feels like survival. Brands that respect how precious a customer's time has become will be rewarded. Strive to remove friction from every interaction. Shorten communications by personalizing them—no need to tell everyone everything, just what each person needs to know right now. Pursue frictionless experiences, knowing this job may never be done. Shave seconds off transaction times. Find ways to save people both time and cognitive effort, because extra thoughts take extra time. Caveat: Save people from meaningless friction, but don't be afraid to add in meaningful friction. Sometimes we need to stop and appreciate the moment, understand the significance and consequence of an action, or just step away for a minute of reflection. As the great Ferris Bueller once said, "Life moves pretty fast. If you don't stop and look around once in a while, you could miss it."

3. Understand Ultimate Intent and Create Memorable Moments

Humans have a set of shared aspirations that cross cultures and generations. We want to feel connected to each other (to family, friends, and colleagues). We want to learn and grow throughout our lives. We want to get things done and feel a sense of accomplishment. We want to be entertained (at appropriate times). We want to express ourselves creatively. We want to stay well, and we want the people we care about to stay well. These six aspirations—connection, learning, accomplishment, entertainment, creative expression, and wellness—are consistent human needs. These are the ways that people create meaning in their lives. They are also how people create a sense of identity. It's how we establish our place in the world. Ultimately, people buy products and services to create meaning in their lives and to reinforce identity. When a teenager buys a new smartphone, the brand and color reflect their identity. The product is a gateway to creativity, self-expression, connection, entertainment, learning, accomplishment, and personal wellness.

Use technology to aim higher. Help people to build a stronger sense of self by offering customized offerings and personalized experiences. Help people to create more meaning in their lives. For example, a cloud-connected photo frame connects grandparents to grandchildren halfway around the world, a provenance chain connects an environmentally concerned buyer to the fair-trade, sustainable origin stories of their purchases, and an AI diet coach helps people feel the accomplishment of hitting their weight-loss goals.

4. Design Highly Responsive Business Operations That Coordinate Human and Machine Intelligence

Automate and semi-automate business processes and implement data-driven decision-making to boost operational efficiency, speed service, reduce operational costs, and make your business more responsive to customer needs. Invest cost savings in future innovation, give some back to shareholders, and pass some on to customers as price reductions to stoke delight and fuel future growth.

5. Create Innovative Products, Services, Experiences, and Transformations That Solve Problems for People

Use technology to elevate your product offerings. Create more impact in people's lives by turning products and services into experiences and transformations. Create memorable moments throughout the customer experience. Research shows that if businesses deliver above-average service—memorable moments—just once somewhere along the way, and again at the very end of an experience, customer perception of that brand soars.

6. Elevate Human Work

Use automation technologies—AI, robotics, Blockchains, and sensors—to free your workers from low-value, repetitive, and dangerous work. Provide them with the training they need to contribute to your organization at a higher level. Elevate their roles so they can perform more meaningful and rewarding work.

Key Strategic Discussions You Must Drive to Determine Next Steps

Now that you have a bold vision for the future and are excited about the possibilities that the six technologies in this book present, it's time to take action and lead your teams to discuss, formulate, and execute a fresh set of strategies. Here are some of the main strategic discussions you'll need to drive to determine next steps.

Automation Strategy

Automation will reshape every business in the 2020s. Artificial intelligence will automate tasks that involve prediction, optimization, vision, and diagnosis. Robots will automate routine physical tasks. Blockchain will automate transactions, contracts, and other exchanges of value, streamline collaboration, and automate away intermediaries.

Automation strategies should start with an automation philosophy. Decide which business goals you're optimizing for, and using the automation goal hierarchy, aim as high as you can.

Build your human-machine partnership strategy, a strategy to build high-functioning teams of people, AI, and robots working together. For every business process, determine which tasks are best done by AI, which are best done by robots, and which are best done by humans.

Sensor Strategy

Develop a sensor strategy to get eyes on your business and build a digital model that exactly mirrors physical operations. Use sensors to detect key "business events" and manage the hand-off of tasks between AIs, robots, and humans. For example, a robot uses sensors to spot a spill on the factory floor and alerts a janitor, or an airport sensor detects a plane arriving at a gate, updates flight tracking systems, and alerts the gate staff to prepare for the arrival of passengers. Plot out all these business events and build a strategy to detect each one using sensors and AI. A sensor strategy is a key component of every automation strategy.

Augmentation Strategy

Use technology to augment your employees' capabilities and elevate their work. Determine how collaborative AI, voice agents, cobots, and augmented reality platforms can provide assistance to different types of worker.

Build a collaborative AI strategy. Inspired by the way generative AI boosts the creativity and productivity of designers, find ways to use AI to augment and support the capabilities of every employee. Use AI to generate thousands of potential options and then narrow them down and present the best options to employees. AI augments the judgment and intuition of employees and helps them make better decisions, faster. Consider the role of natural language processing to support knowledge workers, summarizing, translating, or analyzing the sentiment of text.

Build a digital voice strategy. Decide where chatbots and personal assistants make sense in your organization. Consider chatbots for first-line customer support but also for employees. For example, voice assistants might make employee travel arrangements and schedule meetings. Plan with the expectation that voice platforms will evolve rapidly in the next several years, meaning their utility and relevance will only increase over time.

Consider ways to create hybrid workers that operate as a combination of digital intelligence, human experience, and human physicality. Pilot trials of AR workers, learn from their experiences, and be ready to embrace the technology the moment it matures.

Employee Engagement Strategy

Communication is a vital part of automation. Build a comprehensive employee communications strategy to support your automation projects and build an AI-oriented culture. Link automation to the mission and explain how machines will help everyone at the company to fulfill your corporate purpose. Involve employees in the development of AI that they will be working with. When they have a hand in its creation and understand its operation and limitations, they will more readily accept it as a co-worker. Be honest about the expected extent of automation or employees will be suspicious that they're next. Explain your philosophy on automation. Link the need for automation to the threat posed by competition and *The Innovation Ultimatum*. Position AI and robots as competitive allies and assistants that free workers from routine work so they can aim higher and achieve more. Be clear on the unique value that humans provide to the organization and explain what skills workers possess that make them "robot-proof." Workers need to understand the limits of automation and to feel valued for the unique values they bring. History shows that looms get smashed when people feel their livelihoods are threatened. Communicate, communicate, communicate.

Build a modern culture of innovation. Educate employees on the exciting possibilities presented by technology. Buy them a copy of this book. Boost technology literacy at all levels of the company, from CEO on down. Familiarize employees with the exciting new possibilities presented by these six technologies Share success stories from early deployments to get employees excited about the future and to inspire ideation on new ways technology can automate processes and augment employee performance. Help employees to understand the *Innovation Ultimatum*, the imperative to innovate or fade away. Encourage them to imagine new products, new channels, new customer experiences, new employee experiences, and new ways to do business. Empower them to make plans that drive the business forward. Fund innovation. Allow employees to share in the financial results of automation adoption. Reward role models that take informed risks. Celebrate successful business transformation. Take time to honor the past but keep employees' eyes firmly on the future.

Retraining Strategy

Retrain all displaced employees, either to take on higher value roles within your organization or so they can thrive elsewhere. Upskilling may be cheaper than rehiring and onboarding. More importantly, remember that every one of your employees is watching how you treat workers displaced by automation. Invest heavily in those that are affected, even if you know that ultimately they will be leaving the organization. If you don't, you risk stoking a culture of fear in employees that remain. They will sabotage further change, become disengaged, and retard innovation efforts. Also, it's just the right thing to do.

Blockchain Strategy

Beyond the automation of value exchange, Blockchains have value to create digital provenance and to shape behaviors by aligning incentives. Be ready to add transparency to your supply chain. Origin stories will be demanded in many product categories, either by wary brands you supply, or by concerned consumers. Push your platform suppliers for supply chain management systems that use distributed ledger technology to ensure the provenance of your supplies. Set expectations with your suppliers that transparency and traceability demands are coming. Decide how you might use token economics to align incentives with business partners and other entities.

Consider opportunities to decentralize work where it makes sense. Use Blockchains to distribute value creation in an open source project that uses tokens to incentivize contributions. By distributing risk and reward, you may be able to get projects off the ground that would not otherwise find the funding and support they need for success.

Product and Service Innovation Strategy

PricewaterhouseCoopers predicts AI will create more jobs than it destroys. Most of these new jobs arise from the creation of new AI-based products and services and the increased demand they will create. Smart, connected products will deliver significantly more value than their dumb predecessors. Drive strategic discussions with your teams to discuss how each of the technologies listed in this book (not just AI) could take your product line to the next level. Specifically, determine how you will embrace personalization and customization throughout your product line. Determine how you will not just make your products frictionless to buy, but also frictionless to use. Hold strategic discussions on how to innovate and elevate your business model: use products to deliver services, services to create experiences, and experiences to create transformations. If necessary, create subdivisions chartered with building innovative services, experiences and transformations that are delivered around your core products. Discuss the strategic impact of one-hour, one-dollar local delivery and how that might signal the end of ownership for some products and shift customers toward a rental model.

Data Strategy

Whoever has the best data wins. Leaders should drive specific strategic discussions around the data ultimatum: What data is needed to drive future innovation, and how do you get it? What sensors do you need to gather data? What data is needed to train artificial intelligence, now and in the future? What is your data-driven decision-making strategy? What data is needed to inform automated decision-making? How can you present data visually to support human-made decisions? What data already exists in company silos? How do you unify that data and make it available to those who need it? What data do you need to buy, and what partnerships are needed to get it? What data is needed to support product innovation efforts and to elevate your business model? What data do you need to support your personalization and customization efforts? What data can be monetized, and with whom? Do you need to evolve your data privacy policy? What's your data spiral strategy? How do you ensure the quality of data, and ensure it's available to those that need it? Crawford del Prete, president of global market intelligence company IDC, allowed me to include this great quote from him: "By 2021, data will no longer be viewed as "oil", but as water. It is essential to life, but needs to be accessible and clean."

Security Strategy

This book focuses primarily on the positive potential of technology to do good in the world. But like any other tool, technology can be used both for good and bad. Most sci-fi literature is dystopian and entire shelves of bookstores are devoted to cyber-security. With this book, I wanted to offer a counterbalance to these negative narratives and paint a picture of the good that technology can do. That does not imply we should not be thoughtful and vigilant when deploying new technology. Security and safety are vital considerations for any innovation strategy. When defining the future that we want to build, we must also define the future we wish to avoid. To this end, every leader should ensure the creation of a robust security strategy.

As every company becomes a data company, all data becomes mission critical and needs to be treated as such. The six technologies in this book build bridges between the digital and physical worlds. When objects, people, and infrastructure become connected, they become an attack surface to a hacker. Smart objects connected infrastructure, sensors, robots, drones, and other autonomous machines turn digital threats into physical threats. Push vendors for end-to-end security solutions, even for low-cost devices that integrate cheap computing and sensors. Cyber-criminals find and exploit the weakest link. Don't open your business to hackers to save a few cents per unit. Even sensors must be properly secured. Don't let hackers spy on your business or spoof your sensors with false data that causes your business systems to behave incorrectly. Hybrid workers, who rely on digital intelligence and work instructions delivered through augmented reality, must be secured to stop criminals hacking their perception and guiding them to perform tasks they shouldn't. Build a security strategy that comprehends all of these factors.

Final Thoughts and Encouragement for Tomorrow's Leaders

As you lead business transformation, automate with intention, augment talent to elevate work, and deploy technology in service of improving the human condition, strive to create more meaning in people's lives and boost human-to-human connection. If you do, customers and the market will reward you, no matter what line of business you are in.

A sweeping panorama of possibility lies in front of every business. In the 2020s, new technology will transform entire industries and solve previously impossible problems. Don't be limited by the past. Nintendo evolved from a playing card company to become the video-game powerhouse it is today. They embraced technology to fulfill their core purpose (enabling play) in new ways. You can too.

You are limited only by your creativity and your ability to inspire others to drive change. The same is true of all your competitors. In a time of great possibility, those with the strongest sense of purpose and the greatest will to drive change will prevail. To sit at the nexus of extreme competitive pressure and powerful positive purpose is to be at the heart of *The Innovation Ultimatum*.

ACKNOWLEDGMENTS

Thanks to my wonderful parents, Mike and Andrea Brown, for teaching me the importance of a quality education and for making many sacrifices to ensure that I got one. Their love, steadfast support, and encouragement makes a difference to me every day.

This book would not have been possible without those who shaped my career, opened doors for me, and encouraged me to stride through them. Thanks to Rob Sheppard for hiring me into my first proper job. A special thanks to Stuart Robinson who pushed me to explore a career beyond engineering, despite my instincts at the time. Without his insistence that I expand my own views on what was possible for me, my life would not have turned out the way it has. If only everyone could have a Stuart Robinson to help them challenge self-imposed limits and redefine their identities. Thank you to all those people who saw a glimmer of potential in me, took a chance, and placed me in challenging roles that took me to new places: Matt Haller, Dan Russell, Jim Pappas, Pat Gelsinger, Larry Shoop, Mike Green, and Dr. Genevieve Bell. Larry taught me how to take my communication and emcee skills to the next level. Mike taught me the importance of humility and grace. Genevieve taught me to always look at the world through the lens of people first. Thanks to all those who helped to shape my career and encourage me to be more.

Special thanks to Terry Scalzo, who put me on the path to become a keynote speaker. While I was emceeing an event for Terry, he pointed to a speaker on stage and asked me a life-changing question: "Why don't *you* do this, Steve? You'd be great at it." Sometimes we can change some-one's life with a single sentence. At the time, Terry could have had no idea that he was shifting my own sense of self and putting me on an exciting new path. Thanks, Terry. Thanks also to Shannon Smith. Shannon also had a powerful effect on me with a single sentence, helping me to let go of my self-imposed identity as a Spock-like logical engineering type, and instead to see myself as a creative force. Our words have impact on those around us.

Extra special thanks to the author of this book's Foreword, Brian David Johnson. As Intel's first futurist, Brian took a chance on me to provide sabbatical coverage for him. His belief in me, his friendship, his support, and his infectious good spirit have had a major impact on my life. I would not have a successful career as a futurist had it not been for his generosity. Thank you, Brian.

Writing a book is a serious undertaking. I couldn't have written *The Innovation Ultimatum* without the constant encouragement and support of friends and family. In particular, I'd like to thank a few key people who had a powerful impact on me. This book would have stayed a work-in-progress forever without them. Thank you to Jeff Gaus and Ken Thrasher for constantly and consistently checking in with me to ask how the book was progressing. Sometimes you just need someone to hold you accountable and remind you to keep pushing forward. You also need people who believe in you more than you believe in yourself, who tell you they are proud of you, and that you can do it. Thanks to Tony Postlethwaite for being a constant supporter—your cheerleading meant the world to me when I needed it most. And a very special thanks to Robby Swinnen, my friend of more than 25 years. Robby is also a talented and sought-after executive coach. He quickly helped me to identify mental barriers, set my sights firmly on goals, and get the book finished. Thank you, Robby, for your friendship, support, and kindness. Thanks also to the powerhouse Ginger Johnson, a fellow professional speaker, for connecting me with Wiley.

I wrote this book hoping to enlighten, entertain, and inspire an audience. While aimed at business leaders (where "leader" is defined by a person's ability to inspire others to lead change, not by positional power), I also wanted to make sure this book was accessible and thought-provoking to anyone who picked it up with an interest in the future. To stay focused on that segment of my audience, I wrote with one particular person in mind, Lyle Becker. Lyle is one of my most ardent followers on social media. He's passionate about the future and fascinated with the potential of technology. Lyle is also 102 years old. May we all sustain such curiosity and passion into our twilight years.

Finally, thanks to my amazing wife, Kristin. For many, many months, Kristin helped me to dedicate a couple of thousand hours to re-searching and writing this book. Her constant support, encouragement, and unconditional love gave me the courage I needed to leave Intel, go it alone, build a successful speaking business, and write this book. Thank you, my love. I couldn't ask for a better companion and champion.

ABOUT THE AUTHOR

As the former futurist and chief evangelist at Intel Corporation, Steve Brown has more than 30 years of experience in high tech, half of that time spent in strategic planning roles where he imagined and built plans for a world 5, 10, and 15 years in the future.

After leaving Intel in 2016, Steve built his own company, Possibility and Purpose, which encourages businesses to understand the exciting potential of technology—including artificial intelligence, Blockchains, and augmented reality—and to embrace those technologies to fulfill their corporate purpose in new ways. Steve encourages companies to build a better future for people by creating exciting new products and services, optimizing operations, innovating business models, empowering employees, delighting customers, boosting sustainability, and elevating work.

Now a sought-after keynote speaker, Steve brings his experience in engineering, business, and communications to help audiences understand how automation and other technology will reshape industries, transform the future of work, and improve our lives.

Steve has been featured on *CNN*, *BBC*, *Bloomberg* TV, and in the *Wall Street Journal* and *Wired* magazine, among many other media outlets. He holds bachelor of science and master of engineering degrees in micro-electronic systems engineering from Manchester University. He was born in the UK and became a U.S. citizen in 2008. Steve lives with his wife in Portland, Oregon. Also known as The Bald Futurist, Steve can be reached through his website at baldfuturist.com.

Whether speaking about the future of work, doing a deep dive on artificial intelligence and Blockchain, or discussing flying cars, Steve inspires his audiences to think beyond the status quo and to reimagine their businesses (and their lives) for the better. His book takes readers beyond the content shared in his keynote presentations. It offers a deep dive into the technologies that will shape the next decade and shares fascinating stories that illustrate the profound ways technology can be used to improve people's lives.

INDEX

Note: Page numbers followed by *f* refer to figures.